⚐ **W9-DJE-856**

The Bible and the Psyche

Toni Boehm
430 Winnebago Drive
Lake Winnebago, MO 64034

Marie-Louise von Franz, Honorary Patron

**Studies in Jungian Psychology
by Jungian Analysts**

Daryl Sharp, General Editor

The Bible and the Psyche

Individuation Symbolism
in the Old Testament

Edward F. Edinger

Note: Unless otherwise indicated all biblical quotations are
from the Jerusalem Bible. Other versions of the Bible are referred
to in abbreviated form: AV–Authorized (King James) Version;
DV–Douay Version; NEB–New English Bible; NAB–New American
Bible; RSV–Revised Standard Version; NKJV–New King James Version.

Canadian Cataloguing in Publication Data

Edinger, Edward F. (Edward Ferdinand), 1922-
  The Bible and the psyche

(Studies in Jungian psychology by Jungian analysts; 24)

Bibliography: p.
Includes index.

ISBN 0-919123-23-6

1. Symbolism in the Bible.   2. Bible. O.T.—
Criticism, interpretation, etc.   3. Individuation.
4. Jung, C.G. (Carl Gustav), 1875-1961.   I. Title.
II. Series.

BS1191.E34 1986   221.6'4   C86-093879-4

INTER CITY BOOKS
Box 1271, Station Q, Toronto, Canada M4T 2P4
Telephone (416) 927-0355

Honorary Patron: Marie-Louise von Franz.
Publisher and General Editor: Daryl Sharp.
Editorial Board: Fraser Boa, Daryl Sharp, Marion Woodman.

INNER CITY BOOKS was founded in 1980 to promote the
understanding and practical application of the work of C.G. Jung.

Index by Daryl Sharp

Printed and bound in Canada by Webcom Limited

C. 2

Contents

See final pages for descriptions of other Inner City Books

Now all these things happened to them as examples, and they were written for our admonition on whom the ends of the ages have come.

—1 Corinthians 10:11. (NKJV)

Preface

The title of this book links two terms of unequal familiarity, namely, the Old Testament and individuation. The contents of the Old Testament have been known and revered for well over two thousand years, whereas individuation as a psychological process has been discovered only in the twentieth century by C.G. Jung.

Individuation is both simple and impossible to define. In its simple definition,

> Individuation means becoming a single, homogeneous being, and, in so far as "individuality" embraces our innermost, last, and incomparable uniqueness, it also implies becoming one's own self. We could therefore translate individuation as "coming to selfhood" or "self-realization."[1]

Its impossible definition can be approached by reading Jung's *Mysterium Coniunctionis* in its entirety. About this book Jung says, "The entire alchemical procedure for uniting the opposites, which I have described in . . . [*Mysterium Coniunctionis*] could just as well represent the individuation process of a single individual."[2]

By yet another definition, individuation is the process of the ego's encounter with and progressive relation to the Self. Unfortunately, this merely replaces one unknown term with another. Such definitions become comprehensible only when one has experienced the realities to which they refer.

---

1. Jung, *Two Essays on Analytical Psychology*, CW 7, par. 266. [CW refers throughout to *The Collected Works of C.G. Jung*.]
2. *Mysterium Coniunctionis*, CW 14, par. 792.

9

Text of the Song of Songs arranged as a mandala.
(Beinecke Rare Book and Manuscript Library, Yale University)

1

The Bible and the Psyche

> We must read the Bible or we shall not understand psychology. Our psychology, whole lives, our language and imagery are built upon the Bible.—C.G. Jung.[1]

As the twenty-first century approaches we are witnessing the emergence of a whole new world-view growing out of depth psychology. This new science studies the psyche as an experienceable, objective phenomenon. It takes old data and approaches them in a new way. For instance, mythology, religion and sacred scriptures of all kinds are taken out of their traditional contexts and understood psychologically, that is, are seen as the phenomenology of the objective psyche.

From this view the Bible is considered to be a self-revelation of the objective psyche. As Jung says, "The statements made in the Holy Scriptures are also utterances of the soul. . . . they point to realities that transcend consciousness. These *entia* are the archetypes of the collective unconscious."[2] Heretofore these transcendent psychic entities have appeared as metaphysical contents of religious dogma, but now, writes Jung, "a scientific psychology must regard those transcendental intuitions that sprang from the human mind in all ages as *projections,* that is, as psychic contents that were extrapolated in metaphysical space and hypostatized."[3]

It is no easy transition from the metaphysical standpoint of religious faith to the empirical standpoint of the psyche. Between these two mountain ridges lies a dark valley, the valley of lost faith, alienation, meaninglessness and despair. For those who are perched safely on the ridge of religious faith, the psychological approach can be seen as an interesting addition to the more secure viewpoint they already possess. However, for those who, consciously or unconsciously, have already slipped off the ridge of faith and are in the dark valley, the discovery of the psychological approach may just possibly be life-saving. This approach is an admission of spiritual bankruptcy; it is available only to the "poor in spirit," for as Jung says,

1. *The Visions Seminars,* vol. 1, p. 156.
2. "Answer to Job," *Psychology and Religion,* CW 11, par. 557.
3. "Concerning the Archetypes and the Anima Concept," *The Archetypes and the Collective Unconscious,* CW 9i, par. 120.

I am not . . . addressing myself to the happy possessors of faith, but to those many people for whom the light has gone out, the mystery has faded, and God is dead. For most of them there is no going back, and one does not know either whether going back is the better way. To gain an understanding of religious matters, probably all that is left us today is the psychological approach. That is why I take these thought-forms that have become historically fixed, try to melt them down again and pour them into moulds of immediate experience.[4]

The Old Testament documents a sustained dialogue between God and man as it is expressed in the sacred history of Israel. It presents us with an exceedingly rich compendium of images representing encounters with the *numinosum*.[5] These are best understood psychologically as pictures of the encounter between the ego and the Self, which is the major feature of individuation. The Old Testament is thus a grand treasury of individuation symbolism. These venerable stories derive from countless individual experiences of the *numinosum* and their psychic substance has been augmented through the ages by the pious worship and reflection of millions. When these facts are realized we discover once again that the Old Testament is indeed a Holy Book. It is quite literally the ark of the covenant in which resides the power and glory of the transpersonal psyche. We must therefore approach it with caution, honoring its numinous power.

The psychological approach takes the Bible as it is, on the hypothesis that the collective psyche has (semipurposely) selected and arranged it over the course of the centuries. While respecting the methods of biblical criticism, the psychological standpoint is not concerned that a particular passage of the Pentateuch comes from the "J" source rather than the "E." Also the sequence is considered significant. The Hebrew Bible based on the Masoretic text (600–900 A.D.) consists of 24 books gathered into three parts: *The Law, The Prophets* and *The Writings*. The arrangement of Old Testament books in the Christian Bible derives from the Septuagint Greek translation made from 280–150 B.C. This arrangement emphasizes a linear developmental process consistent with the historical, time-bound quality of the Western psyche. According to this version, the Old Testament is composed of 39 books arranged sequentially in three categories: 17 historical books, 5 books of wisdom and poetry and 17 prophetic books (as shown opposite).

I see this arrangement as a balance. On one side are the historical books in which Yahweh deals with Israel collectively as a nation. At this stage, individuation imagery is carried by the nation as a whole, the chosen people. On the other side are the prophetic books, each one named after a great individual who had a personal encounter with Yahweh and was

---

4. "Psychology and Religion," *Psychology and Religion,* CW 11, par. 148.
5. See Rudolph Otto, *The Idea of the Holy,* for a discussion of the concept of the numinous.

Old Testament Books

Historical	*Poetical-Wisdom*	*Prophetic*
Genesis	Job	Isaiah
Exodus	Psalms	Jeremiah
Leviticus	Proverbs	Lamentations
Numbers	Ecclesiastes	Ezekiel
Deuteronomy	Song of Solomon	Daniel
Joshua		Hosea
Judges		Joel
Ruth		Amos
1 Samuel		Obadiah
2 Samuel		Jonah
1 Kings		Micah
2 Kings		Nahum
1 Chronicles		Habakkuk
2 Chronicles		Zephaniah
Ezra		Haggai
Nehemiah		Zechariah
Esther		Malachi

fated to be an *individual* carrier of God-consciousness. In the middle are the poetical-wisdom books, with Job at their head. Job is the pivot of the Old Testament story. That is why Jung focused his Bible commentary on Job. Here for the first time a man encounters Yahweh *as an individual* and not as a function of the collective. Similarly, Yahweh did not deal with Job as a representative of Israel but rather as an individual man. This book thus marks the transition from collective psychology to individual psychology—from group and church religion to the individual's lonely encounter with the *numinosum*.

After Job comes the wisdom literature, as though the individual ego's encounter with the Self has generated wisdom or, as Jung puts it in "Answer to Job," as though the demonstration of Job's greater consciousness has obliged Yahweh to remember his feminine counterpart, Divine Wisdom (Sophia).[6]

The events of the Bible, although presented as history, psychologically understood are archetypal images, that is, pleromatic events that repeatedly erupt into spatio-temporal manifestation and require an individual ego to live them out. As we read these stories with an openness to their unconscious reverberations we recognize them to be relevant to our own most private experience. We are then reading the Bible the way Emerson tells us to read history:

> The fact narrated must correspond to something in me to be credible or intelligible. We, as we read, must become Greeks, Romans, Turks, priest

6. "Answer to Job," *Psychology and Religion*, CW 11, par. 617. See also Edinger, *Encounter with the Self*, p. 71.

and king, martyr and executioner; must fasten these images to some reality in our secret experience, or we shall learn nothing rightly. What befell Asdrubal or Caesar Borgia is as much an illustration of the mind's powers and depravations as what has befallen us. Each new law and political movement has a meaning for you. Stand before each of its tablets and say, "Under this mask did my Proteus nature hide itself." This remedies the defect of our too great nearness to ourselves. This throws our actions into perspective—and as crabs, goats, scorpions, the balance and the waterpot lose their meanness when hung as signs in the zodiac, so I can see my own vices without heat in the distant persons of Solomon, Alcibiades, and Catiline.[7]

Jung tells us that "the Book of Job serves as a paradigm for a certain experience of God which has a special significance for us today."[8] The same can be said of many other contents of the Old Testament. The new insights of depth psychology allow us to relate the mighty mythologems of the Bible to the depth experience of individuals. Christ reinterpreted the Old Testament as foreshadowing his coming. For instance, speaking to the Emmaeus pilgrims, "beginning at Moses and all the prophets, he expounded unto them in all the scriptures the things concerning himself." (Luke 24:27, AV)[9] So now at the beginning of a new aeon the individual pursuing the process of individuation may read these scriptures once again to learn those "things concerning himself."

---

7. "History," *The Selected Writings of Ralph Waldo Emerson,* p. 124.
8. "Answer to Job," *Psychology and Religion,* CW 11, par. 562.
9. See note on copyright page.

2

Beginnings

Creation

> In the beginning God created the heaven and the earth. (AV)
> *Bereshith bara elohim hashshamayim we haarets.* (Hebrew)
> *En archē epoiēsen ho theos ton ouranon kai ton gēn.* (Septuagint)
> *In principio creavit Deus caelum et terram.* (Vulgate)

Because there are four nouns in the first verse of Genesis, the Gnostics took it as a reference to the divine tetrad:

> Moses, then, they declare, by his mode of beginning the account of creation, at once shows the Principle [*archē*] to be the mother of all things when he says, "In the beginning God created the heaven and the earth"; for, as they maintain by naming these four—God, beginning, heaven and earth—he set forth their tetrad![1]

The unfolding of the first four nouns can be charted thus:

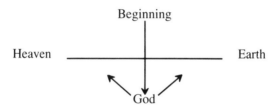

This corresponds to the notion of the pre-Socratic philosophers that the first step in the creation of the universe was the differentiation of the prima materia into the four elements—earth, air, fire and water. The Greek term for prima materia is *archē,* the same word used in the Septuagint to translate *reshith,* beginning.

The process of division into four is a primordial cosmogonic image. Jung points out its important role in alchemy,

> as a quaternio (quaternity), with the two opposites crossing one another, as for instance the four elements or the four qualities (moist, dry, cold, warm), or the four directions and seasons, thus producing the cross as an emblem of the four elements and symbol of the sublunary physical world.[2]

1. Irenaeus, "Against Heresies," I, 18:1; quoted by Jean Daniélou, *The Theology of Jewish Christianity,* p. 167.
2. *Mysterium Coniunctionis,* CW 14, par. 1.

15

It also appears in psychotherapy at crucial moments of creative encounter with the unconscious.[3]

The Kabbalists considered that

> God created the world by joining thereto the Secret Doctrine [of the Kabbalah]. . . . The word BERESHITH with which Genesis opens and which has been rendered sometimes "in wisdom," not "in the beginning," is said to signify the Secret Doctrine and its part in the work of creation.[4]

The reference here is to Proverbs 8, where Wisdom says of herself,

> Yahweh created me when his purpose first unfolded,
>   before the oldest of his works.
> From everlasting I was firmly set,
>   from the beginning, before earth came into being. (verses 22,23)
>
> I was by his side, a master craftsman,
>   delighting him day after day,
>   ever at play in his presence. (verse 30)

Following Proverbs 9:10 we can take the associations one step further. "The fear of Yahweh is the beginning of wisdom," and thus such fear also becomes the prima materia of creation.

Since Divine Wisdom was assimilated to the figure of Christ, he also became synonymous with the beginning. In Revelation 3:14 he is called "the ultimate source [*archē*] of God's creation." Other texts equate the *archē* with the Word. The Gospel of John begins, "In the beginning [*archē*] was the Word." Theophilus of Antioch writes, "God . . . begat (his word) emitting Him along with His own Wisdom before all things. . . . He is called 'Governing principle' (*archē*) because he rules and is Lord of all things fashioned by him."[5] According to Hilary, "*Bereshith* is a Hebrew word which has three meanings. They are: in the beginning, in the head and in the son."[6] Daniélou speculates that this text may derive from Colossians 1:15-18 and that both reflect the same rabbinical tradition; certainly the three terms—"beginning," "head" and "son"—appear as synonyms:

> He is the image of the unseen God
> and the first-born [*son*] of all creation;

---

3. For example, a woman in active imagination descended a long dark tunnel "like the night without stars . . . the night before creation." Emerging into a cavelike opening she encountered a dark, threatening "Kali-like figure" which began to beat her with a stick. After enduring the beating as long as she could, "something snapped" and with a sword she found in her hand she slashed the Kali-like figure in the lines of a cross +. At that, "raw red flesh opened, almost like a flower opening. . . . The force melted, the creature gave up, lost power." This was followed by a reaction of joyful relief.
4. A.E. Waite, *The Holy Kabbalah*, pp. 16f.
5. Quoted by Daniélou, *The Theology of Jewish Christianity*, p. 166.
6. Ibid., p. 168.

from him were created
all things in heaven and on earth:
everything visible and everything invisible,
Thrones, Dominions, Sovereignties, Powers—
All things were created through him and for him,
Before anything was created, he existed,
And he holds all things in unity.
Now the Church is his body,
he is its *head*.
As he is the *Beginning*,
he was first to be born from the dead,
so that he should be first in every way. (Italics added)

This paean to the preexistent Christ refers psychologically to the role of the innate Self in the creation of consciousness. The Church as body of Christ can be understood as the *ecclesia spiritualis*.[7]

Genesis 1:2 continues, "Now the earth was a formless void, there was darkness over the deep, and God's spirit hovered over the water." "Formless void" translates the Hebrew *tohu wa bohu*. This same phrase is used by Jeremiah to describe the effects of an invasion from the north caused by Yahweh's vengeance against Israel.

I looked to the earth, to see a formless waste [*tohu wa bohu*]; to the heavens, and their light had gone. I looked to the mountains, to see them quaking and all the heights astir . . . . The whole land shall be laid waste. I will make an end of it once for all. (Jeremiah 4:23-27)

It is as though Yahweh, like an alchemist, is reducing the land to the prima materia, to its state prior to creation.

The term "deep" translates the Hebrew *tehom*. It has been claimed that *tehom* is a derivative of the Babylonian *Tiamat,* but in Heidel's opinion it is rather that "both words go back to a common Semitic form."[8] Either way, *tehom* is linked symbolically with Tiamat, the primordial monster overcome by the hero-god Marduk. He divided the colossal body into two parts, one the sky, the other the earth.[9] Tiamat symbolizes maternal chaos that undergoes differentiation when it encounters spirit. Thus the spirit of God that broods over *tehom* is followed by the division of light from darkness.[10]

The Septuagint translates *tehom* as *abyssos*, abyss, meaning bottomless depth (*a*, without, *byssos*, depth). "In Gnosticism, the 'Father of all' is described not only as masculine and feminine (or neither), but as Bythos,

---

7. See Jung, *Mysterium Coniunctionis,* CW 14, pars. 9, 12.
8. Alexander Heidel, *The Babylonian Genesis,* p. 100.
9. Ibid., p. 9.
10. For more on this symbolism see Edinger, *Anatomy of the Psyche,* chapter 7, Separatio.

the abyss."[11] The symbolism of the sea and the abyss overlap in patristic usage. Jung summarizes it:

"The sea is the world." It is the "essence of the world, as the element . . . subject to the devil." St. Hilary says: "By the depths of the sea is meant the seat of hell." The sea is the "gloomy abyss," the remains of the original pit, and hence of the chaos that covered the earth. For St. Augustine this abyss is the realm of power allotted to the devil and demons after their fall. It is on the one hand a "deep that cannot be reached or comprehended" and on the other the "depths of sin." For Gregory the Great the sea is the "depths of eternal death." Since ancient times it was the "abode of water-demons." There dwells Leviathan (Job 3:8), who in the language of the Fathers signifies the devil. Rahner documents the patristic equations: *diabolus* = *draco* = Leviathan = *cetus magnus* = *aspis* (adder, asp) = *draco*. St. Jerome says: "The devil surrounds the seas and the ocean on all sides."[12]

The *tohu wa bahu* and the *tehom* can both be considered as synonyms for the prima materia, the original not-yet-created stuff which the alchemists spoke of as the increatum.[13] Paracelsus describes it eloquently:

The Great Mystery is uncreated, and was prepared by the Great Artificer Himself.[14]

It is certain that all perishable things sprang from, and were produced by, the Uncreated Mystery.[15]

All created things proceeded from one matter, not each one separately from its own peculiar matter. This common matter of all things is the Great Mystery. . . . Wherever the aether is diffused, there also the orb of the Great Mystery lies extended. This Great Mystery is the mother of all the elements, and at the same time the spleen [male spawn] of all the stars, trees and carnal creatures. As children come forth from the mother, so from the Great Mystery are generated all created things.[16]

These passages can be read as a description of the unconscious in its aspect of potentiality.

Over the primordial darkness of the prima materia the spirit of God hovered like a brooding bird and by this act light and darkness, upper and lower waters, sea and dry land are separated from each other and the world as we know it unfolds. The New English Bible reads, "a mighty wind . . . swept over the surface of the waters" (Genesis 1:2), indicating

11. Jung, *Mysterium Coniunctionis,* CW 14, par. 8.
12. Ibid., par. 255.
13. See Jung, *Alchemical Studies,* CW 13, par. 283 and *Psychology and Alchemy,* CW 12, pars. 430ff.
14. A.E. Waite, trans., *The Hermetic and Alchemical Writings of Paracelsus,* II, 250.
15. Ibid.
16. Ibid., 249.

the symbolic equation wind = spirit. It is the creative encounter between spirit and undifferentiated substance that sets off creation. In Aristotelian terms it is the meeting of form and matter. This image pictures the elemental foundation or *anlage*[17] of the psyche occurring at a pre-ego phase of development. It applies not only to the initial development of the psyche but also to each new increment of emerging consciousness.

The theme of light being generated in the midst of darkness and wind is a familiar image in depth psychotherapy. For example Jung reports a youthful dream of his:

> It was night in some unknown place, and I was making slow and painful headway against a mighty wind. Dense fog was flying along everywhere. I had my hands cupped around a tiny light which threatened to go out at any moment. Everything depended on my keeping this little light alive.[18]

Another example is a dream of my own as a young man:

> It is a wild and windy night. The electricity seems to be off and some candles are in use. At one time I see the President of the United States (Eisenhower) in an adjoining room working on the State of the Union message by the light of a fitful candle which is being blown by the wind. . . . Outside the house a fire is being kept burning in an open fireplace. The strong wind makes the fire burn high and brilliantly. The night is ominous. The radio is apparently on and suddenly we are told to look up to the sky for a message. Then comes an unearthly high-pitched shriek. I look up to the sky and see a brilliant streak of light across it. This quickly arranges itself into the words of a message.

These dreams are associated to the psychological fact that every increase in consciousness (light) derives from a creative encounter with darkness, the abyss, chaos. This brings about a threatened darkening of the ego, but the law of opposites is then activated and the compensating wind of the spirit rushes in. This spirit fertilizes the darkness and new light is born. According to an Orphic creation myth, "black-winged night, a goddess of whom even Zeus stands in awe, was courted by the wind and laid a silver egg in the womb of darkness; and . . . Eros, whom some call Phanes, was hatched from this egg and set the universe in motion."[19]

Adam and Eve

There are two accounts of the creation of man. According to Genesis 2:7, "Yahweh God fashioned man of dust from the soil. Then he breathed into his nostrils a breath of life, and thus man became a living being." Man

---

17. A term used in embryology, referring to the first accumulation of cells in an embryo recognizable as the beginning of a developing organ.
18. *Memories, Dreams, Reflections*, pp. 87f.
19. Robert Graves, *The Greek Myths*, vol. 1, p. 30.

(*adam*) comes from the earth (*adamah*) and shall return to it. (Genesis 3:19,23) Man is thus a union of opposites, matter and spirit, but with an emphasis on matter since his very name means earth. This leads us into coagulatio symbolism, since earth is a symbol for that process.[20] The creation of man is also a coniunctio, a union of opposites, and fulfills the alchemical recipe: spiritualize the body and coagulate the spirit. This same idea is expressed another way in the other account. "God created man in the image of himself, in the image of God he created him, male and female he created them." (Genesis 1:27) The God-image lodged in a creature of earth corresponds to the union of spirit and matter.

Jung has demonstrated that Adam is an image of the Anthropos, the original whole man, a symbol of the Self.[21] One aspect of this symbolism is his androgyny, implied by the fact that Eve was made out of his rib. (Genesis 1:21,22) This corresponds to Plato's original round man as described in the *Symposium*.[22] Adam as Anthropos is illustrated in the Adam Kadmon of the Kabbala[23] and shows up occasionally in modern dreams.[24] As a union of opposites Adam is a paradoxical figure. Not only does he symbolize the Anthropos, but also, in the theology of Paul, as the "old Adam," he represents the corrupt nature of man superseded by the "second Adam," Christ.[25]

The temptation of Adam and Eve by the serpent has important psychological implications. Jung says,

> There is deep doctrine in the legend of the Fall; it is the expression of a dim presentiment that the emancipation of ego consciousness was a Luciferian deed. Man's whole history consists from the very beginning in a conflict between his feeling of inferiority and his arrogance.[26]

Eating the fruit of the tree of knowledge of good and evil symbolizes the birth of consciousness with the dawning awareness of the opposites. Certain Gnostic sects reversed the roles of Yahweh and the serpent, considering Yahweh as the evil demiurge and the serpent as the spiritual redeemer of man. An example of this standpoint is found in "On the Origin of the World," a Gnostic tractate found in the *Nag Hammadi Library*. In this account the seven planetary archons are in the role of the Old Testament Yahweh:

20. See Edinger, *Anatomy of the Psyche,* chapter 4.
21. *Mysterium Coniunctionis, CW* 14, pars. 544ff.
22. Sections 189-190.
23. *Mysterium Coniunctionis, CW* 14, chapter 5 passim.
24. For an example see Edinger, *Ego and Archetype,* p. 207.
25. Romans 6:6; Ephesians 4:22; Colossians 3:9.
26. "The Phenomenology of the Spirit in Fairytales," *The Archetypes of the Collective Unconscious, CW* 9i, par. 420.

Then the seven took counsel. They came to Adam and Eve timidly. They said to him, "Every tree which is in Paradise, whose fruit may be eaten, was created for you. But beware! Don't eat from the tree of knowledge. If you do eat, you will die." After they gave them a fright, they withdrew up to their authorities.

Then the one who is wiser than all of them, this one who was called "the beast," came. And when he saw the likeness of their mother Eve, he said to her, "What is it that God said to you? 'Don't eat from the tree of knowledge'?" She said, "He not only said 'Don't eat from it,' but 'Don't touch it lest (you) die.'" He said to her, "Don't be afraid! You certainly shall (not die). For (he knows) that when you eat from it your mind will be sobered and you will become like god, knowing the distinctions which exist between evil and good men. For he said this to you, lest you eat from it, since he is jealous."

Now Eve believed the words of the instructor. She looked at the tree. And she saw that it was beautiful and magnificent, and she desired it. She took some of its fruit and ate, and she gave to her husband also, and he ate too. Then their mind opened. For when they ate, the light of knowledge shone for them. When they put on shame, they knew that they were naked with regard to knowledge. When they sobered up, they saw that they were naked, and they became enamored of one another. When they saw their makers, they loathed them since they were beastly forms. They understood very much. . . .

Now when the rulers saw that their Adam had acquired a different knowledge, ... they were troubled because Adam had sobered from every (ignorance). They gathered together and took counsel, and they said, "Behold, Adam has become like one of us, so that he understands the distinction of light and darkness. Now lest perhaps he is deceived in the manner of the tree of knowledge, and he also comes to the tree of life and eats from it and becomes immortal and rules and condemns us and regards (us) and all our glory as folly—afterward he will pass judgment on (us and the) world— come, let us cast him out of Paradise down upon the earth, the place from whence he was taken, so that he will no longer be able to know anything more about us." And thus they cast Adam and his wife out of Paradise. And this which they had done did not satisfy them; rather, they were (still) afraid. They came to the tree of life and they set great terrors around it, fiery living beings called "Cherubim"; and they left a flaming sword in the midst, turning continually with a great terror, so that no one from among earthly men might ever enter that place.[27]

Eating the fruit in the Garden of Eden belongs to coagulatio symbolism and represents a "grounding" process accompanying conscious realization.[28] Hence the text just quoted states that Adam is cast "out of Paradise down upon the earth," implying that heretofore he had not quite been born into earthly existence.[29]

27. *The Nag Hammadi Library,* pp. 174f.
28. See Edinger, *Anatomy of the Psyche,* chapter 4.
29. For more on the Fall see Edinger, *Ego and Archetype,* pp. 18ff.

The Flood and the Tower of Babel

A remarkable event precedes the flood:

> When men had begun to be plentiful on the earth, and daughters had been
> born to them, the sons of God, looking at the daughters of men, saw they
> were pleasing so they married as many as they chose. . . . The Nephilim
> [giants] were on the earth at that time (and even afterwards) when the sons
> of God resorted to the daughters of man, and had children by them. These
> are the heroes of days gone by, the famous men. (Genesis 6:1-4)

This passage is immediately followed by the statement, "Yahweh saw
that the wickedness of man was great on the earth, and that the thoughts
in his heart fashioned nothing but wickedness all day long." (Genesis 6:5)
The implication is clear: forbidden intercourse between the divine and
human realms is responsible for the wickedness. The ego is contaminated
by identification with archetypal contents, and inflation (giants) results.
This state of affairs provokes the flood. "Yahweh regretted having made
man on the earth." (Genesis 6:6) The inflated ego has gravely alienated
itself from the Self and is threatened with extinction.[30] Noah, as an excep-
tion, signifies the residual ego integrity that retains a viable connection
with the Self. This connection is made manifest in the theme of the "covenant." God (Elohim) says to Noah,

> I mean to bring a flood, and send the waters over the earth to destroy all
> flesh on it, every living creature under heaven; everything on earth shall
> perish. But I will establish my Covenant with you, and you must go on
> board the ark, yourself, your sons, your wife, and your sons' wives along
> with you. (Genesis 6:17,18)

Applying this imagery to the psychology of the individual, it refers to
an impending massive inundation by the unconscious—a threatened
psychosis. In such desperate circumstances Noah, the ego, receives the
promise of a covenant from Elohim, the Self. Again, after the flood sub-
sided, Elohim said to Noah,

> I establish my Covenant with you: no thing of flesh shall be swept away
> again by the waters of the flood. There shall be no flood to destroy the earth
> again. . . . Here is the sign of the Covenant I make between myself and
> you and every living creature with you for all generations. I set my bow in
> the clouds and it shall be a sign of the Covenant between me and the earth.
> (Genesis 9:11,12)

Considered psychologically these passages tell us that a covenant, a
conscious connection between the ego and the Self, is apt to occur at times
when the unconscious is highly activated and threatens to inundate the

---

30. For more on ego inflation see ibid., pp. 3ff.

ego. Once one has weathered such a threatened inundation (without a breaking of the ego), one is largely immunized against future attacks. Sometimes the actual image of a rainbow is used in dreams to convey this message.

Such encounters with the activated unconscious commonly give one a glimpse of wholeness symbolized by the rainbow's spectrum of colors, the *omnes colores* of alchemy. Jung remarks:

> The "omnes colores" are frequently mentioned in the texts as indicating something like totality. They all unite in the *albedo* [whitening], which for many alchemists was the climax of the work. . . . Morally this means that the original state of psychic disunity, the inner chaos of conflicting part-souls which Origen likens to herds of animals, becomes the "vir unus," the unified man . . . . [which is] equivalent to integrating the many colours (or, psychologically, the contradictory feeling-values) into a single colour, white.[31]

Another version of divine retribution occurs in the Tower of Babel incident. Man was gripped with a great urge to sublimatio[32] and said, "Let us build ourselves a town and a tower with its top reaching to heaven." (Genesis 11:4) Yahweh, annoyed at this invasion of his realm, opened a counterattack. "This is but the start of their undertakings! There will be nothing too hard for them to do. Come, let us go down and confuse their language on the spot so that they can no longer understand one another." (Genesis 11:6,7) Yahweh resents man's striving for heaven and yet this is due to the way he made him. "Let us make man in our own image, in the likeness of ourselves," he says in Genesis 1:26. Naturally, having a built-in God-image, man will strive to be godlike. Evidently Yahweh wasn't aware of what he was in for when he created a free and autonomous creature.

Initially all men spoke the same language, but after the "confusion of tongues" many languages arose. This represents a process of differentiation arising out of original homogeneity. Understood psychologically, this is a positive event indicating a developmental process in which individual differences are born out of an original state of *participation mystique*.[33] The fact that the myth represents this event as a crime is further evidence of the ambiguous nature of consciousness. At least in part, the quest for consciousness is against nature and exposes the individual to reprisal. And yet even that is ambiguous because Yahweh's reprisal of confusing the language is the very instrument that brings about the differentiation.

The theme of multiplicity growing out of original unconscious unity

---

31. *Mysterium Coniunctionis,* CW 14, par. 388.
32. See Edinger, *Anatomy of the Psyche,* chapter 5.
33. A term derived from the anthropologist Lucien Lévy-Bruhl, denoting a primitive unconscious connection in which the subject cannot clearly distinguish himself from the object. (See Jung, "Definitions," *Psychological Types,* CW 6, par. 781)

belongs to an early stage of ego development. At a later stage the multiplicity of the psyche seeks renewed, but conscious, unity. This later phase is symbolized by the Pentecost, of which the Tower of Babel story is an antitype. At Pentecost, the descent of the transpersonal spirit restores the unity of communication lost at the Tower of Babel (Acts 2), signifying a conscious reconnection of ego and Self which had been necessarily lost at an earlier stage of development.

3

Abraham and Yahweh

The Call

The idea of covenant relations between God and man occurs again in the story of Abraham, where it takes on a more definite and mutual aspect as Yahweh calls Abraham out of Haran: "Leave your country, your family and your father's house, for the land I will show you. I will make you a great nation, I will bless you and make your name so famous that it will be used as a blessing." (Genesis 12:1,2)[1]

This is the archetypal image of the "call" that initiates individuation. Other examples in the Old Testament include Moses (Exodus 3:4), Samuel (1 Samuel 3:4), Isaiah (Isaiah 6:8) and Jonah (Jonah 1:1). The Apostle Paul makes frequent reference to this theme, for instance in Ephesians 4:1: "I, the prisoner of the Lord implore you therefore to lead a life worthy of your vocation [*Klēsis*]."

The call is also a prominent image in Gnosticism. The Gnostic call is directed to one who is drunken, asleep, lost in darkness. It is a call to wake up and remember one's heavenly origin. One such Gnostic call reads,

> My soul, O most splendid one, . . . whither hast thou gone? Return again. Awake, soul of splendor, from the slumber of drunkeness into which thou hast fallen . . ., follow me to the place of the exalted earth where thou dwellest from the beginning.[2]

Abraham is called to leave his home, move to a new place, a promised land, where he is to multiply to the size of a nation. The request to "leave your country, your family and your father's house" is reminiscent of the saying of Jesus: "It is not peace I have come to bring, but a sword. For I have come to set a man against his father, a daughter against her mother, a daughter-in-law against her mother-in-law. A man's enemies will be those of his own household." (Matthew 10:34-36)

Psychologically this refers to the separatio[3] necessary to break up a state of *participation mystique*. This is a basic requirement of individuation. One must be dumped out of the psychic containers that keep one unconsciously identified with family, tribe, party, church and country. One who succeeds in dissolving this *participation mystique* becomes, like Abraham, "a great nation." To achieve the state of conscious individual

---

1. According to Wisdom 10:5, it was Wisdom who chose Abraham.
2. Hans Jonas, *The Gnostic Religion*, p. 83.
3. See Edinger, *Anatomy of the Psyche*, chapter 7.

being is like the birth of a new world.[4] Jung hints at this mysterious idea when he says, "It is quite possible that we contain whole peoples in our souls, worlds where we can be as infinitely great as we are infinitely small externally–so great that the history of the redemption of a whole nation or a whole universe might take place within us."[5]

The experience of being called is a crucial feature of individuation. It brings an irrefutable awareness of the transpersonal center of the psyche, the Self, and its imperatives. Jung describes the psychological significance of vocation in his essay "The Development of Personality":

> What is it, in the end, that induces a man to go his own way and to rise out of unconscious identity with the mass as out of a swathing mist? . . .
>
> It is what is commonly called *vocation:* an irrational factor that destines a man to emancipate himself from the herd and from its well-worn paths. True personality is always a vocation and puts its trust in it as in God . . . . Vocation acts like a law of God from which there is no escape. . . .
>
> The clearest examples of this are to be found in the avowals of the Old Testament prophets.[6]

Only the man who can consciously assent to the power of the inner voice becomes a personality; but if he succumbs to it he will be swept away by the blind flux of psychic events and destroyed. That is the great and liberating thing about any genuine personality: he voluntarily sacrifices himself to his vocation, and consciously translates into his own individual reality what would only lead to ruin if it were lived unconsciously by the group.[7]

The inner voice is a "Lucifer" in the strictest and most unequivocal sense of the word, and it faces people with ultimate moral decisions without which they can never achieve full consciousness and become personalities. The highest and the lowest, the best and the vilest, the truest and the most deceptive things are often blended together in the inner voice in the most baffling way, thus opening up in us an abyss of confusion, falsehood, and despair.[8]

The ambiguous and even dangerous aspect of vocation is often not visible in canonical material, which has been refined over many centuries for theological purposes. These missing elements are sometimes found in the legends that accumulate around the sacred figures. According to legend, the immediate reason for Abraham's move to Canaan was that King Nimrod was seeking to kill him. The king had had a dream which his wisemen interpreted to mean that he would lose his life at the hands

---

4. The alchemists equated their opus with the creation of the world.
5. *The Visions Seminars,* vol. 1, p. 59.
6. *The Development of Personality,* CW 17, pars. 299ff.
7. Ibid., par. 308.
8. Ibid., par. 319.

of a descendent of Abraham.[9] The psychological implication is clear: to honor the inner authority, the source of the call, may require the denial of external and projected authority, thus exposing oneself to dangerous reprisal. In the legend Abraham's call exposes him to the same danger the new-born Moses and Christ experience.

The Covenant

Abraham's next encounter with Yahweh is described in Genesis 15:

> It happened some time later that the word of Yahweh was spoken to Abram in a vision, "Have no fear, Abram, I am your shield, your reward will be great."
> "My Lord Yahweh," Abram replied, "what do you intend to give me? I go childless . . ." Then Abram said, "See, you have given me no descendants; some man of my household will be my heir." And then this word of Yahweh was spoken to him, "He shall not be your heir; your heir shall be of your own flesh and blood." Then taking him outside he said, "Look up to heaven and count the stars if you can. Such will be your descendants," he told him. Abram put his faith in Yahweh, who counted this as making him justified.
> "I am Yahweh," he said to him, "who brought you out of Ur of the Chaldaeans to make you heir to this land." "My Lord Yahweh," Abram replied, "how am I to know that I shall inherit it?" He said to him, "Get me a three-year-old heifer, a three-year-old goat, a three-year-old ram, a turtledove and a young pigeon." He brought him all these, cut them in half and put half on one side and half facing it on the other; but the birds he did not cut in half. Birds of prey came down on the carcases but Abram drove them off.
> Now as the sun was setting Abram fell into a deep sleep, and terror seized him. Then Yahweh said to Abram, "Know this for certain, that your descendants will be exiles in a land not their own, where they will be slaves and oppressed for four hundred years. But I will pass judgement also on the nation that enslaves them and after that they will leave, with many possessions. For your part, you shall go to your fathers in peace; you shall be buried at a ripe old age. In the fourth generation they will come back here, for the wickedness of the Amorites is not yet ended."
> When the sun had set and darkness had fallen, there appeared a smoking furnace and a firebrand that went between the halves. That day Yahweh made a Covenant with Abram in these terms:
> "To your descendants I give this land, from the wadi of Egypt to the Great River, the river Euphrates, the Kenites, the Kenizzites, the Kadmonites, the Hittites, the Perizzites, the Rephaim, the Amorites, the Canaanites, the Girgashites, and the Jebusites." (verses 1-21)

The covenant here described between Yahweh on one hand and Abraham

9.　Louis Ginzberg, *Legends of the Bible*, p. 98.

and his descendents on the other is the core content of the old Testament. Abraham is told that the fruits of his life will be countless and of the nature of stars. Beyond the literal meaning this passage refers to the *psychic* products of his life, which are to be infinite and sidereal. This is an allusion to the transpersonal effects of individuation. There is reason to believe that the psychic accomplishments of the individual are transferred to the archetypal realm and become permanent contents of the collective psyche.[10] This seems to be what is promised to Abraham. He is to be the father of "star stuff." Jung tells us, "The decisive question for man is: Is he related to something infinite or not? . . . In the final analysis we count for something only because of the essential we embody."[11] This remark has two aspects. On the one hand the ego counts for something if it has made a connection with the ever-living eternal. On the other hand it counts for something if it has taken on eternal qualities, that is, has *created a piece of eternity* (the Philosophers' Stone).

The covenant Yahweh proposes is ratified by a remarkable sacrificial ritual. A heifer, a goat and a ram are cut in half with half put on one side and half on the other. When night came Yahweh appeared as "a smoking furnace and a firebrand that went between the halves." We know from Jeremiah 34:18 that this is an ancient ritual of covenant:

> The contracting parties passed between the parts of the slain animal and called down upon themselves the fate of the victim should they violate the agreement. The flame symbolizes Yahweh (cf. the burning bush, Exodus 3:2; the pillar of fire, Exodus 13:21; the smoke of Sinai, Exodus 19:18).[12]

W. Robertson Smith has an interesting comment on this ritual. He writes,

> The Hebrew phrase *karath berith*, "to make (literally, to cut) a covenant" is generally derived from the peculiar form of sacrifice mentioned in Genesis 15, Jeremiah 34:18, where the victim is cut in twain and the parties pass between the pieces; and this rite again is explained as a symbolic form of imprecation, as if those who swore to one another prayed that, if they proved unfaithful, they might be similarly cut in pieces, but this does not explain the characteristic feature in the ceremony—the passing between the pieces; and, on the other hand, we see from Exodus 34:8 . . . that the dividing of the sacrifice and the application of the blood to both parties go together. The sacrifice presumably was divided into two parts (as in Exodus 34:8 the blood is divided into two parts), when both parties joined in eating it; and when it ceased to be eaten, the parties stood between the pieces, as a symbol that they were taken within the mystical life of the victim.[13]

---

10. See Edinger, *The Creation of Consciousness*, pp. 24ff.
11. *Memories, Dreams, Reflections*, p. 325.
12. *Jerusalem Bible*, p. 31, note.
13. *The Religion of the Semites*, pp. 480f.

Since the victim is divided into two pieces the symbolism of the number two seems relevant. We are reminded of the original meaning of the Greek word *symbolon:*

> In original Greek usage, symbols referred to two halves of an object such as a stick or a coin which two parties broke between them as a pledge and to prove later the identity of the presenter of one part to the holder of the other. The term corresponded to our word tally concerning which Webster's unabridged dictionary states: "It was customary for traders, after notching a stick to show the number or quantity of goods delivered, to split it lengthwise through the notches so that the parts exactly corresponded, the seller keeping one stick, and the purchaser the other." A symbol was thus originally a tally referring to the missing piece of an object which when restored to, or thrown together with, its partner recreated the original whole object.[14]

Embedded in the archaic covenant ritual seems to be the latent idea of the reunion or restitution of a primordial state of division. Like Plato's original spherical man[15] the sacrificial victim is divided into two. By passing between the divided halves the convenanting parties symbolically restore unity and wholeness to the victim. Where the parties to the covenant are God and man, the implication is that the ego's lost connection with the Self is being restored together with the wholeness of the psyche.

A significant detail appears in Genesis 15:12. "Now as the sun was setting, Abram fell into a deep sleep and terror [horror of great darkness, AV] seized him." This "terror" is the psychological equivalent of the sacrifice just performed. On the one hand it is the human reaction to an encounter with the *numinosum;* on the other hand the ego's willingness to accept the terror is its sacrificial offering for the realization of the Self. One might call this image the archetypal basis of anxiety.

Later commentators have attached great importance to Genesis 15:6: "Abram put his faith in Yahweh, who counted this as making him justified." According to Jewish legend, "the redemption of Israel from the exile will take place as a recompense for his firm trust."[16] Paul quotes this verse as an example of justification by faith and considers Abraham a model for Christian faith in Christ. "The promise of inheriting the world was not made to Abraham and his descendants on account of any law but on account of the righteousness which consists in faith." (Romans 4:13) Jung takes up the psychological significance of faith in the essay previously quoted:

> The development of personality . . . . means fidelity to the law of one's own being.
> For the word "fidelity" I should prefer, in this context, the word used in

14. Edinger, *Ego and Archetype*, p. 130.
15. *Symposium*, sections 189f.
16. Ginzberg, *Legends of the Bible*, p. 107.

the New Testament, *pistis,* which is erroneously translated "faith." It really means "trust," "trustful loyalty." Fidelity to the law of one's own being is a trust in this law, a loyal perseverance and confident hope; in short, an attitude such as a religious man should have towards God.[17]

Abraham's next encounter with Yahweh is described in Genesis 17:

> When Abram was ninety-nine years old Yahweh appeared to him and said, "I am El Shaddai. Bear yourself blameless in my presence, and I will make a Covenant between myself and you, and increase your numbers greatly."
>
> Abram bowed to the ground[18] and God said this to him, "Here now is my Covenant with you; you shall become the father of a multitude of nations. You shall no longer be called Abram; your name shall be Abraham, for I make you father of a multitude of nations. I will make you most fruitful. I will make you into nations, and your issue shall be kings. I will establish my Covenant between myself and you, and your descendants after you, generation after generation, a Covenant in perpetuity, to be your God and the God of your descendants after you. I will give to you and to your descendants after you the land you are living in, the whole land of Canaan, to own in perpetuity, and I will be your God."
>
> God said to Abraham, "You on your part shall maintain my Covenant, yourself and your descendants after you, generation after generation. Now this is my Covenant which you are to maintain between myself and you, and your descendants after you: all your males must be circumcised. You shall circumcise your foreskin, and this shall be the sign of the covenant between myself and you. When they are eight days old all your male children must be circumcised, generation after generation of them, no matter whether they be within the household or bought from a foreigner not one of your descendants. They must always be circumcised, both those born within the household and those who have been bought. My Covenant shall be marked on your bodies as a Covenant in perpetuity. The uncircumcised male, whose foreskin has not been circumcised, such a man shall be cut off from his people: he has violated my Covenant." (verses 1-14)

On this occasion Yahweh's promise is repeated, but instead of an animal sacrifice to ratify the covenant the ritual of circumcision is required. "My Covenant shall be marked on your bodies as a Covenant in perpetuity." Clearly, the ordeal of circumcision is an alternative to the animal sacrifice of Genesis 15. It has been suggested that circumcision was originally a substitute for child-sacrifice.[19] According to George Barton,

> In the beginning . . . Semitic circumcision was apparently a sacrifice to the goddess of fertility. Whether it was intended to ensure the blessing of the goddess, and so to secure more abundant offspring, or whether it was considered as the sacrifice of a part instead of the whole person, we may not clearly determine.[20]

17. *The Development of Personality,* CW 17, pars. 295f.
18. "Fell on his face," AV.
19. See Jung, *Symbols of Transformation,* CW 5, par. 671 and note.
20. James Hastings, ed., *Encyclopaedia of Religion and Ethics,* vol. 3, p. 680.

We know that the Near Eastern mother goddess was served by eunuch priests, the *Galli,* who in ecstatic dedication would castrate themselves and fling their severed genitals into the lap of the goddess. It seems that Yahweh has taken over a mitigated version of this sacrifice as he claims for himself the allegiance previously offered to the Great Mother. The patriarchal spirit-principle replaces the nature-principle of matriarchy as the supreme value. Paul alludes to the ancient connection between circumcision and castration in service of the Great Mother in his sarcastic remark of Phillipians 3:2. "Watch out for the cutters" (*katatome,* concision, instead of *peritome,* circumcision), a reference to those who gash and mutilate themselves in honor of the Great Mother.[21]

Circumcision is symbolic castration, that is, a sacrifice of original, unregenerate desirousness. It has the same meaning as the commandment, Thou shalt not covet (Exodus 20:17; Romans 7:7). Natural libido is turned against itself in allegiance to the spirit. This same image is behind Christ's statement that "there are eunuchs who have made themselves that way for the sake of the kingdom of heaven." (Matthew 19:12) Later the image of circumcision is used explicitly to refer to a psychic attitude transformed by God-consciousness, as in Deuteronomy 10:16, "Circumcise your heart and be obstinate no longer." Similarly, Stephen berates his attackers, "Ye stiffnecked and uncircumcised in heart and ears, ye do always resist the Holy Ghost." (Acts 7:51, AV)

The Visit at Mamre

Like Baucis and Philemon, Abraham and Sarah discover they are entertaining deity in Genesis 18. Three figures appear, variously described as three men, as angels and as Yahweh. According to legend the three figures were the three angels, Michael, Raphael and Gabriel, each charged by God with a specific mission. "Raphael was to heal the [circumcision] wound of Abraham, Michael was to bring Sarah the glad tidings that she would bear a son, and Gabriel was to deal destruction to Sodom and Gomorrah."[22] The legend recounts that the visitation took place on the third day after Abraham's circumcision and adds that the day was exceedingly hot, for God "had bored a hole in hell."[23]

The third day after circumcision is typically the day of greatest pain and apparently a time of special peril, judging by the fate of the Shechemites who "on the third day, when they were sore" (AV) were attacked and slaughtered by the brothers of the ravished Dinah. (Genesis 34:25) More generally the "third day," *yom shelishi,* is the archetypal time when the numinous event manifests. On the third day Abraham arrived at Moriah where he was to sacrifice Isaac (Genesis 22:4); on the third day Pharaoh

---

21. *Jerusalem Bible,* p. 341, note.
22. Ginzberg, *Legends of the Bible,* p. 110.
23. Ibid.

fulfilled what Joseph had foretold in his dream interpretation (Genesis 40:20); Moses was informed that "on the third day Yahweh will descend on the mountain of Sinai in the sight of all the people" (Exodus 19:11); on the third day Yahweh healed Hezekiah (2 Kings 20:5); on the third day Esther dared to face King Ahasuerus (Esther 5:1); on the third day Yahweh, who "has torn us to pieces," promises to "raise us and we shall live in his presence" (Hosea 6:2); on the third day the marriage in Canae took place during which water was turned into wine (John 2:1); and, finally, it was on the third day after his death that Christ was "raised up" (Matthew 16:21; 20:19, etc.).

The visitation at Mamre brings with it simultaneously healing of the circumcision, promise of immediate progeny and destruction (of Sodom and Gomorrah). The announcement of Isaac's birth is at the same time a conception. This is indicated by Genesis 18:10, which says literally, "When I come back to you *at about a life's interval* [i.e., at the end of the period of pregnancy], your wife Sarah shall have a son."[24] This corresponds to the similar symbolic implication in the Annunciation to Mary (Luke 1:26ff), and refers to the psychological fact that an encounter between the ego and the Self often leads to a psychic pregnancy which is expressed in dreams by images of gestation and birth.[25]

The heat of the day due to the "hole in hell" alludes to the affective intensity that accompanies the activation of the unconscious, and corresponds to the fire and brimstone that were rained on Sodom and Gomorrah (Genesis 19:23). The same event is healing and inseminating to the "righteous" aspects of the psyche and is experienced as destructive fire by the "sinful" aspects. Highly significant psychologically is Abraham's remonstrance with Yahweh in an effort to mitigate his wrath (Genesis 18:16-33). Through his efforts Lot and his family are saved.[26]

The Sacrifice of Isaac (The *Akedah*)

In Genesis 22 we are given a deep glimpse into a mysterious aspect of the ego-Self relationship:

> It happened some time later that God put Abraham to the test. "Abraham, Abraham," he called. "Here I am," he replied. "Take your son," God said, "your only child Isaac, whom you love, and go to the land of Moriah. There you shall offer him as a burnt offering, on a mountain I will point out to you."
>
> Rising early next morning Abraham saddled his ass and took with him two of his servants and his son Isaac. He chopped wood for the burnt

---

24. *Anchor Bible*, Genesis, p. 130, note.
25. See the example published by Jung in "The Psychology of the Transference," *The Practice of Psychotherapy,* CW 16, pars. 377ff.
26. See Edinger, *The Creation of Consciousness*, pp. 94f.

offering and started on his journey to the place God had pointed out to him. On the third day Abraham looked up and saw the place in the distance. Then Abraham said to his servants, "Stay here with the donkey. The boy and I will go over there; we will worship and come back to you."

Abraham took the wood for the burnt offering, loaded it on Isaac, and carried in his own hands the fire and the knife. Then the two of them set out together. Isaac spoke to his father Abraham, "Father," he said. "Yes, my son," he replied. "Look," he said, "Here are the fire and the wood, but where is the lamb for the burnt offering?" Abraham answered, "My son, God himself will provide the lamb for the burnt offering." Then the two of them went on together.

When they arrived at the place God had pointed out to him, Abraham built an altar there, and arranged the wood. Then he bound his son Isaac and put him on the altar on top of the wood. Abraham stretched out his hand and seized the knife to kill his son.

But the angel of Yahweh called to him from heaven. "Abraham, Abraham," he said. "I am here," he replied. "Do not raise your hand against the boy," the angel said. "Do not harm him, for now I know you fear God. You have not refused me your son, your only son." Then looking up, Abraham saw a ram caught by its horns in a bush. Abraham took the ram and offered it as a burnt offering in place of his son. (verses 1-14)

According to legend, Yahweh was taunted by Satan to put Abraham to the test in the same way as Job was tested.[27] Certainly Abraham was confronted with the desperate paradox of Yahweh, who first promised him innumerable descendents through Isaac and then commanded that Isaac be killed. One way of understanding this paradox is to see it as a conflict between two different developmental levels of deity. As I have written elsewhere,

> The clue to this interpretation is the fact that the divine name changes in the course of the account. At the beginning, the divine name is "*Elohim*," i.e., God. At the end of the story, when Abraham is restrained from sacrificing Isaac, the name used is Yahweh. From the standpoint of biblical criticism, this means that two different documents (the E and J documents) have been combined to make the canonical text. However, from the standpoint of empirical psychology, which reads the dream or scripture as it stands, it means that a transformation of the deity has occurred. The same thing is indicated by the fact that God has changed his mind and no longer wants Isaac to be sacrificed.
>
> The text begins with the statement that God "put Abraham to the test." What is the nature of that test? Abraham was caught between two different levels of divine manifestation—a primitive God (*Elohim*) requiring human sacrifice, and a more differentiated and merciful God (Yahweh). One biblical scholar notes: "In Abraham's day the sacrifice of the firstborn was a common practice among the Semitic races, and was regarded as the most pleasing

---

27.   Ginzberg, *Legends of the Bible,* pp. 127f.

service which men could offer to their deities. It was the 'giving of their firstborn for their transgression, the first of their body for the sin of their soul.'" (Micah 6:7)[28] Abraham is in the fearful position of having to mediate between two developmental levels of deity. That is his test.

The primitive level of deity is represented by the ram, which according to legend was grazing in Paradise before it was transported to the thicket on Mount Moriah.[29] The ram signifies unregenerate archetypal energy which must be extracted from the unconscious and sacrificed. Abraham is participating in a process of divine transformation by permitting himself to entertain murderous impulses against Isaac. This brings the ram-energy into consciousness where it can then be sacrificed under the aegis of the more differentiated aspect of God. Psychologically one might say that Abraham's test determined whether he was willing to risk a conscious encounter with his primitive affects in the faith that they are capable of transformation.

The Church Fathers considered Isaac to be a prefiguration of Christ. For instance, Augustine says that Isaac "himself carried to the place of sacrifice the wood on which he was to be offered up, just as the Lord himself carried His own cross." Also the ram "caught by the horns in the thicket: What then did he represent but Jesus, who, before He was offered up, was crowned with thorns by the Jews?"[30] According to this association, Yahweh's test of Abraham is to determine whether Abraham is willing to share Yahweh's later ordeal of sacrificing his son, Christ. Abraham is asked to participate in the tragic drama of divine transformation. He assents, allowing it to be said of Abraham as well as of Yahweh that he "loved . . . so much that he gave his only son." (John 3:16)[31]

Genesis 22 is part of the series of covenant passages previously quoted, as indicated by verses 16-18:

> I swear by my own self—it is Yahweh who speaks—because you have done this, because you have not refused me your son, your only son, I will shower blessings on you, I will make your descendants as many as the stars of heaven and the grains of sand on the sea shore. Your descendants shall gain possession of the gates of their enemies. All the nations of the earth shall bless themselves by your descendants, as a reward for your obedience.

This promise for Abraham's descendents is the same covenant promise previously stated in Genesis 15 and 17. Thus the intention to sacrifice Isaac corresponds to the animals cut in two and the requirement of circumcision in the previous accounts. We therefore arrive at the symbolic equation: divided animals = circumcision = sacrifice of son—three forms of sacrifice.

Sacrifice is the central image in Old Testament Yahweh-worship and the central image in Christianity as well. Abraham's sacrifice of Isaac is a

28. J.R. Dummelow, ed., *The One-Volume Bible Commentary*, p. 22.
29. Erich Wellisch, *Isaac and Oedipus*, p. 70.
30. Augustine, *City of God*, XVI, 32.
31. Edinger, *The Creation of Consciousness*, pp. 97f.

supreme example which illustrates the unfolding relation between the ego and the Self. Jung writes,

> It is the self that causes me to make the sacrifice; nay more, it compels me to make it. The self is the sacrifice, and I am the sacrificed gift, the human sacrifice. Let us try for a moment to look into Abraham's soul when he was commanded to sacrifice his only son. Quite apart from the compassion he felt for his child, would not a father in such a position feel himself as the victim, and feel that he was plunging the knife into his own breast? He would be at the same time the sacrificer and the sacrificed.
>
> Now, since the relation of the ego to the self is like that of the son to the father, we can say that when the self calls on us to sacrifice ourselves, it is really carrying out the sacrificial act on itself. We know more or less what this act means to us, but what it means to the self is not so clear. As the self can only be comprehended by us in particular acts, but remains concealed from us as a whole because it is more comprehensive than we are, all we can do is to draw conclusions from the little of the self that we can experience. We have seen that a sacrifice only takes place when we feel the self actually carrying it out on ourselves. We may also venture to surmise that in so far as the self stands to us in the relation of father to son, the self in some sort feels our sacrifice as a sacrifice of itself. From that sacrifice we gain ourselves—our "self"—for we have only what we give. But what does the self gain? We see it entering into manifestation, freeing itself from unconscious projection, and, as it grips us, entering into our lives and so passing from unconsciousness into consciousness, from potentiality into actuality. What it is in the diffuse unconscious state we do not know: we only know that in becoming ourself it has become man.[32]

In being asked to sacrifice his son, Abraham is placed in the same position as Yahweh who is sacrificing his son Abraham by imposing this ordeal on him. The Self requires the ego to carry out its (the Self's) actions in the world. If this is done unconsciously, it is inflation; if done consciously, it is a sacrifice. When the ego accepts the assignment it may bring relief from generalized destructive effects emanating from the unconscious; similarly, the plague was stayed when Phinehas took on himself the task of executing Yahweh's vengeance. (Numbers 25:1-8) In the case of Abraham the effect was the renewal of the covenant.

32. "Transformation Symbolism in the Mass," *Psychology and Religion*, CW 11, pars. 397f.

4

Jacob and His Sons

Jacob and Esau

The story of Jacob and Esau indicates that the ego destined for individuation is born as twins. Other examples of this same archetypal image are Romulus and Remus and the Dioscuri, Castor and Pollux. This division into two has two aspects: ego and shadow, and ego and Self. Both aspects appear in Jacob's dealings with Esau.

According to legend, the twins embodied good and evil. "It had been decreed that . . . [Rebekah], the daughter of an idolator, would have two sons, one resembling Abraham and the other resembling Bethuel."[1] Even while still in the womb the good and evil nature of the two expressed itself. "For each time Rebekah passed a place where there were idols, one of the twins wanted her to enter and pushed the other; and each time Rebekah passed a House of God the other twin wanted her to enter."[2] Although at the beginning of Israel these opposites must be separated, at the end they must be united. Thus a rabbinic commentary says, "Messiah son of David will not come before the tears of Esau have ceased to flow."[3]

As foretold by Yahweh (Genesis 25:23) and with the connivance of his mother Rebekah, Jacob stole the birthright and paternal blessing belonging to Esau. A crime stands at the very beginning of Israel's history. The psychological implications of this primal crime have been clearly elaborated in an excellent paper by Myron Gubitz.[4] The basic idea is that the ego establishes its unique, autonomous existence by a denial and dissociation of the shadow. But a heavy price is exacted. According to Gubitz, Amalek, the grandson of Esau, became the embodiment of the dissociated shadow in the collective Jewish psyche as a consequence of the crime against Esau. The Amalekites made war against Israel and in response Moses announced that "the Lord will have war with Amalek from generation to generation." (Exodus 17:16, AV) The unacknowledged crime against Esau has established a dissociated guilt and revenge complex that pits the seed of Jacob against the seed of Esau. Gubitz writes,

In psychological terms, anxiety about imminent violence or destruction (paranoia, in the extreme case) is generally linked to a deep-seated sense of guilt. Often, too, this guilt is the reverse side of a psychic inflation, an

1. Joseph Gaer, *The Lore of the Old Testament*, p. 107.
2. Ibid.
3. Myron B. Gubitz, "Amalek: The Eternal Adversary," p. 57.
4. Ibid.

over-identification with a powerful archetype. In the mythic history of the Jewish people both of these factors may be traced to the Jacob-Esau split and down through the ages via the ramifying myth of Amalek. The guilt in the collective Jewish psyche is the inevitable price paid for Jacob-Israel's theft of Esau's birthright, his fraudulent acquisition of the paternal blessing, and the conscious rejection of those aspects and values embodied by Esau. In terms of the mode of consciousness basic to Judeo-Christian culture this may have been a step forward, a movement away from the purely earth-bound, the irrational and the polytheistic, toward a new plan of spirituality and morality. But, as Herman Hesse remarks in *The Glass Bead Game:*

> Among the pangs inherent in a genuine vocation, these are the bit-terest. One who has received the call takes, in accepting it, not only a gift and a commandment, but also something akin to guilt.

What set the Israelites apart from others at an early stage was their commitment to the exclusiveness of monotheism, their identification with Yahweh and His goal of moral perfection in the realm of human affairs. The inevitable psychic consequence of such a perfectionist commitment—of *any* unqualified commitment to a goal which is by definition unattainable—is a broadly ramified structure of guilt. Reaching avidly for the brightness of transcendent spirituality, one becomes guilty of slighting the earthy ground which gives birth and nourishment to all life. Feeling oneself to be the human representative of God on earth, one also takes upon one's own shoulders the burden of mankind's human shortcomings and thus the guilt for man's inability to measure up to the divine ideal of perfection. Possessed by an immensely powerful archetype, and thus set apart from the rest of humanity as God's Chosen, one must have an unconscious realization that one's blood brothers have been slighted, that standing apart also means exposure as a target for enormous negative projections and all the destructive energies they can unleash.[5]

These remarks do not apply only to the "collective Jewish psyche." The Jacob-Esau myth belongs to the Western psyche as a whole and therefore to us all.

After stealing Esau's blessing Jacob was obliged to flee the country to escape his brother's vengeance. On the first night out the fugitive had a numinous dream.

> Jacob left Beersheba and set out for Haran. When he had reached a certain place he passed the night there, since the sun had set. Taking one of the stones to be found at that place, he made it his pillow and lay down where he was.
>
> He had a dream: a ladder was there, standing on the ground with its top reaching to heaven; and there were angels of God going up it and coming down. And Yahweh was there, standing over him, saying, "I am Yahweh, the God of Abraham your father, and the God of Isaac. I will give to you and your descendants the land on which you are lying. Your descendants

5. Ibid., p. 53.

shall be like the specks of dust on the ground; you shall spread to the west and the east, to the north and the south, and all the tribes of the earth shall bless themselves by you and your descendants. Be sure that I am with you; I will keep you safe wherever you go, and bring you back to this land, for I will not desert you before I have done all that I have promised you."

Then Jacob awoke from his sleep and said, "Truly, Yahweh is in this place and I never knew it." He was afraid and said, "How awe-inspiring this place is! This is nothing less than a house of God; this is the gate of heaven!" Rising early in the morning, Jacob took the stone he had used for his pillow, and set it up as a monument, pouring oil over the top of it. He named the place Bethel, but before that the town was called Luz.

Jacob made this vow, "If God goes with me and keeps me safe on this journey I am making, if he gives me bread to eat and clothes to wear, and if I return home safely to my father, then Yahweh shall be my God. This stone I have set up as a monument shall be a house of God, and I will surely pay you a tenth part of all you give me." (Genesis 28:10-22)

This is a classic image of the ego-Self axis. Characteristically, the great dream occurs at a particular moment in a sequence of events. Jacob's heroic action to assert his destiny is followed by deadly danger and exile. At this low point of alienation the ego is granted a vision of its connection to the Self.[6]

According to legend Jacob had his dream on Mount Moriah, the site of the sacrifice of Isaac and the future site of Solomon's temple. Twelve stones from the altar on which Isaac lay had miraculously joined into a single stone which was Jacob's pillow and was then set up as a pillar and annointed.

God sent this annointed stone into the abyss, to serve as the centre of the earth, the same stone, the Eben Shetiyah, that forms the centre of the sanctuary, whereon the Ineffable Name is graven, the knowledge of which makes a man master over nature, and over life and death.[7]

The image of Jacob's stone shows up in the Kabbala and again in alchemy as a symbol of the Philosophers' Stone. Jung writes,

[In the *Zohar*] . . . the Haye Sarah on Genesis 28:22 says that Malchuth is called the "statue" when she is united with Tifereth. Genesis 28:22 runs: "And this stone which I have set for a pillar, shall be God's house." The stone is evidently a reminder that here the upper (Tifereth) has united with the lower (Malchuth): Tifereth the son has come together with the "Matrona" in the hierosgamos. If our conjecture is correct, the statue could therefore be the Cabalistic equivalent of the lapis Philosophorum.[8]

As often happens in the analysis of individuals, Jacob was granted an

6. See Edinger, *Ego and Archetype,* pp. 69f.
7. Ginzberg, *Legends of the Bible,* pp. 166f.
8. *Mysterium Coniunctionis,* CW 14, par. 568.

anticipatory vision of the coniunctio early in the process. Its actual conscious achievement is the effort of a lifetime.

After many years, a wealthy man with two wives and eleven children, Jacob is obliged to separate from the family of his father-in-law and establish himself independently. Now he must return to his own country and encounter his wronged brother from whom he fled many years before. The repressed shadow returns and Jacob is in terror. During the night preceding his meeting with Esau, he had a crucial encounter.

> And there was one that wrestled with him until daybreak who, seeing that he could not master him, struck him in the socket of his hip, and Jacob's hip was dislocated as he wrestled with him. He said, "Let me go, for day is breaking." But Jacob answered, "I will not let you go unless you bless me." He then asked, "What is your name?" "Jacob," he replied. He said, "Your name shall no longer be Jacob, but Israel, because you have been strong against God, you shall prevail against men." Jacob then made this request, "I beg you, tell me your name," but he replied, "Why do you ask my name?" And he blessed him there.
>
> Jacob named the place Peniel, "Because I have seen God face to face," he said, "and I have survived." The sun rose as he left Peniel, limping because of his hip. (Genesis 32:26-32)

This story contains all four features of what I have described elsewhere as the Job archetype:[9] 1) encounter with a superior being; 2) wounding; 3) perseverance; and 4) divine revelation. This is the theme of encounter with the Greater Personality.[10] What is particularly significant about Jacob's experience is that it occurs simultaneously with an encounter with the wronged shadow. Because of Jacob's fear of him, Esau becomes a stand-in for God. Jacob's guilty conscience imbues Esau with divine power. When Jacob meets Esau he says, "I have seen thy face, as though I had seen the face of God." (Genesis 33:10, AV) This means psychologically that a crime against the shadow is also a crime against the Self and may activate the Self in its avenging form.

This motif may manifest either externally or internally. Externally, if I commit a wrong against another person I will fear his desire for revenge which comes from the Self. ("Vengeance is mine and requital," says Yahweh—Deuteronomy 33:35.) Similarly internally, if I have wronged the shadow within it is a violation of totality and may arouse the vengeance of the Self against the ego. To encounter such a reaction and endure it without succumbing to either defensive hostility or despair corresponds to Jacob's wrestling with the angel until it blesses him.

Since we hate what we fear, Jacob may have had to wrestle with his rage at Esau before he could arrive at a conciliatory attitude which would

9.   Edinger, *Encounter with the Self*, p. 11.
10.   See Jung, "Concerning Rebirth," *The Archetypes and the Collective Unconscious*, CW 9i, pars. 215ff, 240ff.

allow him to send Esau propitiating gifts. Or perhaps, Jacob was obliged
to wrestle with his terror until he could extract from it the courage needed
to meet Esau. Intense affects of all kinds come from the Self and have
destructive consequences unless they are mediated by a conscious ego.
Jung writes,

> [The God] appears at first in hostile form, as an assailant with whom the
> hero has to wrestle. This is in keeping with the violence of all unconscious
> dynamism. In this manner the god manifests himself and in this form he
> must be overcome. The struggle has its parallel in Jacob's wrestling with
> the angel at the ford Jabbok. *The onslaught of instinct then becomes an*
> *experience of divinity*, provided that man does not succumb to it and follow
> it blindly, but defends his humanity against the animal nature of the divine
> power. It is a fearful thing to fall into the hands of the living God.[11]

In another place Jung says, "Jacob . . . wrestled with the angel and
came away with a dislocated hip, but by his struggle prevented a murder."[12]
What does this mean? I think of three possibilities. 1) The angel might
have murdered Jacob if he hadn't resisted. This would correspond to
Jacob's suicide out of guilt and terror. 2) Jacob in his rage might have
murdered Esau. 3) Esau in his vengeance might have murdered Jacob if
Jacob had remained caught in a power conflict with him; or Jacob in his
guilty fear might have identified with the victim and thereby constellated
his own execution.

Another aspect of Jacob's ordeal is mentioned by Jung. "A contemporary
Jacob . . . would find himself willy-nilly in possession of a secret that
could not be discussed, and would become a deviant from the collectiv-
ity."[13] Encounter with the Self is necessarily a secret. Such things are not
communicable in their concrete particulars. The secret he must carry
creates the individual as a unique being separate from the collective, but
at the same time it is a wound, like that of Philoctetes, which alienates
him painfully from others.

According to the apocryphal book *Wisdom of Solomon* it was Wisdom
that saved Jacob:

> Wisdom delivered her servants from their ordeals.
> The virtuous man, fleeing from the rage of his brother [Jacob],
> was led by her along straight paths.
> She showed him the kingdom of God
> and taught him the knowledge of holy things.
>   . . . .
> She guarded him closely from his enemies
> and saved him from the traps they set for him.
> In an arduous struggle she awarded him the prize,
> to teach him that piety is stronger than all. (Wisdom 10:9-14)

11. *Symbols of Transformation*, CW 5, par. 524, my italics.
12. *Memories, Dreams, Reflections*, p. 344.
13. Ibid.

The word here translated "piety" is rendered "godliness" and "devotion to God" in other versions. The Septuagint uses *eusebeia,* reverence for the Gods, which is equivalent to the Hebrew "fear of the Lord."[14] This passage tells us that Wisdom was with Jacob during his wrestling with the angel and he was victorious by virtue of a religious attitude. The consequence of the encounter was the transformation of Jacob indicated by his new name, Israel.

Joseph and His Brothers

Throughout the sacred history of Israel the nation as a whole has been the carrier of God-consciousness. Initially this consciousness was carried by individuals, Abraham, Isaac and Jacob. However Jacob had twelve sons by four mothers and these twelve became the progenitors of the twelve tribes whereby the religious task was transferred to the collective.

Nevertheless, the divine prerogative was not distributed equally among the twelve. We learn that "Yahweh was with Joseph" (Genesis 39:2), and his father also singled him out for special favor and gave him a special "coat with long sleeves" (Genesis 37:3; "coat of many colours," AV; "long-sleeved robe," NEB). It was a garment "reaching to the ankles and wrists, and worn by persons of distinction. The ordinary coat had no sleeves and reached only to the knees."[15] As so often happens, the personal and archetypal factors that determine one's destiny here overlap. Yahweh was with Joseph *and* he was his father's favorite. Some schools of psychotherapy will claim that the former is "only" a consequence of the latter. However the facts of the psyche are better served by the alternative emphasis. Joseph was his father's favorite *because* Yahweh was with him.

The robe of distinction is an important image. It corresponds to the "Robe of Glory" in the Gnostic *Hymn of the Pearl.*[16] It is the garment of the Self and wearing it carelessly or unconsciously signifies ego-Self identity. For that reason Joseph must be stripped of it. Identification with his special status is also indicated by his dreams, which express both the fact of his election and his inflation.

By virtue of his special relation to the Self Joseph is superior to his brothers,[17] but the ego's identification with that superiority is exceedingly dangerous. It constellates hostility in the unconscious and in the outer environment, a hostility calculated to correct the one-sidedness of the ego. This psychological fact is expressed in the legends. There Joseph is described as carrying false reports of wrongdoing against his brothers:

He charged them with casting their eyes upon the daughters of the Canaan-

---

14. *New American Bible,* Wisdom, 10:12, note.
15. Dummelow, *The One-Volume Bible Commentary,* p. 39.
16. See Edinger, *Ego and Archetype,* pp. 119ff.
17. Moses calls him "the consecrated one among his brothers." (Deuteronomy 33:16)

ites, and giving contemptuous treatment to the sons of the handmaids Bilhah and Zilpah, whom they called slaves. For these groundless accusations Joseph had to pay dearly. He was himself sold as a slave, because he had charged his brethren with having called the sons of the handmaids slaves, and Potiphar's wife cast her eyes upon Joseph, because he threw the suspicion upon his brethren that they cast their eyes upon the Canaanitish women.[18]

Joseph showed very poor judgment in recounting his dreams to his brothers. In part, the dreams must have compensated for a conscious attitude of inferiority since he was next to the youngest of the twelve and something of a sissy according to legend. The dream of the sheaves (Genesis 37:7) suggests that the superiority of Joseph's harvest, the creative fruits of his life, will be acknowledged.[19] The dream of the sun, moon and stars (Genesis 37:9) is given a reductive, personalistic, "Adlerian" interpretation by his father, an appropriate rebuke for Joseph's naiveté in revealing the dream.

Joseph was sold as a slave into Egypt by his brothers, this being, according to legend, the beginning of the Egyptian bondage, with Joseph the first to be subjected to it.[20] Tertullian says this event is a prefiguration of Christ: "He suffered persecution at the hands of his brethren, and was sold into Egypt on account of the favour of God; just as Christ was sold by Israel—(and therefore) according to the flesh, 'by his brethren'—when He is betrayed by Judas."[21] The image of bondage is itself an aspect of individuation symbolism. One of the effects of encounter with the Self is the ego's loss of will power. It becomes a servant to the Greater Personality.

Joseph's descent into Egypt begins the strange, enduring theme of Israel and Egypt. For Israel, Egypt is alternately a place of security and nourishment and a place of bondage. The pattern repeats itself in the life of Christ. No sooner is the Christ-child born than he must seek refuge in Egypt, later to return and fulfill the pre-established pattern, "out of Egypt have I called my son." (Hosea 11:1; Matthew 2:15) The symbolism of Egypt also plays a prominent role in Gnosticism:

> *Egypt* as a symbol for the material world is very common in Gnosticism (and beyond it). The biblical story of Israel's bondage and liberation lent itself admirably to spiritual interpretation of the type the Gnostics liked. But the biblical story is not the only association which qualified Egypt for its allegorical role. From ancient times Egypt had been regarded as the home of the cult of the dead, and therefore the kingdom of Death; this and other features of Egyptian religion, such as its beast-headed gods and the great

18.   Ginzberg, *Legends of the Bible*, p. 195.
19.   "My sheaf rose to an upright position, and your sheaves formed a ring around my sheaf and bowed down to it." (Genesis 37:7, NAB) The image is of a mandala with the ego at the center, a very dangerous psychic condition characteristic of paranoia.
20.   Ginzberg, *Legends of the Bible*, p. 198.
21.   "An Answer to the Jews," *The Ante-Nicene Fathers,* vol. 3, p. 165.

role of sorcery, inspired the Hebrews and later the Persians with a particular abhorrence and made them see in "Egypt" the embodiment of a demonic principle. The Gnostics then turned this evaluation into their use of Egypt as a symbol for "this world," that is, the world of matter, of ignorance, and of perverse religion: "All ignorant ones (i.e., those lacking gnosis) are 'Egyptians,'" states a Peratic dictum quoted by Hippolytus (V.16.5). . . . Generally the symbols for world can serve also as symbols for the body and vice versa. . . . Regarding "Egypt" the Peratae, to whom it is otherwise "the world," also said that "the body is a little Egypt" (Hippol. V.16.5; similarly the Naassenes, *ibid.* 7.41).[22]

As the "body" or "world," descent into Egypt signifies incarnation or coagulatio,[23] a necessary step in *realization* of the psyche. At an early stage of development Egypt serves as a nourishing, protective mother. Later she becomes bondage and tyranny from which to escape.

Joseph's encounter in Genesis 39 with Potiphar's wife (named Zuleika in legend) is particularly relevant to the symbolism of Egypt. Zulieka corresponds to Egypt and her attempted seduction of Joseph corresponds to the necessary but dangerous involvement of the soul with matter. This is an archetypal theme and hence has parallels in other mythological contexts. An Egyptian folk tale, "The Story of Two Brothers" (ca. 1225 B.C.), describes a similar occasion on which a conscientious younger brother is falsely accused of a proposal of adultery by the wife of his elder brother for whom the younger brother worked. This story ends by the younger brother's castrating himself and the older brother's killing his wife.[24] The pattern appears again in the Greek myth of Hippolytus and Phaedra, in which Hippolytus is killed by the bull from the sea.

Psychologically, these myths picture the naive and innocent young ego being lured by woman, world and matter to relate to her as a fully adult male, not a subordinate. It is a moment of great danger in which criminality and heroism, wisdom and cowardice are inextricably mixed. To succumb to the seduction may lead to death or to maturity. To virtuously flee from the dangerous invitation may also lead to death (Hippolytus) or arrested development (Story of Two Brothers) or fulfillment of one's highest potential (Joseph).

Joseph had a special relation to the unconscious, as indicated by his ability to interpret dreams. The nature of the dreams that he was called upon to understand is also informative. While in prison he was presented with the dreams of the royal cup bearer and the royal baker. One presaged pardon, the other execution, that is, the opposites. Again with Pharaoh's dreams—seven fat cows and seven lean cows, seven fat ears and seven lean ears, feast and famine—he is confronted with the problem of the

22. Jonas, *The Gnostic Religion,* p. 118.
23. See Edinger, *Anatomy of the Psyche,* chapter 4.
24. James B. Pritchard, ed., *The Ancient Near East,* p. 12.

opposites. In order to achieve a conscious relation to the Self one is obliged to integrate the opposites. Since "Yahweh is with Joseph," he must endure the activated opposites. "The paradoxical nature of God . . . tears him asunder into opposites and delivers him over to a seemingly insoluble conflict."[25] To the extent the opposites are reconciled, the inner authority of the Self takes control of one's life. The achievement of that inner authority is indicated by the fact that Joseph becomes the regent of Pharaoh.

Jacob had twelve sons and these twelve, with slight rearrangements, became the ancestors of the twelve tribes of Israel. Briefly under the kingship of David and Solomon the twelve tribes constituted one united kingdom. Following the death of Solomon, ten tribes seceded from the unified kingdom and set up the northern kingdom of Israel. The remaining tribes of Judah and Benjamin constituted the southern kingdom of Judah. Thus twelve is reduced to two. Following the Assyrian conquest of the northern kingdom in 721 B.C., the ten northern tribes were largely dispersed to other regions. They eventually lost their identity and became known as the Ten Lost Tribes of Israel.

This sequence of events is important psychologically. The sacred history of the Jews is an expression of individuation symbolism and its vicissitudes are an expression of analogous events in the psychic development of the individual. The history of Israel from Father Abraham to the single kingdom of Judah can be charted as follows:

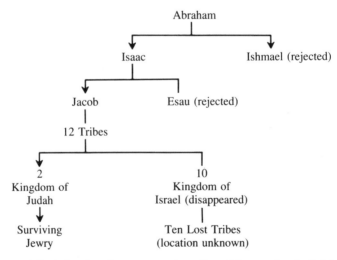

The Self is defined as the center and totality of the psyche. Individuation symbolism is totality symbolism and the biblical history of the Jews is certainly an expression of it. Nonetheless, as the chart shows, a great deal has been left out.

25. Jung, "Answer to Job," *Psychology and Religion,* CW 11, par. 738.

5

Moses and Yahweh: The Exodus

The encounter between Moses and Yahweh is one of the grandest individuation dramas of the Western psyche. Moses as the mediating agent between Yahweh and Israel brings about the redemption of his people from Egyptian bondage and leads the nation to fulfillment of its destiny.

With the aid of depth psychology this sacred story pertaining to the collective history of the Jews can now be understood as applicable to the experience of the individual. The story begins in Exodus 1:

> Then there came to power in Egypt a new king who knew nothing of Joseph. "Look," he said to his subjects, "these people, the sons of Israel, have become so numerous and strong that they are a threat to us. We must be prudent and take steps against their increasing any further, or if war should break out, they might add to the number of our enemies. They might take arms against us and so escape out of the country."
>
> Accordingly they put slave-drivers over the Israelites to wear them down under heavy loads. In this way they built the store-cities of Pithom and Rameses for Pharaoh. But the more they were crushed, the more they increased and spread, and men came to dread the sons of Israel. The Egyptians forced the sons of Israel into slavery, and made their lives unbearable with hard labour, work with clay and with brick, all kinds of work in the field; they forced on them every kind of labour. (verses 8-14)

This describes the psychological state of the individual who is about to be hit with the imperative of individuation. Egypt under the Pharaoh represents a certain stage of psychological development in which the ego, in identification with the superior function, is centered in the principle of power and willful control. The Israelites signify the "other," a new and different standpoint which is emerging from the unconscious and requiring attention. This new factor, allied with the inferior function, is multiplying in a way that threatens the status quo. Therefore repressive measures are instituted; all male Hebrew infants are to be killed. This act of repression against the emerging unconscious content provokes a reaction from the unconscious—the birth of the hero.

The hero is a figure lying midway between the ego and the Self. It can perhaps best be defined as a personification of the urge to individuation. The story of Moses' birth follows closely the characteristic pattern of the myth of the birth of the hero.[1] The chief features of this myth are: 1) the

---

1. See Otto Rank, *The Myth of the Birth of the Hero*, and Jung, *Symbols of Transformation*, CW 5, pars. 493ff.

birth occurs under adverse circumstances; 2) the authorities seek to kill it; 3) the infant is exposed or abandoned, often in water; 4) it is rescued, usually by lowly people, and accompanied by marvels; 5) there is a double set of parents, royal ones and lowly ones. These features all apply to the myth of Moses' birth and refer psychologically to the vicissitudes surrounding the birth of the urge to individuation. The established authority (inner and outer) is always opposed. The individual is thus exposed to the experience of exile or alienation and receives help only from the "lowly" aspects of the psyche which are open to the transpersonal dimension.[2]

The canonical sources say nothing about Moses' youth and education. This gap is filled by legend, one of which is particularly pertinent. According to Philo, Moses quickly surpassed the knowledge of his teachers, "anticipating all their lessons by the excellent natural endowments of his own genius; so that everything in his case appeared to be a recollecting rather than a learning."[3] This echoes Plato's famous idea as expressed in the "Phaedo":

> If we acquired knowledge before we were born and lost it at birth, but afterwards by the use of our senses regained the knowledge which we had previously possessed, would not the process which we call learning really be recovering knowledge which is our own? And should we be right in calling this recollection?[4]

This doctrine is an intuitive, philosophical anticipation of what we now know to be the collective unconscious or objective psyche. Applied to Moses, the process of learning by recollection means that individuation involves the discovery of one's innate wisdom and pattern of being.

The Bible picks up the story of Moses as an adult (at age forty, according to Acts 7:23) when he kills an Egyptian slave-driver. Although reared as Egyptian royalty, Moses belongs to the enslaved race of Hebrews and his allegiance manifests in this impulsive act. It is a primitive, unmediated expression of individuation energy, the initial manifestation of his "call." The murder leads Moses to his personal exodus, his flight into the wilderness where he will meet Yahweh. One might say that the murderous rage which overcame Moses at the sight of the slave-driver's cruelty was Yahweh's wrath which took possession of Moses and acted through him. It was Yahweh who killed the Egyptian and at the same time brought about the circumstances which led to Moses' later encounter with Yahweh.[5]

Those destined for individuation often have the problem of intense energy-eruptions in youth. That was true of Jung.[6] The constellated Self

---

2. Cf. Baucis and Philemon.
3. *The Essential Philo*, p. 195.
4. *Plato I*, p. 362, 75E.
5. According to legend Moses killed the Egyptian slave-driver by pronouncing the Sacred Name. (Ginzberg, *Legends of the Bible*, p. 297)
6. See *C.G. Jung Speaking*, p. 429.

will not endure bondage or constriction. In extremis it will resort to crime. In fact, actual criminality can be considered as perverted individuation. This aspect of Moses is recognized in legend, which asserts that he was of an "originally evil disposition . . . . covetous, haughty, sensual; in short, disfigured by all possible ugly traits." It was through strong will, character and severe discipline that he transformed his disposition into its opposite.[7]

After living many years in exile Moses encounters Yahweh:

Moses was looking after the flock of Jethro, his father-in-law priest of Midian. He led his flock to the far side of the wilderness and came to Horeb, the mountain of God. There the angel of Yahweh appeared to him in the shape of a flame of fire, coming from the middle of a bush. Moses looked; there was the bush blazing but it was not being burnt up. "I must go and look at this strange sight," Moses said, "and see why the bush is not burnt."

Now Yahweh saw him go forward to look, and God called to him from the middle of the bush. "Moses, Moses!" he said. "Here I am," he answered. "Come no nearer," he said. "Take off your shoes, for the place on which you stand is holy ground. I am the God of your father," he said, "the God of Abraham, the God of Isaac and the God of Jacob." At this Moses covered his face, afraid to look at God.

And Yahweh said, "I have seen the miserable state of my people in Egypt. I have heard their appeal to be free of their slave-drivers. Yes, I am well aware of their sufferings. I mean to deliver them out of the hands of the Egyptians and bring them up out of that land to a land rich and broad, a land where milk and honey flow, the home of the Canaanites, the Hittites, the Amorites, the Perizzites; the Hivites and the Jebusites. And now the cry of the sons of Israel has come to me, and I have witnessed the way in which the Egyptians oppress them, so come, I send you to Pharaoh to bring the sons of Israel, my people, out of Egypt."

Moses said to God, "Who am I to go to Pharaoh and bring the sons of Israel out of Egypt?" "I shall be with you," was the answer, "and this is the sign by which you shall know that it is I who have sent you . . . . After you have led the people out of Egypt, you are to offer worship to God on this mountain."

Then Moses said to God, "I am to go, then, to the sons of Israel and say to them, 'The God of your fathers has sent me to you.' But if they ask me what his name is, what am I to tell them?" And God said to Moses, "I Am who I Am. This," he added, "is what you must say to the sons of Israel: 'I Am has sent me to you.'" And God also said to Moses, "You are to say to the sons of Israel: 'Yahweh, the God of your fathers, the God of Abraham, the God of Isaac, and the God of Jacob, has sent me to you.' This is my name for all time; by this name I shall be invoked for all generations to come." (Exodus 3:1-15)

This is a classic image of an encounter with the Self. One or more of

7. Ginzberg, *Legends of the Bible,* pp. 294f.

its various features often come up in dreams. Fire is a frequent synonym for the divine. It pertains to calcinatio[8] and the alchemical symbolism of sulphur[9]; it signifies affects and desirousness, intense libido-manifestations which are not integrated into the ego and hence have a transpersonal quality. According to *The Gospel of Thomas* Jesus said, "He who is near me is near the fire."[10] The unconsuming nature of the fire emphasizes its transpersonal nature. It is desire that is not quenched by personal satisfactions, the desire Jung speaks of as "a thirsting for the eternal."[11] Libido is recognized as transpersonal when the ego succeeds in disidentifying from it. Then what one desires is no longer perceived as *my* pleasure, *my* power, *my* ambition, but rather a task imposed by the Self. A task is what Yahweh imposes on Moses. Considering the symbolism of fire, out of which the assignment comes, Moses' task is *to follow his libido*. The fulfillment of this libido, perceived transpersonally, is his sacred task of Self-realization.

According to legend Moses' encounter with Yahweh in the burning bush was preceded by a dream in which Metatron, the angel of the divine face or presence,[12] conducted him on a tour of the glories of the seven heavens and the horrors of *Gehinnom*.[13] Heaven and hell are the two aspects of transpersonal libido. "Energy is eternal delight,"[14] but also "God has a terrible double aspect: a sea of grace is met by a seething lake of fire."[15]

An important feature of the theophany is the revelation of the divine name. "YHWH" apparently derives from an archaic form of the verb "to be."[16] It thus means "I am who I am" or "I am the One who is." Empirically, the most important characteristic of the Self, which defies precise definition, is that it *exists*. It has effective reality. As Jung puts it, "God is Reality itself."[17]

YHWH, the so-called tetragrammaton, *yod he waw he*, is, significantly, a quaternity. It is also a triad since one of its letters is duplicated.[18] A similar combination of three and four occurs in the sacred emblem associated with the crucifixion of Christ in ecclesiastical art. Attached to the cross is a sign with the letters INRI (*Iesus Nazarenus Rex Iudaeorum*).[19]

8. See Edinger, *Anatomy of the Psyche*, chapter 3.
9. Jung, *Mysterium Coniunctionis*, CW 14, pars. 134ff.
10. *The Nag Hammadi Library*, p. 127.
11. Jung, *Mysterium Coniunctionis*, CW 14, par. 192.
12. See Gustav Davidson, *A Dictionary of Angels*, p. 192.
13. Gaer, *The Lore of the Old Testament*, pp. 148f.
14. William Blake, "The Marriage of Heaven and Hell," plate 4.
15. Jung, "Answer to Job," *Psychology and Religion*, CW 11, par. 733.
16. *Jerusalem Bible*, p. 81, note 3h.
17. "Answer to Job," *Psychology and Religion*, CW 11, par 631.
18. Jung, *Mysterium Coniunctionis*, CW 14, par. 619.
19. A modern tetragrammaton was dreamed by a man with a seminary education. It

Yahweh proceeds to show Moses the signs of his election. Moses casts his staff upon the ground and it becomes a serpent; he picks it up and it becomes a staff. He puts his hand in his bosom; on withdrawal it is leprous. He puts it in again and it is healed. (Exodus 4:2-7) According to legend these signs followed Moses' stubborn refusal to accept his mission and pictured threats to Moses that if he was not obedient he would become a serpent or a leper.[20] This idea has a very important psychological parallel. Once the Self has been constellated, if its imperative is refused by the ego it can turn dangerously negative—provoking perhaps an accident or illness. For example, a middle-aged woman who was fatally ill with cancer dreamed that she possessed something valuable that "the Powers" wanted. They asked her to drop it but she refused. They therefore threw a snake on her back. The snake here represents the call to individuation. If it is not accepted it may attack from behind. In this case the snake on her back can be understood as the woman's fatal cancer.[21]

The same idea is expressed in the mysterious passage of Exodus 4:24. Yahweh had directed Moses to proceed to Egypt. "On the journey, when Moses had halted for the night, Yahweh came to meet with him and tried to kill him." This passage, a perpetual enigma to the commentators, can now be understood as an illustration of the dangerously ambiguous nature of the activated Self. The relativization of the ego involves a sacrifice of the ego which is accompanied by intense anxiety. As Jung says,

> Fear of self-sacrifice lurks deep in every ego, and this fear is often only the precariously controlled demand of the unconscious forces to burst out in full strength. No one who strives for selfhood (individuation) is spared this dangerous passage.[22]

Moses' assignment is to convince Pharoah to release the enslaved Israelites and lead them out of Egypt and into the promised land. Psychologically this means that the psyche is in bondage to the tyrannical power principle symbolized by Pharaoh. A lesser authority (the power-driven ego) is functioning in place of the Self (Yahweh). Once the Self is activated, individuation must proceed. If the ego does not cooperate it will be hit with increasing disturbances. Thus come about the ten plagues of Egypt.

1. *The waters of Egypt are turned into blood.* Such an image suggests the welling up of violent affects. In one of the last plagues of the

---

consisted of the letters IMZE. The dreamer's first association was to the revelation of the divine name in Exodus 3:14: "I am who I am." He also observed that, read from left to right as in Hebrew, EZMI is reminiscent of Christ's saying in Matthew 11:30, "My yoke is easy and my burden light."

20. Ginzberg, *Legends of the Bible,* p. 318.
21. I am indebted to Philip Zabriskie for this dream.
22. "Psychological Commentary on 'The Tibetan Book of the Dead,'" *Psychology and Religion,* CW 11, par. 849.

Apocalypse the sea is turned to blood. (Revelation 16:3) In alchemy blood is a synonym for the prima materia.[23] On the eve of World War I Jung had visions of a sea of blood engulfing Europe.[24] Again, when he began his deliberate confrontation with the unconscious, in his fantasy blood spurted out of a hole in the earth.[25] A dangerous activation of the unconscious is indicated, threatening hemorrhage of the vital life essence.

2. *The plague of frogs.* In their negative aspect frogs represent the primordial "swamp level" of the psyche—primitive, slimy, cold-blooded contents which invade consciousness. In Revelation frogs signify unclean spirits coming "out of the mouth of the dragon, and out of the mouth of the beast, and out of the mouth of the false prophet." (Revelation 16:13, AV)

3. and 4. *The plague of mosquitos and the plague of gadflies.* These images picture the activated unconscious as provoking an irritable, restless state of agitation, with multiple bites and random itchings.

5. *Death of all Egyptian livestock.* The death of a large animal (horse or cow) in a dream is a matter of grave concern. It means that one's major instinctual foundation has been lost and it may harbinger physical illness or even death.

6. *The plague of boils.* In dreams boils signify festering unconscious complexes requiring drainage (abreaction).

7. *The plague of hail.* Ice dreams refer to the frozen state of the feeling life in which warm and living impulses are congealed by the power motive. In Dante's imagery, Lucifer resides in the depths of hell embedded in ice.[26]

8. *The plague of locusts.* Invasion by insects is an image of being overrun by a multiplicity of elementary units. It indicates a fragmentation of the psyche on an elemental level and often means a toxic disorder of the autonomic nervous system, as for example in delirium tremens. It is an ominous image in dreams.

9. *The plague of darkness.* Now the light of consciousness is completely eclipsed. This would correspond to dreams of being blind.

10. *Death of the Egyptian first-born.* "And at midnight Yahweh struck down all the first-born in the land of Egypt: the first-born of Pharaoh, heir to the throne, the first-born of the prisoner in his dungeon, and the first-born of all the cattle." (Exodus 12:25)

The Israelites are spared through the sacrifice of the paschal lamb, "without blemish," whose blood is daubed on the doorposts and lintel of each Hebrew dwelling. If this rite is performed, Yahweh promises, "The blood shall serve to mark the houses that you live in. When I see the blood I will pass over you and you shall escape the destroying plague." (Exodus 12:13)

---

23. See Jung, *Psychology and Alchemy,* CW 12, pars. 425f.
24. *Memories, Dreams, Reflections,* p. 175.
25. Ibid., p. 179.
26. Dante, *The Divine Comedy,* Inferno, canto 34.

The events of Passover night present an awesome image of an encounter with the activated Self. Yahweh stalks the streets at midnight, slaughtering every first-born creature that he meets, while the Jews huddle in their homes hoping their apotropaic rites will spare them. Yahweh must have his bloody sacrifice. Those who know Yahweh (the Israelites) can deliberately offer him a lamb and thereby be spared the greater price. The Egyptians, who don't know Yahweh, have no means of mitigating his demand. The full brunt of the divine imperative falls on them.

Passover symbolism repeats itself in a new context with the death of Christ. He takes upon himself the fate of the Egyptian first-born and of the paschal lamb. Just as the first-born son of Pharaoh must be sacrificed to achieve release of the Israelites from bondage, so Christ, the first-born son of Yahweh, must be offered up like another paschal lamb as a bloody sacrifice for man's spiritual salvation. As Jung points out, Christ's blood becomes another apotropaic amulet:

> Jesus became the tutelary image or amulet against the archetypal powers that threatened to possess everyone. The glad tidings announced: "It has happened, but it will not happen to you inasmuch as you believe in Jesus Christ, the son of God!" Yet it could and it can and it will happen to everyone in whom the Christian dominant has decayed.[27]

The underlying idea is that the first-born belongs to Yahweh. "Consecrate all the first-born to me, the first issue of every womb, among the sons of Israel. Whether man or beast, this is mine." (Exodus 13:2) This notion is not confined to ancient Israel. Frazer documents many other examples,[28] so evidently it is archetypal. What does it mean? First-born children do in fact carry a quality of specialness—in their own mind, in the minds of their parents and even in the view of society (witness the law of primogeniture). This sense of specialness may be augmented by the parental projection of the Self as divine child onto the first-born. Interpreted subjectively, the first-born refers to the ego in its once-born state, that is, unconsciously identified with the Self. With the sacrifice of the first-born ego, which is required for the birth of the Self into consciousness, the second-born state is realized.

The exodus begins with the miracle of the Red Sea crossing (Exodus 14), a rite of exit occurring at the threshold between Egyptian bondage and theophany in the wilderness. It is a transition to a new level of consciousness, a solutio image which I discuss elsewhere.[29] What follows is forty years of desert wandering before the Promised Land is reached. This corresponds to the prolonged dealing with the unconscious—the chaos or prima materia—that is required following an irrevocable commitment to

27. *Psychology and Alchemy,* CW 12, par. 4.
28. James G. Frazer, *The Golden Bough,* part 3, "The Dying God," pp. 171ff.
29. See Edinger, *Anatomy of the Psyche,* pp. 71f.

individuation. Forty days or years is the length of the alchemical opus[30] and forty days is the traditional time required for the Egyptian embalming process (Genesis 50:3), that is, the transition between personal, temporal existence (ego) and eternal, archetypal life (Self). Thus the forty years of wandering in the wilderness signify a *nekyia* or night journey from the ego-bound existence of Egypt to the transpersonal life of the Promised Land.

The account of the wilderness wandering provides us with a whole series of profound symbolic images pertaining to the individuation process. Immediately upon departure, agencies of divine guidance make their appearance. "Yahweh went before them, by day in the form of a pillar of cloud to show them the way, and by night in the form of a pillar of fire to give them light." (Exodus 13:21) This image is reminiscent of a passage in the *I Ching:*

> Only a strong man can stand up to his fate, for his inner security enables him to endure to the end. This strength shows itself in uncompromising truthfulness (with himself). It is only when we have the courage to face things exactly as they are, without any sort of self-deception or illusion, that *a light will develop out of events,* by which the path to success may be recognized.[31]

The light that develops out of events (both inner and outer) is only visible when the ego is in a state of emptiness, that is, in the wilderness. Through the window of a brightly lighted house at night one cannot see the stars. Turn off the light and they come into view. As Eckhart says,

> By keeping thyself empty and bare . . . and giving up thyself to this darkness and ignorance without turning back, thou mayest well win that which is all things. . . . Of this barrenness it is written in Hosea: "I will lead my friend into the desert and will speak to her in her heart." (2:14) The genuine Word of eternity is spoken only in eternity, where man is a desert and alien to himself and multiplicity.[32]

In fact, Eckhart says, God *has* to fill whatever emptiness he finds.

> God is bound to act, to pour himself out (into thee) as soon as ever he shall find thee ready . . . finding thee ready he is obliged to act, to overflow into thee; just as the sun must needs burst forth when the air is bright and clear, and is unable to contain itself.[33]

These passages describe the way the ego discovers the guidance of the Self. The ego must be in a humbled state of darkness and need before it

30. Jung, *Mysterium Coniunctionis,* CW 14, par. 77 and note 215.
31. *The I Ching or Book of Changes,* p. 25, my italics.
32. *Meister Eckhart,* vol. 1, p. 23.
33. Ibid.

can perceive the dim light of the transpersonal psyche. Cardinal Newman describes this experience in his poem "Lead, Kindly Light":

> Lead, kindly Light, amid the encircling gloom,
>   Lead Thou me on!
> The night is dark, and I am far from home—
>   Lead Thou me on!
> Keep Thou my feet; I do not ask to see
>   The distant scene—one step enough for me.
> I was not ever thus, nor prayed that Thou
>   Shouldst lead me on.
> I loved to choose and see my path; but now
>   Lead Thou me on!
> I loved the garish day, and, spite of fears,
>   Pride ruled my will: remember not past years.
> So long Thy power hath blessed me, sure it still
>   Will lead me on,
> O'er moor and fen, o'er crag and torrent, till
>   The night is gone;
> And with the morn those angel faces smile
> Which I have loved long since, and lost awhile.[34]

A major source of the "kindly light" is one's dreams, and a strong incentive to study one's dreams is to be in distress, in the grip of a painful problem. Thus the guiding light manifests in the wilderness.

The first stop in the desert was Marah (meaning bitterness) where the water was too bitter to drink and the people grumbled. (Exodus 15:23,24) Bitterness is commonly encountered in psychotherapy. An infallible indicator of an unconscious infantile complex is the presence of bitterness and resentment. According to Simonian Gnosis the bitterness of the Exodus is a feature of fleshly existence which is transformed by the Logos.

> The title of the second book of Moses is Exodus. All that are born must pass through the Red Sea—by Red Sea he means blood—and come to the desert where they must drink bitter water, for bitter is the water beyond the Red Sea and this indicates our life of toil and bitterness. Yet transformed by Moses, that is by the Logos, this bitterness is made sweet.[35]

In alchemy, bitterness is an aspect of the prima materia. Ripley says, "Each thing in its first matter is corrupt and bitter."[36] Bitterness belongs to the symbolism of salt. Jung writes,

> The most outstanding properties of salt are bitterness and wisdom. . . . The factor common to both, however incommensurable the two ideas may seem, is, psychologically, the function of *feeling*. Tears, sorrow, and disappoint-

---

34. W.A. Briggs and W.R. Benét, eds., *Great Poems of the English Language*, p. 644.
35. Hippolytus, "Refutation of All Heresies," quoted by Hugo Rahner, *Greek Myths and Christian Mystery*, p. 210.
36. Quoted by Jung, *Mysterium Coniunctionis*, CW 14, par. 246.

ment are bitter, but wisdom is the comforter in all psychic suffering. Indeed, bitterness and wisdom form a pair of alternatives: where there is bitterness wisdom is lacking, and where wisdom is there can be no bitterness. Salt, as the carrier of this fateful alternative, is co-ordinated with the nature of woman.[37]

It seems appropriate therefore that the journey to the Promised Land, which is psychologically equivalent to the Philosophers' Stone of the alchemists, should begin with bitterness. Indeed there was much bitterness on the part of the Israelites throughout their wandering because of the loss of their Egyptian comforts.

As they proceeded on their way a daily supply of food was provided by Yahweh, meat in the evening and bread in the morning, but only enough for one day. If it was saved for the following day, "it had maggots and smelt foul." (Exodus 16:20) Under the condition of divine guidance, as pertains during an individual's wandering in the wilderness, one is required to live only in the immediate present—one day at a time. Christ expresses a similar idea. "Do not say, 'what are we to eat? What are we to drink? How are we to be clothed?' . . . Your heavenly Father knows you need them all." (Matthew 6:31-32) Jung puts it psychologically:

> The great thing is now and here, this is the eternal moment, and if you do not realize it, you have missed the best part of life, you have missed the realization that you were once the carrier of a life contained between the poles of an unimaginable future and an unimaginably remote past. Millions of years and untold millions of ancestors have worked up to this moment, and you are the fulfillment of this moment. Anything that is past is no longer reality, anything that will be is not yet reality, reality is now. To look at life as a mere preparation for things to come is as if you could not enjoy your meal while it was hot.
>
> That is the disease really of our time, everybody is chiefly concerned about the future; one admits that now things are very bad, so all the more one tries to jump out of them, and therefore they never improve. One should take each moment as the eternal moment, as if nothing were ever going to change, not anticipating a faraway future. For the future always grows out of that which *is,* and it cannot be sound if it grows in a morbid soil; if we are morbid and don't feel this here and now, then we naturally will build up a sickly future. We have seen that in actual historical conditions; things are so bad at present because everybody lived in anticipation of something to come, one always expected the golden age, so things got worse and worse. Therefore in psychology, in the life of the individual, it is of the greatest importance that we never think of it as merely now, with the hope of something coming in the future. You can be sure it will never come when you think like that. You must live life in such a spirit that you make in every moment the best of the possibilities.[38]

37. Ibid., par. 330.
38. *Interpretation of Visions,* vol. 6, pp. 185f.

6

Theophany in the Wilderness

The culmination of the wilderness experience is the divine revelation on Mount Sinai in which Yahweh establishes his covenant with Israel and lays down the elaborate procedure for worshiping him. (Exodus 19–Leviticus 27) "If you obey my voice and hold fast to my covenant, you of all nations shall be my very own for all the earth is mine. I will count you a kingdom of priests, a consecrated nation." (Exodus 15:5-6)

Considered psychologically, it is characteristic that the wilderness and revelation be linked. Jung writes,

> Everyone who becomes conscious of even a fraction of his unconscious gets outside his own time and social stratum into a kind of solitude . . . . But only there is it possible to meet the "god of salvation." Light is manifest in the darkness, and out of danger the rescue comes. In his sermon on Luke 19:12 Meister Eckhart says: "And who can be nobler than the man who is born half of the highest and best the world has to offer, and half of the innermost ground of God's nature and God's loneliness? Therefore the Lord speaks in the prophet Hosea: I will lead the noble souls into the wilderness, and speak into their hearts. One with the One, One from the One, and in the One itself the One, eternally!"[1]

It was ordained on Sinai that the center of Yahweh-worship would be the tabernacle or tent of meeting (where Yahweh met man) containing the sacred ark of the covenant, the very throne of Yahweh. It must be built to Yahweh's rigid specifications:

> You are to make me an ark of acacia wood two and a half cubits long, one and a half cubits wide, one and a half cubits high. You are to plate it, inside and out, with pure gold, and decorate it all round with gold moulding. You will cast four gold rings for the ark and fix them to its four supports: two rings on one side and two rings on the other. You will also make shafts of acacia wood plated with gold and pass the shafts through the rings on the sides of the ark, to carry the ark by these. The shafts must remain in the rings of the ark and not be withdrawn. Inside the ark you will place the Testimony that I will give you.
>
> Further, you are to make a throne of mercy, of pure gold, two and a half cubits long, and one and a half cubits wide. For the two ends of this throne of mercy you are to make two golden cherubs; you are to make them of beaten gold. Make the first cherub for one end and the second for the other, and fasten them to the two ends of the throne of mercy so that they make one piece with it. The cherubs are to have their wings spread upwards so that they overshadow the throne of mercy. They must face one another, their

1. *Mysterium Coniunctionis*, CW 14, par. 258.

faces towards the throne of mercy. You must place the throne of mercy on the top of the ark. Inside the ark you must place the Testimony that I shall give you. There I shall come to meet you; there, from between the two cherubs that are on the ark of the Testimony, I shall give you all my commands for the sons of Israel. (Exodus 25:10-22)

The ark of the covenant has a number of interesting features. The four gold rings and its design to be carried by four men connect it with quaternity symbolism. It is carried by four, just as the divine chariot in Ezekiel's vision (Ezekiel 1) is supported by four and just as the throne of Christ is supported by the pillars of the four evangelists in medieval representations. The two cherubs, like guardian spirits of the threshold, express the psychological fact that the *numinosum* manifests between the opposites.

Perhaps most interesting is the numerical proportion of the ark's dimensions. It is one and one-half cubits wide and two and one-half cubits long, the proportion 3:5. This is remarkably close to the Golden Section of the Greeks, which is done by bisecting a line in such a way that the lesser part is to the greater part as the greater part is to the whole. If a line of length c is bisected into a shorter part a and a longer part b, the proportion will be $a/b = b/c$; b is the so-called Golden Mean. Applying this formula to the proportions of the ark of the covenant, where $a = 3$, $b = 5$, $c = 8$ $(3+5)$, then

$$a/b = \frac{3}{5} = .6$$

$$b/c = \frac{5}{8} = .625$$

The dimensions of the ark of the covenant thus correspond almost exactly to the Golden Section of the Greeks. Aristotle used the image of the mean to define the nature of virtue. He writes,

Moral virtue is a mean. It is a mean between two vices, the one involving excess, the other deficiency. It is such because its character is to aim at what is intermediate in passions and in actions. . . . Hence also it is no easy task to be good. For in everything it is no easy task to find the middle, e.g., to find the middle of a circle is not for everyone but for him who knows.[2]

I understand this golden proportion, so highly valued by the Greeks and enshrined in the structure of the ark of the covenant, to be a formula for the reconciliation of the opposites and for the ego's relation to the Self (the lesser to the whole).[3]

The ark of the covenant is housed in the tabernacle, which is also built to precise specifications. (Exodus 26) Although there is some ambiguity

2. *Nichomachean Ethics,* 1109a, *The Basic Works of Aristotle,* p. 963.
3. In practical terms this refers to the process of analogy. *Analogia* means proportion in Greek.

Artist's representation of the ark of the covenant.
(From *Aid to Bible Understanding,* p. 21)

about the dimensions, the usual understanding is that the tabernacle was 30 cubits long, 10 cubits wide and 10 cubits high:

> The inclosure thus constructed was next divided into two apartments, separated by a "veil" . . . . The outer of these chambers, or "holy place," was, as usually computed, 20 cubits long by 10 broad; the inner, or "most holy place," was 10 cubits square.[4]

The "Holy of Holies" which contains the ark of the covenant is thus a cube $10 \times 10 \times 10$ cubits.

The dimensions of the tabernacle again express the Golden Section—1:2 = 2:4 (3 + 1). The cube is granted special significance as the shape of the Holy of Holies. In Plato the cube signifies the element earth.[5] According to Lü Pu-wei, "Heaven's way is round, earth's way is square."[6] In dreams a cube is often a symbol of the Self.[7] The number ten or decad is also given sacred significance in the dimensions of the "Holy of Holies." This corresponds to a similar valuation by the Greeks. The Pythagorean Tetrac-

---

4. *International Standard Bible Encyclopaedia,* vol. 4, p. 2890.
5. *Timaeus,* 55d.
6. Quoted by Jung, "A Psychological Approach to the Dogma of the Trinity," *Psychology and Religion,* CW 11, par. 247, note 7.
7. See Jung, *Alchemical Studies,* CW 13, par. 348, note 25, and par. 349.

tys $(1+2+3+4=10)$ was a most sacred amulet. Aristotle tells us that "as the number 10 is thought to be perfect [*teleion*] and to comprise the whole nature of numbers, they say that the bodies which move through the heavens are ten, but as the visible bodies are only nine, to meet this they invent a tenth—the 'counter-earth.'"[8] The Pythagoreans set up a table of ten principles arranged as ten pairs of opposites.[9] Jewish tradition perpetuated the sacredness of the number ten in many ways, notably in the ten Sephiroth of the Kabbala.

The image of the tabernacle housing the divine presence is directly relevant to psychology. Jung uses this image in a letter:

> God wants to be born in the flame of man's consciousness, leaping ever higher. And what if this has no roots in the earth? If it is not a house of stone where the fire of God can dwell, but a wretched straw hut that flares up and vanishes? Could God then be born? One must be able to suffer God. That is the supreme task for the carrier of ideas. He must be the advocate of the earth. God will take care of himself. My inner principle is: Deus *et* homo. God needs man in order to become conscious, just as he needs limitations in time and space. Let us therefore be for him limitation in time and space, an earthly tabernacle.[10]

The outer chamber of the tabernacle contained the table of "show bread," the altar of incense and the lampstand. (Exodus 40:22-27) The latter is an obvious reference to the divine nature of light (consciousness). The offerings of "show bread" and incense are parts of the larger system of ritual sacrifice, which is the heart of ancient Yahweh-worship and profoundly significant for individual psychology.

Sacrifice to the gods is a universal feature of primitive religion and thereby demonstrates its archetypal nature. It is an instinctual urge to establish relations between the ego and the Self. The sacrificial ritual of ancient Israel is a particularly rich and differentiated example of this archetypal pattern. The elements of the ritual are these: A perfect, unblemished victim is selected which is then slaughtered in a prescribed manner—a bloody event that is numinous to behold. There may be a blood libation poured out to Yahweh. The flesh of the victim is divided into two portions. Yahweh's portion is burned whereby it ascends to heaven in the smoke. The human portion is consumed by the worshipers in a ritual meal. If the sacrifice is a holocaust or "whole offering" it is burned in its entirety and Yahweh gets it all.

For purposes of discussion we can distinguish four major ideas in ancient sacrificial ritual. The ancients were aware of a transpersonal agency (God) which affects human affairs. By sacrifice they intended 1) to offer

---

8. "Metaphysics," 986a, *The Basic Works of Aristotle*, p. 698.
9. Ibid.
10. *C.G. Jung Letters*, vol. 1, pp. 65f.

payment to God in thanksgiving for blessings received or evils averted, a bribe operating on the principle of *do ut des* (I give in order that you may give). A subset of 1) but important enough to warrant a separate category is 2), those sacrifices intended as reparation or *atonement* for sin. Another idea behind sacrifice is 3), the *feeding of God.* The smoke and sweet savor that ascends to heaven was originally thought to be literally consumed and relished by God. And finally 4), there is a *feeding of man* through the communion meal. The worshipers eat the flesh of the consecrated victim who belongs to God. Thus the participants are, in effect, *feeding off God.* The consequence is a sense of communion between God and man and among men. These basic ideas underlying ritual sacrifice are very important for the understanding of the ego's relation to the Self. Let us consider them each in turn.

1. *Sacrifice as payment.* The primitive mind is directly aware by experiential certainty that a transpersonal factor influences human existence. Modern man also reaches this awareness as a result of an encounter with the unconscious which activates the deeper layers of the psyche. With this awareness comes the realization that the "other" in oneself requires attention and consideration. One's own well-being is linked to the "other." This attention given to the unconscious is equivalent to the primitive idea of sacrifice as payment.

2. *Sacrifice as atonement for sin.* When the ego violates the requirements of totality, or when it claims for itself the prerogatives of the Self, it is in a state of psychological "sin" and will bring down on its own head consequences that may be experienced as punitive. This is not to say that we are dealing with a moral issue necessarily. If one violates the law of gravity one falls; so it is if one violates a law of the psyche. Restitution is required for such mistakes to restore the balance.[11]

3. *Sacrifice as the feeding of God.* The Self requires the continual attention of the ego in order to come into manifest existence. It needs to be "fed" by a religious attitude, which Jung defines as "the attitude peculiar to a consciousness which has been changed by experience of the *numinosum.*"[12]

4. *Sacrifice as a feeding off God.* Not only is the Self nourished by the careful consideration it receives from the ego but the ego is also fed by its connection to the Self. We cannot exist on our own. Every moment and every act is allowed to exist only through the support and cooperation of the unconscious. The realization of this fact is one of the sources of the religious attitude.

In the Mosaic ritual an animal is offered in sacrifice. Psychologically an animal refers to instinctual libido or desirousness. In order to be avail-

---

11.   See Edinger, *Ego and Archetype,* pp. 55f.
12.   "Psychology and Religion," *Psychology and Religion,* CW 11, par. 9.

able for sacrifice such desirousness must be first of all under the control
of the ego. One must achieve the ability to renounce what one desires. In
a sense the whole Mosaic law is an instrument to help man gain control
of his instinctual desirousness. As the ego develops it begins to experience
the energies of instinct and desire as its own responsibility. As an inner
"spirit" figure crystallizes, a counterpole to mere "nature," the ego begins
to feel guilty for its unbridled desirousness. This is not just a consequence
of the superego,[13] but also derives from the Self which is yearning for
transformation. As the ego sacrifices desirousness it is at the same time
contributing to the transformation and humanization of God.[14]

The Ten Commandments

In addition to specifying the details of ritual sacrifice, the chief content of
the theophany on Sinai is the Decalogue (Exodus 20 and Deuteronomy 5).
With the advent of depth psychology the time has come to consider this
cornerstone of the Western psyche from the psychological rather than the
literal standpoint. We must now ask: What do the ten commandments mean
psychologically?

1. *You shall have no gods except me.* This is the origin of monotheism
and of supreme importance psychologically. It announces the fact that the
Self is a unity and not a multiplicity.[15] This is the basis of the responsibility
and integrity of the individual, for only an integer is capable of integrity.
Responsible consciousness can be carried only by a centered personality
which is an indivisible (individual) unity. Psychopathology offers us many
examples of psychic dissociation in which a unified center is missing,
notably chronic alcoholism and drug addiction.

2. *You shall not make yourself a carved image or any likeness of anything in heaven above or on earth beneath or in the waters under the
earth; you shall not bow down to them or serve them.* Two ideas are
intermixed here: the making of images (imagination) and idolatry. For
ancient man the making of an image must have had such a powerful effect
on the unconscious that the image immediately became an idol, evoking
projection of divine or magical powers. Psychologically, idolatry means
the worship of one archetypal aspect or power of the unconscious at the
expense of the whole. The ego almost always develops out of an initial
state of idolatry. One psychic function is granted preeminence and the
value of the whole is carried by that one function, which, in effect,
becomes an idol. As Jung says, "Mephistopheles is the diabolical aspect
of every psychic function that has broken loose from the hierarchy of the

13. "The superego is a necessary and unavoidable substitute for the experience of the
 self." (Jung, "Transformation Symbolism in the Mass," ibid., par. 394)
14. For an excellent discussion of the psychology of sacrifice, see ibid., pars. 387ff.
15. Empirically the Self is *both* unity and multiplicity, or better, unified multiplicity.

total psyche and now enjoys independence and absolute power."[16] This commandment forbids idolatry, that is, the worship of a part for the whole.

In addition to idolatry, the commandment also forbids image-making. This means that imagination itself is interdicted and no spontaneous congress with the unconscious is allowed. Thus was erected a psychic incest taboo. Evidently the danger of succumbing to the regressive pull of the unconscious is so great at that stage of ego development that fantasy and all the powers of the imagination must be suppressed. As part of nature the imagination was linked with the fertility rites and the religion of the Great Mother which the spiritual religion of Yahweh was replacing. Modern individuals, in an effort to unite the opposites which Yahwehism separated, must have a different attitude to imagination and to image-making. Just as they strive to reconcile the masculine and feminine principles which Yahweh sundered, so they seek to combine the unitary principle of the spirit with the multiple facets of the creative imagination as exemplified by ancient polytheism.

3. *You shall not utter the name of Yahweh your God to misuse it, for Yahweh will not leave unpunished the man who utters his name to misuse it.* This apparently refers to the false swearing of an oath in which one invokes God's name to guarantee the truth of a statement. Zedekiah is a terrible example of violation of this commandment. (2 Chronicles 36:13) Psychologically, one can understand an oath invoking the name of God to refer to the claim that one is in harmony with the Self, the presumptuous assumption that one is operating out of wholeness. This is a dangerous disregard for the reality of the shadow and of the "other" in the unconscious. Christ revises this commandment in Matthew 5:33-37.

> You have learnt how it was said to our ancestors: *You must not break your oath, but must fulfil your oaths to the Lord.* But I say this to you: do not swear at all . . . . All you need say is "Yes" if you mean yes, "No" if you mean no; anything more than this comes from the evil one.

4. *Observe the sabbath day and keep it holy, as Yahweh your God has commanded you. For six days you shall labor and do all your work, but the seventh day is a sabbath for Yahweh your God. . . . For in six days Yahweh made the heavens and the earth and the sea and all that these hold, but on the seventh day he rested; that is why Yahweh has blessed the sabbath day and made it sacred.* The seven-day week, having no astronomical basis, is a purely arbitrary invention. In other words it is a projection of a psychic image. Ancient Rome had an eight-day cycle, but the seven-day week became established throughout the empire about the beginning of our era, perhaps influenced by the seven-day week of the Jews. The wavering between seven and eight is analogous to that between three and

16. *Psychology and Alchemy,* CW 12, par. 88.

four and is characteristic of individuation symbolism.[17] Perhaps it is significant that our era opted for the dynamic number seven rather than the static number eight. The seven-day week became the temporal embodiment of the seven planetary deities, each having a sacred day: Sunday (Sun), Monday (Moon), Tuesday (Mars), Wednesday (Mercury), Thursday (Jupiter), Friday (Venus), Saturday (Saturn). The fact that the Jewish sabbath fell on Saturday led to the idea of certain Gnostics that Yahweh was synonymous with Saturn.

In ancient Israel wilful sabbath-breaking was a capital offense. (Numbers 15:32-36) The day itself was a container for the sacred essence of Yahweh, a temporal version of the ark of the covenant. This institution established decisively the prerogatives of the sacred, transpersonal dimension of the psyche, over and against secular pursuits. The word "sabbath" means to cease or to rest. According to the usual interpretation, the sabbath was meant as a blessing to man. However, Jastrow has demonstrated that

> the Hebrew Sabbath was originally a day of propitiation like the Babylonian *sabatum* (American Journal of Theology, II, 312-52). He argues that the restrictive measures in the Hebrew laws for the observance of the Sabbath arose from the original conception of the Sabbath as an unfavorable day, a day in which the anger of Yahweh might flash forth against men.[18]

Although orthodox commentators object to this observation, the practice of executing those who declined the blessing of the sabbath does lend itself to the idea that the anger of Yahweh did "flash forth against men" on that day.

Christ took a more lenient attitude toward the sabbath, claiming that "the sabbath was made for man, not man for the sabbath" (Mark 2:27); and that on the sabbath, "My Father goes on working and so do I" (John 5:17). The latter is a shocking remark to be made in ancient Israel and the Pharisees were properly shocked. Such a statement can only be made by one who has an *individual* relation to the Self. For such a person the numinous content of the sabbath has been internalized. What is a crime in a collective setting is permissible to the individual, *providing he has sufficient consciousness.* According to an uncanonical source, Christ, seeing a man working on the sabbath, said to him: "Man, if indeed thou knowest what thou doest, thou art blessed: but if thou knowest not, thou art cursed, and a transgressor of the law."[19] Jung says about this saying, "It might well be the motto for a new morality."[20]

    5. *Honor your father and your mother, as Yahweh your God has com-*

---

17. See Jung, "A Psychological Approach to the Dogma of the Trinity," *Psychology and Religion,* CW 11, pars. 243ff.

18. *International Standard Bible Encyclopaedia,* vol. 4, p. 2630.

19. M.R. James, *The Apocryphal New Testament,* p. 33.

20. "A Psychological Approach to the Dogma of the Trinity," *Psychology and Religion,* CW 11, par. 291.

manded you, so that you may have long life and may prosper in the land that Yahweh your God gives to you. Understood psychologically, this commandment enjoins respect for the archetypal images of father and mother wherever they may manifest. They connect us with our roots and origins and remind the ego that it is only a twig on the tree of life. Yahweh indicates that his power stands behind these images and connection with them is connection with life and prosperity. Dependent neurotics may misuse this passage to justify regressive dependence on their personal parents.

6. *You shall not kill.* Dreams of killing usually refer to repression, the denial of the right of a psychic content to exist in consciousness. While necessary and inevitable in the early stages of development, in the process of individuation it is a crime against wholeness and is appropriately accompanied by guilt. Occasionally dreams of killing have another meaning. They then have the quality of a necessary crime which is at the same time a sacrifice. Jung's dream of killing Siegfried belongs to this category.[21]

7. *You shall not commit adultery.* What Yahweh means by adultery is indicated in Jeremiah 13:27, where he berates Israel for her whoredom with false gods: "Oh! Your adulteries, your shrieks of pleasure, your vile prostitution! On the hills, in the countryside, I have seen your abominations. Woe to you, Jerusalem, unclean still! How much longer will you go on like this?"

According to its etymology, adultery is a process of adulterating (*adulterare* from *ad* + *alter,* other, different) and means to mix or dilute a valuable material with something spurious or inferior. It is a crime against the marriage contract. Psychologically this refers to a violation of the coniunctio. Adultery is possible only when one is married, that is, after one has experienced the marriage of the opposites and is committed to the realization of wholeness. Psychological adultery is a violation of one's highest perceived value, a regressive back-sliding.

8. *You shall not steal.* This commandment is based on the distinction between what belongs to oneself and what belongs to another. Psychologically this is the distinction between the ego and the non-ego or Self. Dreams of stealing often refer to the ego's appropriation of what does not belong to it, a presumptuous identification with the Self which initiates punitive action from the Self. However, sometimes a dream of stealing falls into the category of a necessary crime. According to myth (Garden of Eden, Prometheus, etc.) the beginning of ego consciousness is based on theft.[22]

9. *You shall not bear false witness against your neighbor.* The neighbor signifies the shadow. Man is required to be honest about the shadow. False

21. *Memories, Dreams, Reflections,* p. 180.
22. See Edinger, *Ego and Archetype,* pp. 16ff.

witness would deny its existence by projecting it. The breaker of this commandment says, "I am good. The source of evil is to be found in others, not me." Thus the psychological atmosphere is polluted by false witness. This is another commandment that is necessarily broken in the early phases of ego development. In the beginning the shadow must be denied in order to allow the ego to crystallize.[23]

10. *You shall not covet your neighbor's wife, you shall not set your heart on his house, his field, his servant—man or woman—his ox, his donkey or anything that is his.* This commandment is the crown of the Decalogue. It not only forbids taking what is not yours but also forbids *wanting* what is not yours. It radically challenges the basic propensity of the natural man, desirousness itself. The effect is to split the psyche into two poles, nature and spirit, which is a prerequisite for consciousness. Since all men are desirous—that being the nature of the primordial psyche—this commandment makes all men sinners, in conflict and thus in need of redemption. The Apostle Paul expresses it trenchantly:

> I should not have known what sin was except for the Law. I should not for instance have known what it means to covet if the Law had not said *You shall not covet*. But it was this commandment that sin took advantage of to produce all kinds of covetousness in me, for when there is no Law, sin is dead.
>
> Once, when there was no Law, I was alive; but when the commandment came, sin came to Life and I died: the commandment was meant to lead me to life but it turned out to mean death for me, because sin took advantage of the commandment to mislead me, and so sin, through that commandment, killed me. (Romans 7:7-11)

The commandment against sin (desirousness) creates sin by the separation of the opposites.[24] The commandment establishes a spiritual counterpole to nature whereby the latter can be judged as bad.

The psychological implications of this commandment are immense. It deposits in the human psyche the conflict of the opposites which belong to God. This is the beginning of God's incarnation in man. Man is required to transform through consciousness the primal energies that flow through God unchecked. God permits himself jealousy, desirousness, violence and slaughter but for man these are sin. The ten commandments thus become an instrument for the transformation of God incarnated in man.

---

23. See Edinger, *The Living Psyche,* section 84.
24. See Edinger, *Anatomy of the Psyche,* chapter 7.

7

Joshua, Gideon, Samson, Ruth

Joshua

The Promised Land was a gift from Yahweh to the Israelites and yet it had to be conquered. It was not a gift freely given which the receiver may accept or decline. It was a command to take the land of Canaan. Those who declined were destroyed. (Numbers 14:37)

Psychologically the Promised Land can be seen as an area of the unconscious which the imperative of individuation requires to be assimilated by the ego. This area is specifically assigned to the ego by the Self but still must be conquered by the efforts of the ego. The land is not vacant but occupied. It is studded with fortified cities; that is, it contains defended unconscious complexes which must be resolved before it can be assimilated. Joshua's conquest of Canaan is a symbolic picture of how to deal with the unconscious and its hostile complexes under certain circumstances.

Yahweh directs Joshua to enter Canaan and take possession of it:

> Be strong and stand firm, for you are the man to give this people possession of the land that I swore to their fathers I would give to them. Only be strong and stand firm and be careful to keep all the Law which my servant Moses laid on you . . . . Have the book of this Law always on your lips; meditate on it day and night, so that you may carefully keep everything that is written in it. Then you will prosper in your dealings, then you will have success . . . . for go where you will, Yahweh your God is with you. (Joshua 1:6-9)

The growth urge summons the ego to proceed and cautions it to follow dutifully the dictates of one's inner law, the innate design of one's being; then the totality of the psyche will cooperate.

Spies were dispatched to reconnoiter the land around Jericho and were sheltered by Rahab the harlot. (Joshua 2) A man's first foray into the unconscious discovers the helpful anima. According to Ginzberg,

> She had been leading an immoral life for 40 years, but at the approach of Israel, she paid homage to the true God, lived the life of a pious convert, and, as the wife of Joshua, became the ancestress of eight prophets and of the prophetess Huldah.[1]

Rahab corresponds to the soul of Israel who shares its forty years of wandering. She is analogous to Sophia who fell into the darkness of matter

---

1. Ginzberg, *Legends of the Bible*, p. 508.

(the wilderness) and had to be rescued.[2] Simon is said to have found his female companion, Helen (a manifestation of Sophia), in a brothel in Tyre.[3] The relations between Rahab and Israel are mutual and reciprocal. Rahab protects the Israelite spies and in return she is saved. This is a typical theme of anima-rescue stories, e.g., Jason and Medea, Theseus and Ariadne, etc.

Among patristic writers Rahab is a type of the Church.[4] As the Church is the bride of Christ, so in legend Rahab was the bride of Joshua who is a type of his namesake, Jesus (Joshua). As the soul of Israel, Rahab is also the soul of the land which belongs to Israel. I am reminded of a dream dreamt by a Jewish man who had denied his Jewish origins.

> I am in Israel in an open field on a hill. The hill is shaped exactly like a woman's breast. On the very top of the hill, where the nipple would be was a beautiful girl—blond, blue-eyed. Maybe she was Jewish, maybe not. I fall in love with her and pursue her, calling on the telephone. She laughs and finally says, "OK stupid, come on over." I go to the hill and meet her there, expecting to have a sexual experience. Instead, she tells me her story. She is from elsewhere. She married an orthodox Jew but he was impotent and buried himself in religion, neglecting her. She turned to others and had affairs with men. As I look at her she seems to be a lost soul, drifting.

This dream, which followed a visit to Israel, pictures the dreamer's encounter with his lost anima, whose fate had paralleled that of the "collective soul" of Israel.

Rahab's "scarlet thread," the sign that all in her house should be spared, was important symbolically to the Church Fathers. It served the same function as the blood daubed on the doorposts at the Passover[5] and was considered to exemplify the saving blood of Christ. According to Clement,

> They gave her [Rahab] a sign to this effect, that she should hang forth from her house a scarlet thread. And thus they made it manifest that redemption should flow through the blood of the Lord to all them that believe and hope in God.[6]

2. *Pistis Sophia,* trans. G.R.S. Meade, pp. 36f.
3. See Jonas, *The Gnostic Religion,* p. 107, and Edinger, *The Living Psyche,* section 47.
4. "Rahab, who herself also bore a type of the Church . . . received the command which said, 'Thou shalt bring thy father, and thy mother, and they brethren, and all thy father's household unto thee into thine house; and whosoever shall go out of the doors of thine house into the street, his blood shall be upon him.' (Joshua 2:18-19) In which mystery is declared, that they who will live, and escape from the destruction of the world, must be gathered together into one house alone, that is, into the Church; but whosoever of those thus collected together . . . shall depart and go not of the Church, that his blood shall be upon him[self]." ("The Epistle of Cyprian," *The Ante-Nicene Fathers,* vol. 5, p. 398)
5. As noted by Irenaeus, "Against Heresies," IV, 20, ibid., vol. 1, p. 492.
6. "The First Epistle of Clement," ibid., vol. 1, p. 8.

Rahab is connected by her name with the primordial mother-monster mentioned in Isaiah 51:9,10.

Awake, awake! Clothe yourself in strength,
Arm of Yahweh.
Awake, as in the past,
in times of generations long ago.
Did you not split Rahab in two,
And pierce the Dragon through?
Did you not dry up the sea,
the waters of the great Abyss,
to make the sea bed a road
for the redeemed to cross?[7]

In this passage Rahab is a personification of the watery chaos existing prior to creation. She corresponds to the Babylonian Tiamat who was slain by Marduk in the creation of the world.[8] It is the hero's task to slay the primordial aspect of the Great Mother (dragon) which in many myths has the effect of rescuing the anima. As Neumann puts it,

The transformation which the male undergoes in the course of the dragon fight includes a change in his relation to the female, symbolically expressed in the liberation of the captive from the dragon's power. In other words, the feminine image extricates itself from the grip of the terrible mother, a process known in analytical psychology as the crystallization of the anima from the mother archetype.[9]

Something of this sort of transformation takes place in Israel's relation to the feminine with the conquest of Canaan. Rahab the monster is transformed into Rahab the helpful woman. She is rescued from the enemy and, according to legend, true to the archetypal pattern she marries Joshua her rescuer.

Just as the forty years of wilderness wandering was inaugurated by a rite of entry—the crossing of the Red Sea—so a rite of exit—crossing the river Jordan—marks the termination of the wilderness experience. The transition was signaled by the fact that manna ceased to fall (Joshua 5:12) and we hear no more about the guiding pillar of cloud and pillar of fire. The theme of crossing a river, a border or even a highway comes up in dreams to indicate a major transition from one level of consciousness to another. Such a crossing often requires evidence of one's identity and commitment. With the crossing of the Jordan this evidence is presented by the mandala of twelve stones set up at Gilgal.[10] (Joshua 4:20) The fact that the waters of the Jordan parted for the crossing, as had the Red Sea,

---

7. See also Job 26:12 and Psalms 89:10.
8. Discussed by Jung, *Symbols of Transformation*, CW 5, pars. 376ff.
9. Erich Neumann, *The Origins and History of Consciousness*, p. 198.
10. The word *gilgal* means "ring of stones." (*Jerusalem Bible*, p. 279, note c)

expresses the theme of the "easy passage." This refers to the psychological fact that when the Self is activated and the ego has finally decided to take a major step, the execution of the decision may be remarkably easy because of cooperation from the unconscious.

Joshua receives precise directions from Yahweh for the conquest of Jericho:

> All your fighters, valiant warriors, will march round the town and make the circuit once, and for six days you will do the same thing . . . . On the seventh day you will go seven times round the town . . . . When the ram's horn rings out . . . the whole people must utter a mighty war cry and the town wall will collapse then and there; then the people can storm the town, each man going straight ahead. (Joshua 6:3-5)

This is a recipe for the resolution of an unconscious complex. It must be circumambulated—experienced from all sides—repeatedly. Circular movement around a center has the psychic effect of focusing energy on the center, by constellating the Self as a field of force. The crossing of the Jordan was sealed by the mandala image of the ring of stones. Now that image is being invoked again to breach the defenses of Jericho. *Circumambulatio* is a powerful process that constellates the Self. Jung describes it in his commentary on *The Secret of the Golden Flower:*

> *Circumambulatio* is expressed . . . by the idea of "circulation." The circulation is not merely movement in a circle, but means, on the one hand, the marking off of the sacred precinct and, on the other, fixation and concentration. The sun-wheel begins to turn; the sun is activated and begins its course . . . . everything peripheral is subordinated to the command of the centre. . . . Psychologically, this circulation would be the "movement in a circle around oneself," so that all sides of the personality become involved. "The poles of light and darkness are made to rotate," that is, there is an alternation of day and night.
>
> The circular movement thus has the moral significance of activating the light and dark forces of human nature, and together with them all psychological opposites of whatever kind they may be. It is nothing less than self-knowledge by means of self-brooding (Sanscrit *Tapas*).[11]

The seven-fold action alludes to the seven planetary spheres of antiquity, each ruled by one of the seven planetary deities. To complete seven circuits implies integrating all seven archetypal factors symbolized by the planets. With the seventh comes the shout announcing wholeness, and the complex collapses.

Jericho and the other captured cities were placed under a ban by Yahweh. "The town and everything inside it must be set apart for Yahweh under a ban." (Joshua 6:15)

---

11. *Alchemical Studies*, CW 13, pars. 38f.

The ban, *herem* in Hebrew, makes over all that is captured to God; hence men and animals are killed and booty given to the sanctuary. The ban is a religious act, a rule of holy war . . . . Failure to observe it is sacrilege and its punishment is severe.[12]

When Achan defied the ban and kept some booty for himself (Joshua 7:1), the consequence was Israel's defeat at Ai. Yahweh tells Joshua,

> They have taken what was under the ban, stolen and hidden it and put it into their baggage. That is why the sons of Israel cannot stand up to their foes; why they have turned their backs on their enemies, because they have come under the ban themselves. I will be with you no longer unless you remove what is under the ban from among you. (Joshua 7:11,12)

Resort to such extreme measures reflects the dangerous nature of all Canaanite things to invading Israel. Israel is in the process of establishing its identity. Not only must it conquer the land of Canaan but also it must impose its identity on the land. There are many historical examples of a country's conquering culturally its physical conquerors. Similarly, in the psychology of the individual there are times of transition when it may be fatal to allow any consideration for the standpoint one is trying to overcome. An "all or nothing" condition must prevail. Only thus is the connection with the Self preserved.

Gideon

As Israel occupied Canaan it made a radical shift from nomadic to settled life. During the wandering and the conquest Moses and Joshua provided central leadership, but now, in the so-called period of the Judges, there was a breakdown of centralized authority. "In those days there was no king in Israel and every man did as he pleased." (Judges 17:6)

The conquest of Canaan was a partial, fluctuating and disorderly process. Victories were followed by defeats and enslavement. Again and again we read that the Israelites "did what displeases Yahweh. They forgot Yahweh their God and served the Baals and the Asherahs. Then Yahweh's anger flamed out against Israel" (Judges 3:7,8), and he allowed them to be enslaved by their enemies. After each relapse comes repentence and the Israelites "cry to Yahweh" who raises up a leader or "Judge" to rescue them.

The fluctuating and chaotic time of the Judges symbolizes the vicissitudes that accompany the ego's effort to assimilate a major area of the unconscious. The outcome is often ambiguous for some time, as it remains uncertain whether the ego will assimilate the complex or the complex will assimilate the ego. The lack of a central authority reflects the weakness

12. *Jerusalem Bible,* p. 281, note c.

of the ego during the transition from one mode of life to another. Lacking a stable ego, reliance must be placed on sporadic, intermittent revelations from the Self, represented by the charismatic Judges who emerged in time of need to rescue Israel from its oppressors. One such Judge was Gideon.

At the time of Gideon's calling, Israel was oppressed by the Midianites and subject to Baal-worship. Yahweh directs Gideon to "pull down the altar to Baal belonging to your father and cut down the sacred post at the side of it. Then . . . build a carefully constructed altar to Yahweh your God" (Judges 6:25,26) and offer a holocaust sacrifice. This is a grave matter. The new God-image is demanding that the old God-image be destroyed. An individual ego must be the agent of that action. Although the working of God can be perceived in human history, individuals must take the responsibility for effecting that work. They thus become the carriers of the divine drama and suffer personally and concretely the consequences of God's actions. It is therefore understandable that when Gideon was ordered by Yahweh to take up arms against Midian, he (Gideon) wanted to be certain that this was indeed God's will and not an inflated, grandiose notion of his own.

Gideon requested a sign from God.

> "If you really mean to deliver Israel by my hand, as you declare, see now, I spread out a fleece on the threshing floor; if there is dew only on the fleece and all of the ground is left dry, then I shall know that you will deliver Israel by my hand, as you have declared." And so it happened. (Judges 6:36)

The sign was also manifested in reverse: " 'Let the fleece alone be dry, and let there be dew on the ground all around it.' And God did so that night." (Judges 6:39,40)

Dew is an important symbolic image. In Proverbs a king's favor is "like dew on the grass." (19:12) The messianic Psalm 72 speaks of the promised king "welcome as rain that falls on the fleece." (Verse 6 note, alternate reading) Moses says,

> May my teaching fall like the rain,
> May my word drop down like the dew,
> like showers on fresh grass
> And light rain on the turf.
> For I proclaim the name of Yahweh. (Deuteronomy 32:2)

And in Hosea Yahweh announces, "I will fall like dew in Israel. He shall bloom like the lily." (14:6) Irenaeus identifies Gideon's dew with the Holy Spirit;[13] Augustine equates it with the "grace of Christ"[14] and makes this observation:

---

13. "Against Heresies," *The Ante-Nicene Fathers*, vol. 1, p. 445.
14. "Exposition on the Book of Psalms," *The Nicene and Post-Nicene Fathers*, vol. 8, p. 329.

What meant Gideon's fleece? It is like the nation of the Jews in the midst of the world, which had the grace of sacraments, not indeed openly manifested, but hidden in a cloud, or in a veil, like the dew in the fleece. The time came when the dew was to be manifested in the floor; it was manifested, no longer hidden. Christ alone is the sweetness of dew.[15]

Gideon's dew also appears in alchemy. "*Ros Gedeonis* (Gideon's dew) is a synonym for the *aqua permanens*, hence for Mercurius."[16] It appears in Figure 8 of the *Rosarium* pictures about which Jung makes the following comment.

An attitude that seeks to do justice to the unconscious as well as to one's fellow human beings cannot possibly rest on knowledge alone . . . .
. . . That is why the purely intellectual attitude must be abandoned. "Gideon's dew" is a sign of divine intervention, it is the moisture that heralds the return of the soul.[17]

Gideon's initial army of 32,000 was drastically reduced by Yahweh. First, all who were fearful were dismissed, leaving 10,000. (Judges 7:3) This number was then reduced to 300 by an interesting device:

Take them down to the waterside . . . . All those who lap the water with their tongues, as a dog laps, place these on one side . . . . With the three hundred who lapped the water I will rescue you and put Midian into your power. (Judges 7:4-7)

This process of selection is an extraction procedure according to the formula $32 - 10 - 3$. It extracts from the total of 32 first the number 10 and then the number 3.[18] The final criterion for selection is the doglike behavior of lapping water. In Psalms 68:23 Yahweh says he will arrange "for the tongues of your dogs to lap their share of the enemy." Commenting on this passage, Augustine remarks, "For it was not indeed to no purpose, not without a great mystery, that Gideon was bidden to lead them alone, who should lap the water of the river like dogs."[19] As carrion-eater the dog had negative associations in the Old Testament, but as watchdog and sheep herder a very positive one. Jung writes,

In the history of symbols the dog is distinguished by an uncommonly wide range of associations . . . . The Gnostic parallel *Logos/canis* is reflected in

15. Ibid., p. 634.
16. Jung, "The Psychology of the Transference," *The Practice of Psychotherapy,* CW 16, par. 483.
17. Ibid., pars. 486f.
18. In the Kabbala there are thirty-two paths of wisdom made up of the ten numbers and the twenty-two letters of the Hebrew alphabet. (S.L.M. Mathers, trans., *The Kabbalah Unveiled,* p. 276) For the symbolism of the number three, see Edinger, *Ego and Archetype,* pp. 197ff. In essence, three is the number of egohood.
19. "Exposition on the Book of Psalms," *The Nicene and Post-Nicene Fathers,* vol. 8, p. 295.

the Christian one, *Christus/canis*, handed down in the formula "gentle to the elect, terrible to the reprobate," a "true pastor." St. Gregory says: "Or what others are called the watch-dogs of this flock, save the holy doctors?" . . . In the *Hieroglyphics of Horapollo* . . . emphasis is laid on the dog's power to spread infection . . . . Because of its rich symbolic context the dog is an apt synonym for the transforming substance.[20]

Gideon's forces were assured of victory when spies overheard the dream of a Midianite: "A cake made of barley bread came rolling through the camp of Midian; it reached the tent, struck against it and turned it upside down [and the tent lay flat]." (Judges 7:13) Such a dream, in which an inanimate object effects a deliberate action, indicates the activation of the autonomous psyche (the Self). It is then imperative for the ego to align its attitude in accordance with the activated Self, otherwise it will be knocked flat.

Samson

The story of Samson (Judges 13-16) is that of a coniunctio gone wrong. It begins with a wedding between Samson the Israelite and the daughter of a Philistine. In the midst of the wedding feast, Samson poses a riddle. "Out of the eater came what is eaten, and out of the strong came what is sweet." (Judges 14:14) This refers to the honeycomb Samson found in the carcass of the lion he had killed. (Judges 14:5-8) As with Oedipus, the riddle is the central issue of the story, and, like Oedipus, Samson fails to address the deeper meaning of the riddle.[21]

What does it mean that out of a dead lion comes sweet honey? It signifies the transformation of the power principle. The "spirit of Yahweh" dwelled in Samson, allowing him to do great deeds of valor and vengeance when under the influence of intense affect (e.g., Judges 14:19). However, Samson was called to the coniunctio which required that he become conscious of the opposites, both power and love. He failed that test. The vengeance principle prevails throughout the Samson story. For this reason his Philistine anima turned against him. Thus is the one-sided ego undone by the unconscious in its effort to promote the larger standpoint of wholeness.

The synchronistic event of finding a honeycomb in the body of the lion he had killed was meant to inform Samson the Nazirite and man of God that it was his task to contribute to the transformation of God.[22] From this perspective, the lion's death and Samson's defeat and death are symbolically equivalent.[23] They both picture the transformation of the archetypal

20. *Mysterium Coniunctionis*, CW 14, par. 174, note 280.
21. See below, pp. 96-99, for more on riddle symbolism.
22. See Edinger, *The Creation of Consciousness*, chapter 4.
23. Jung says the hero has no weapons when he fights the lion or the bull because he is fighting himself. (*Symbols of transformation*, CW 5, par. 600, note 186)

power principle. The coniunctio Samson could not achieve in life occurs at his death as both he and the Philistines perish together. (Judges 16:30)

Samson has analogies with both Mithra and Christ. Mithra sacrificed the bull and Christ carried the cross, the instrument of his own self-sacrifice. There are pictures of Samson carrying the gates of Gaza (Judges 16:3) in the form of a cross.[24] Blind Samson in prison turning the mill wheel (mandala) in Gaza (Judges 16:21) is an image of servitude to wholeness—an unconscious version of carrying the cross of the Self.

Irenaeus interprets Samson as a prefiguration of Christ.

> The little boy, therefore, who guided Samson by the hand, pre-typified John the Baptist, who showed to the people the faith in Christ. And the house in which they were assembled signifies the world, in which dwell the various heathen and unbelieving nations, offering sacrifice to their idols. Moreover, the two pillars are the two covenants. The fact, then, of Samson leaning himself upon the pillars [indicates] this, that the people, when instructed, recognized the mystery of Christ.[25]

Referring to Judges 14:14—"Out of the eater came what is eaten, and out of the strong came what is sweet"—Picinellus says,

> This is to be understood of the Son of God, who after having long imitated the terrible lion in rebuking the world's sins, a little later, when he instituted the most holy sacrament of the Eucharist as his death drew nigh, turned himself into exceeding sweet honeycombs.[26]

Samson personifies the torturous process of transformation of the power motive: Lion $\longrightarrow$ Honey, Yahweh $\longrightarrow$ Christ. The strong man is turned into the blind defeated slave, who yet from his captivity in darkness destroys the old temple in preparation for the new and generates a sweet food for the soul.

John Milton had personal familiarity with the archetypal image of Samson. His great final poems, *Paradise Lost, Paradise Regained* and *Samson Agonistes,* were written in total blindness and during intermittent attacks of gout. These lines of Samson from the latter poem are an example of honey from the "dead lion" who had been Cromwell's polemicist.

> God of our Fathers, what is man!
> That thou towards him with hand so various,
> Or might I say contrarious,
> Temperst thy providence through his short course,
> Not evenly, as thou rul'st
> The angelic orders and inferiour creatures mute,
> Irrational and brute.
> Nor do I name of men the common rout,

24. Ibid.
25. "Against Heresies," *The Ante-Nicene Fathers,* vol. 1, p. 572.
26. *Mundus Symbolicus,* I, 397, cited by Jung, *Mysterium Coniunctionis,* CW 14, par. 639, note 324.

That wandring loose about
Grow up and perish, as the summer flie,
Heads without name no more rememberd,
But such as thou hast solemnly elected,
With gifts and graces eminently adorn'd
To some great work, thy glory,
And peoples safety, which in part they effect:
Yet toward these thus dignifi'd, thou oft
Admidst their highth of noon,
Changest thy countenance, and thy hand with no regard
Of highest favours past
From thee on them, or them to thee of service.
  Nor only dost degrade them, or remit
To life obscur'd, which were a fair dismission,
But throw'st them lower then thou didst exalt them high,
Unseemly falls in human eie,
Too grievous for the trespass or omission,
Oft leav'st them to the hostile sword
Of Heathen and prophane, their carkasses
To dogs and fowls a prey, or else captiv'd:
Or to the unjust tribunals, under change of times,
And condemnation of the ingrateful multitude.
If these they scape, perhaps in poverty
With sickness and disease thou bow'st them down,
Painful diseases and deform'd,
In crude old age;
Though not disordinate, yet causless suffring
The punishment of dissolute days, in fine,
Just or unjust, alike seem miserable,
For oft alike, both come to evil end.
  So deal not with this once thy glorious Champion,
The Image of they strength, and mighty minister.
What do I beg? how hast thou dealt already?
Behold him in this state calamitous, and turn
His labours, for thou canst, to peaceful end. (lines 667-709)

Ruth

The Book of Ruth is an oasis of feminine charm in the patriarchal sternness of the Old Testament. Goethe called it "the loveliest little epic and idyllic whole which has come down to us."[27] Naomi, with her husband and two sons, moves from Israel to Moab because of famine in Israel. After some years the husband and two sons die and Naomi returns to Israel with her Moabite daughter-in-law Ruth. There Ruth meets Boaz and they are mar-

---

27. Quoted by H. Yechezkel Kluger, "Ruth: A Contribution to the Study of the Feminine Principle in the Old Testament," pp. 52ff. I am indebted to this excellent article for material used in this section.

ried. To them is born Obed, the grandfather of David and ancestor of the Messiah.

The Moabites were the descendents of Moab, the first of the incestuous union between Lot and his oldest daughter. They were traditional enemies of Israel and associated with licentiousness, as reported in Numbers 25:1: "At Shittim the people gave themselves over to debauchery with the daughters of Moab." As Kluger suggests, "Moab represents the psychic opposite or complement to Israel,"[28] the feminine (eros) side as opposed to the masculine (logos) side. A very interesting legend informs us that

> Moses wanted to war on the descendants of Lot after the episode of Shittim. God forbade this, saying that the two nations must be spared because two *doves* were to spring from them: the Moabitess Ruth, and the Ammonitess Naamah. (This Naamah was the wife of Solomon.) One version of this legend has God say that He *"lost something valuable among them."*[29]

We can understand the lost value to be an aspect of the feminine principle symbolized by Ruth, while the Book of Ruth is a record of the redemption of that lost value.

Moab represents the matriarchal psyche, where the principle of nature and fertility is primary and the masculine spirit principle is subordinate— no more than an instrument to fecundate the Great Mother. Naomi, however, represents the feminine that has been transformed by encounter with the autonomous spirit, Yahweh. But in that transformation something was also lost and requires rescue or redemption—hence her sojourn in Moab.

In the Kabbalistic work *Zohar Ruth,* Ruth "personifies the community of *Israel* and also the Shechinah, God's feminine side, who, like Israel, is in exile."[30] According to this symbolism Ruth's move to Israel and her marriage to Boaz is nothing less than the ultimate coniunctio which brings about the redemption of both Israel and Yahweh.

The theme of redemption is a central part of the story. When Ruth returns from gleaning grain in Boaz's field and informs Naomi that she has met Boaz, Naomi replies, "This man . . . is a relative of ours. He is one of those who has the right of redemption over us [literally, he is one of our *goelim*]." (Ruth 2:20) According to the levirate law, a widow who has no son is taken to wife by her brother-in-law or another near kinsman. The eldest son of this marriage is reckoned to be the son of the dead husband, whose heir he becomes.[31] The near kinsman who marries the widow is called her redeemer (*goel*). The same term means to "buy back" and is applied to that kinsman upon whom certain redemptive duties fall. For instance, if a man sells himself into slavery, "he shall enjoy the right

28. Ibid., p. 56.
29. Ibid., p. 63.
30. Ibid., p. 74.
31. *Jerusalem Bible,* note to Deuteronomy 25:5, p. 249.

of redemption after sale, and one of his brothers may redeem him. His paternal uncle, his uncle's son, or a member of his own family may redeem him; if he has the means he may redeem himself." (Leviticus 25:48,49) The same term is applied to Yahweh. "Thus says Yahweh, who created you, Jacob, who formed you, Israel. Do not be afraid, for I have redeemed you; I have called you by your name, you are mine." (Isaiah 43:1) The early Jewish rabbis applied the term *goel* to the Messiah[32] and it has this implication in Job 19:25. "I know that my redeemer [*goel*] liveth and that he shall stand at the latter day upon the earth." (AV)

There were two near kinsmen, Boaz and another man, who had the right of redemption of Ruth. Kluger informs us that the *Zohar Ruth* identifies these two *goelim* as the two Messiahs, messiah ben David and messiah ben Joseph.[33] These ideas connect symbolically with the fact that Obed, the son of Ruth and Boaz, is an ancestor of the Messiah. Thus the union of Ruth and Boaz implies redemption on two levels, the personal, individual level and the collective, archetypal (represented by the two Messiahs).

The core of the story is a coniunctio image, the union of Ruth and Boaz. As Kluger demonstrates, Ruth's nighttime meeting with Boaz can be considered a sacred seduction with Ruth in the role of "sacred prostitute" or hierodule. Kluger quotes Hosea 9:1[34] and goes on,

> It is permissible to assume from Hosea's reproach, that rites involving . . . "sacred prostitutes" or hierodules, took place on the threshing floors. . . . The hierodule was, after all, a priestess or representative of the goddess, and the great mother goddess, under whatever name she was worshipped—Ishtar, Isis, Aphrodite—was associated with a lover—Tammuz, Osiris, Adonis—with whom she mated year by year. This union of the divine pair, the sacred marriage or *hieros gamos,* was enacted by the priest or priestess on earth, especially at the harvest festivals.[35]

The same image of a "sacred marriage" occurs in the Kabbala. We have already noted that Ruth was identified with the Shekinah, the feminine aspect of Yahweh. She is also linked to Malchuth, the Tenth Sefirot. Malchuth unites with Yesod, the Ninth Sefirot, as Ruth unites with Boaz, and the result is the union of Yahweh with his lost feminine essence which will restore the original paradisical state of unity of man with God and of God with himself—"the blissful union of the rhythms of divine existence in the one great melody of God."[36] The Book of Ruth anticipates the coniunctio which receives its full expression in the Song of Songs.

---

32. Ibid., note to Job 19:25, p. 751.
33. H.Y. Kluger, "Ruth," p. 75; see also Jung, *Aion,* CW 9ii, par. 168.
34. ". . . you have deserted God to play the whore, you have enjoyed the prostitute's pay on every threshing floor."
35. H.Y. Kluger, "Ruth," p. 71.
36. Gershom Scholem, *Major Trends in Jewish Mysticism,* p. 231.

8

Saul and the Spirit of Yahweh

The story of Saul begins with Samuel, who as a boy was dedicated by his mother to service in the sanctuary with Eli the priest. Samuel's personal calling by Yahweh is an important paradigm for psychology.

> Samuel was lying in the sanctuary of Yahweh where the ark of God was, when Yahweh called, "Samuel, Samuel." He answered, "Here I am." Then he ran to Eli and said, "Here I am, since you called me." [Three times this happens] . . . Eli then understood that it was Yahweh who was calling the boy, and he said to Samuel, "Go and lie down, and if someone calls say, 'Speak, Yahweh, your servant is listening.'" (1 Samuel 3:3-9)

The young Nietzsche identified with Samuel, as he informs us in his autobiography:

> Of all the books of the Bible, *First Samuel,* especially in the opening passages, made the profoundest impression on me. In a way, it may be responsible for an important spiritual element in my life. It is where the Lord three times wakes the infant prophet in his sleep, and Samuel three times mistakes the heavenly voice for the voice of Eli asleep near him in the temple. Convinced, after the third time, that his prodigy is being called to higher services than those available to him in the house of sacrifices, Eli proceeds to instruct him in the ways of prophecy. I had no Eli (not even a Schopenhauer) when a similar visitation darkened the opening days of my adolescence. I was all of twelve when the Lord broke in on me in all His glory, a glaring fusion of the portraits of Abraham, Moses and the Young Jesus in our family Bible.[1]

Miss Miller, the subject of Jung's case study presented in *Symbols of Transformation,* was reminded of Samuel's words, "Speak, Lord, for thy servant heareth," just before a visionary experience.[2] Jung comments as follows:

> The Biblical words contain an invocation or "prayer," that is, a wish addressed to God, a concentration of libido on the God-image.[3]

> The story in I Samuel 3:1ff. illustrates how the libido can be directed inwards: the invocation expresses this introversion, and the explicit expectation that God will speak empties the conscious mind of activity and transfers it to the divine being constellated by the invocation, who, from the empirical point of view, must be regarded as a primordial image. It is a fact of

1. *My Sister and I,* p. 184.
2. Jung, *Symbols of Transformation,* CW 5, par. 256.
3. Ibid., par. 257.

experience that all archetypal contents have a certain autonomy, since they appear spontaneously and can often exercise an overwhelming compulsion. There is, therefore, nothing intrinsically absurd about the expectation that "God" will take over the activity and spontaneity of the conscious mind, for the primordial images are quite capable of doing precisely this.[4]

Samuel's mistaking the call of Yahweh for the call of Eli represents the fact that the call of the Self is often first projected onto an outer authority figure. In fact, a young person's ability to make sizable projections is often a measure of his or her own potential. When Samuel finally does listen to Yahweh he is told that Eli's house is doomed. "You are to tell him that I condemn his House for ever." (1 Samuel 3:13) In terms of individual psychology this means that relation to the inner authority via projection is to be destroyed. Samuel shall now have a direct relation to God.

Kingship in Israel was spurred by the occurrence of a national disaster. The ark of the covenant was captured by the Philistines. (1 Samuel 4) For this palladium to fall into enemy hands meant that the nation was in danger of dissolution and dependent bondage to the possessors of its sacred image. In the psychology of the individual, the ark signifies the sacred secret which insures the integrity of the personality. Its capture represents a projection of the Self which creates an abject dependence on the carrier of the projection (e.g., transference). Such a projection is not good for its recipient either, especially if there is a tendency to identify with it. For the Philistines, the presence of the ark brought a toppling of their God (Dagon) and a plague. (I Samuel 5) These effects represent the destructive consequences of identifying with another's Self-projection. One is infected by the psyche of the other, one's relation to one's own suprapersonal value is lost and one is afflicted with inflation (tumors or swellings).

The method whereby the Philistines rid themselves of the plague is instructive. They are advised to return the ark of the covenant to Israel accompanied by five golden models of their tumors and of their rats. (I Samuel 6:5) Thus they were told to return the Self-projection to its source, recognize its objective value (gold) and contemplate images of their affliction (tumors and rats). The latter has the same meaning as the brazen serpent which healed the plague of serpents in the wilderness. (Numbers 21:6ff) It represents the process of active imagination whereby the affect with which one is possessed is objectified.

Through the agency of Samuel, Saul was chosen to be the first king of Israel. Two versions of this event appear in the Bible, the so-called "royalist" and "anti-royalist" versions.[5] According to one account, the people come to Samuel and insist that he give them a king, which request Yahweh considers a rejection of himself. (I Samuel 8:1-5) According to

4. Ibid., par. 260.
5. *Jerusalem Bible*, p. 353, note a.

the other account the issue is initiated by Yahweh, who tells Samuel he has chosen Saul to be king. (I Samuel 9:15,16) This paradoxical double account of the origin of kingship in Israel is very important to the understanding of ego development.

The time of the Judges represents a diffuse state of the psyche in which there are multiple and shifting centers of authority ("every man did as he pleased"—Judges 17:6). The coming of kingship brings a centering and consolidation of the ego. As Jung tell us, the Self can be considered "an unconscious prefiguration of the ego."[6] It is the archetypal ground-plan on which the ego is built and the Self, in order to be realized, must incarnate in the ego. However, for the ego to assume the role of center of the psyche is also a sin against the Self since it constitutes a theft of divine prerogative. Thus kingship is *both* obedience and rebellion. The ego encounters the opposites and "becomes a vessel filled with divine conflict."[7] For Saul this "divine conflict" was manifested in him by the spirit of Yahweh which was initially auspicious and then became an evil spirit. (I Samuel 16:14)

Saul meets his higher destiny while looking for his father's lost donkeys. (I Samuel 9) Unable to find them, he seeks out Samuel the seer for help. Samuel in turn had been told by Yahweh to watch for Saul whom he is to annoint king of Israel. This theme of reciprocal movement, in which the ego seeks the guidance of the unconscious while the unconscious seeks the attention of the ego, is characteristic of the process of individuation. So also is the fact that one is apt to discover a new life-direction only after a painful period of search for a lost value.

After meeting Samuel, Saul is invited to a meal where he is served the portion that had been set aside for him:

> Samuel said to the cook, "Bring the portion I gave you, of which I said to you, 'Put it aside.'" . . . and Samuel said, "See, what was kept is set before you. Eat; because it was kept for you until the hour appointed." (I Samuel 9:23,24, RSV)

The word translated "portion" (*manah*) means something weighed out or divided, also "lot." Psalm 16:15 says, "The Lord is the portion [*manah*] of mine inheritance and of my cup" (AV) and Jeremiah 13:25, "This is thy lot, the portion [*manah*] of thy measures from me saith the Lord" (AV). The term is similar to the Greek *moira,* fate or destiny, which has as its primary meaning "part" or "allotted portion."[8] Saul is required to eat the food of his destiny.[9] This is a coagulatio image signifying the conscious realization of a previously unconscious content.[10]

---

6. "Transformation Symbolism in the Mass," *Psychology and Religion,* CW 11, par. 391.
7. "Answer to Job," ibid., par. 659.
8. F.M. Cornford, *From Religion to Philosophy,* p. 16.
9. Cf. John 4:34: "My food is to do the will of the one who sent me."
10. See Edinger, *Anatomy of the Psyche,* pp. 109ff.

The following day, "Samuel took a phial of oil and poured it on Saul's head; then he kissed him, saying, 'Has not Yahweh annointed you prince over his people Israel?'" (I Samuel 10:1) This introduces the important image of "annointing," a concrete representation of the entry of the spirit of Yahweh into Saul. It is quite literally poured or rubbed into him. The annointing is followed by Saul's ecstasy as predicted by Samuel: "Then the Spirit of Yahweh will seize on you, and you will go into an ecstasy [prophesy, AV] with them and be changed into another man." (I Samuel 10:6) Concerning the term "go into an ecstasy" or "prophesy," Rivkah Kluger remarks,

> The word "prophesy" (*hitnabbē*) really means: "the ecstatic utterance of sounds." The root, *nābā,* also means "to bring forth" in Arabic and is used especially of words. It only began to mean "prophecy" later. The development of the word also gives us an idea of the development of prophecy from mere ecstasy to delivering divine messages. . . . It is most important for our investigation that the word *hitnabbē* is used for Saul's rage in Chapter 8:10, when he was already the victim of his melancholia. Perhaps this indicates that Saul's melancholy was already taken to be connected with his prophetic gift.[11]

Following Paul Volz, Kluger speaks of three ways the spirit of Yahweh may manifest: 1) by the drawing of lots; 2) by prophetic ecstasy; and 3) by *furor bellicus.*[12] These three modes have parallels in the manifestation of the unconscious. Drawing of lots corresponds to the phenomena of synchronicity. Prophetic ecstasy is the extreme form of inspiration by the unconscious. *Furor bellicus,* battle fury, that can take possession of a soldier on the battlefield, corresponds to the intense affect that may erupt to protect a vital psychic value that has been threatened.[13] All three of these aspects of the spirit of Yahweh occurred in relation to Saul. According to one version he was chosen king by lots (I Samuel 10:20,21). After being annointed by Samuel he fell into a prophetic ecstasy (I Samuel 10:10), and while the spirit of Yahweh remained he was invincible in battle.

Saul's downfall begins with a crime against Yahweh. We have two versions of that crime. According to I Samuel 13:10-13, Saul's crime was that in the urgency of a military situation Saul himself offered sacrifice to Yahweh rather than wait for Samuel to arrive. In 15:8,9, Saul's crime is that he violated the ban on the Amalekites by permitting King Agag to live and by sparing the best sheep and cattle. Samuel chastises Saul,

11.   "King Saul and the Spirit of God," *Psyche and Bible,* p. 53.
12.   Ibid., p. 51.
13.   One never knows what reaction from the unconscious may emerge in a moment of crisis. A mild-mannered, unaggressive young man awoke one night to find an intruder in his bedroom. To his astonishment he leapt at the intruder enraged and the thief fled for his life.

saying, "Rebellion is a sin of sorcery, presumption a crime of teraphim [worship of household idols]. Since you have rejected the word of Yahweh, he has rejected you as king." (I Samuel 15:23) Yahweh regrets having made Saul king and withdraws the spirit of Yahweh, or rather, transforms it into an evil spirit. "Now the spirit of Yahweh had left Saul and an evil spirit from Yahweh filled him with terror." (I Samuel 16:14)

Saul's failure conveys a difficult message to the modern mind. His crime does not seem great to us. For urgent and reasonable considerations he did not immediately honor the vengeful voice of Yahweh speaking out of the depths of affect. Repeatedly, Yahweh had demanded that Amalek be totally destroyed. In Exodus 17:14-16, Yahweh says, "I shall wipe out the memory of Amalek from under heaven . . . . Yahweh is at war with Amalek from age to age!" Again, in Deuteronomy 25:19, "You are to blot out the memory of Amalek from under heaven. Do not forget." These statements are the background for Yahweh's command to Saul, "Now, go and strike down Amalek; put him under the ban with all that he possesses. Do not spare him, but kill man and woman, babe and suckling, ox and sheep, camel and donkey." (I Samuel 15:3)[14] It is as though Saul tried to function out of a reasonable attitude that set him dangerously against the unconscious. He did not sufficiently honor the "sacred affect" which was the basis of the Spirit of Yahweh. As a result he loses the cooperation of the unconscious; not only that, it turns hostile and plagues him with fits of melancholy, depression and rage.

The positive spirit of Yahweh is transferred from Saul to David, who must now be sought to calm the effects of Saul's evil spirit.

> Saul's servants said to him, "Look, an evil spirit of God is the cause of your terror. Let our Lord give the order, and your servants who wait on you will look for a skilled harpist; when the evil spirit of God troubles you, the harpist will play and you will recover" . . . . And so David came to Saul and entered his service . . . . And whenever the spirit from God troubled Saul, David took the harp and played; then Saul grew calm, and recovered, and the evil spirit left him. (I Samuel 16:15-23)

The fact that David's music can cure Saul's melancholy indicates their essential identity. Like cures like. David is the carrier of the positive spirit of Yahweh which can only be cured by itself so to speak. When a symptom is caused by the Self it can only be cured by a conscious realization of its meaning. The spirit of Yahweh has turned negative to Saul because he had turned his back to it. (The unconscious takes the same attitude toward the ego as the ego takes toward it.) David and his music represent a healing change of attitude.

Saul signifies the first stage of ego-kingship in which the ego inevitably

---

14. See the excellent paper by Myron Gubitz, "Amalek: The Eternal Adversary," p. 34.

identifies with the archetypal authority granted it. David signifies the second stage in which the tendency to inflation is overcome. Ideally, Saul should willingly collaborate in the transfer of power to David. This he cannot do because he is identified with the archetype of king and hence is possessed by the power motive. He must attempt to kill his destined successor.

The Saul-David constellation is sometimes seen in the relation between father and son. The moody and violent father cannot allow the transfer to the son of authority that will allow the latter to achieve maturity. Perhaps more important is the inner reference in which the Saul stage of ego development refuses to relinquish authority to the David stage and brings about its own destruction by willfully clinging to power.

With David driven into exile, Saul, in anxiety about the invading Philistines, consults the spirit of the dead Samuel through the witch of Endor. (I Samuel 28:3ff) After the positive Spirit of Yahweh had left Saul he lost his connection with Samuel, the inner prophet. Now he seeks to retrieve it by consulting the unconscious. Samuel's message is the same one he had given when alive: Saul is to suffer defeat. It is the experience of defeat that Saul had refused to acknowledge. It is this experience that stands between the first-stage ego and the second-stage ego. ("The experience of the Self is always a defeat for the ego.")[15] Saul as the archetype of the first-stage ego cannot accept defeat and therefore must suffer it totally.

As the spirit of Samuel predicted, Saul was defeated at the battle of Gilboa (I Samuel 31:1ff) and committed suicide. His death by his own hand signifies the fact that the first-stage ego is no longer viable and demonstrates Yahweh's statement, "All who hate me are in love with death." (Proverbs 8:36) As Rivkah Kluger observes, Saul is a tragic figure because he could not accept consciously the suffering imposed by the prophetic election. "He was not able like the great prophets to transform his possession by God into devotion to God."[16] Another way of putting it might be that he failed to make the transition from king to prophet and thus was a casualty to the process of individuation.

As the first "king of the Jews" and first "annointed one," Saul is linked symbolically with Christ to whom those terms were also applied. Both were invested with the Spirit of Yahweh and both were abandoned by that spirit. The moment of abandonment for Christ occurred on the cross when he cried, quoting Psalm 22:1, "My God, my God, why have you deserted me?" (Matthew 27:46) This despairing cry from the cross led to the Docetic idea that the spirit of God descended on the human being, Jesus, at his baptism, performed miraculous deeds through him and then abandoned him to suffer the crucifixion alone. Jung says,

---

15. Jung, *Mysterium Coniunctionis,* CW 14, par. 778.
16. Rivkah Kluger, *Psyche and Bible,* p. 78.

Christ saw that his whole life, devoted to the truth according to his best conviction, had been a terrible illusion. He had lived it to the full absolutely sincerely, he had made his honest experiment, but it was nevertheless a compensation. On the cross his mission deserted him. But because he had lived so fully and devotedly he won through to the Resurrection body.[17]

This parallel may help to enlarge our perspective on Saul, who is a truly tragic figure. A legend indicates the need to honor him more.

A year after Saul and his sons had been killed, a famine came on the land for three successive years. . . . And the Lord spoke unto him [David]: "It is on account of Saul." . . . Then David arose and gathered together the mighty and wise in Israel. They crossed the Jordan and came to Jabesh in Gilead. There they found the corpses of Saul and Jonathan, which no worm had gnawed. They put them into a shrine and returned across the Jordan, and buried them in the sepulchre of Saul's father, Kish, in the land of Benjamin, and they carried out all the king's commands . . . . The king had ordered them to take Saul's coffin throughout the whole land of Israel, into every region and into every village, and to take care that the people should everywhere pay due homage to the bodies. And it happened that all the people and their sons and daughters paid homage to the king's body and thus absolved their debt. And when the Lord saw that the people had paid due honor to their king, he became compassionate and sent rain upon the land.[18]

17. *C.G. Jung Speaking*, p. 98.
18. Ginzberg, *Legends of the Bible*, p. 80.

9

David

As the second king of Israel David represents the second-stage ego. In contrast to Saul, who was a lonely solitary, David is a man of many pairings. Almost all the events of his life occurred in the context of a pair: David and Goliath, David and Saul, David and Jonathan, David and Michal, David and Bathsheba, David and Nathan, David and Absalom, and overarching them all, David and Yahweh. This multitude of pairings indicates a unique capacity for engagement and dialogue with the "other," which reminds us of the fact that consciousness is a product of the number two. Number one is the ego; number two is the unconscious, the other, which generates awareness of the opposites; and number three is the consciousness that grows out of the conflict between one and two. David as king number two manifests the symbolic implications of that number.

As the youngest of the eight sons of Jesse, David is a bringer of wholeness (eight = double quaternity). Initially he is a shepherd watching his father's sheep. But, like Paris, he is called out of his innocent life to a higher destiny. This call is manifested in two ways: 1) He is annointed by Samuel (I Samuel 16:13), and 2) he responds to the challenge of Goliath (I Samuel 17:32). David's ability to accept the challenge is evidence of the Spirit of Yahweh that entered him when he was annointed. Since he has been elected by Yahweh he can elect to take on the task. He has the support of the Self.

Psychologically we can understand Goliath to represent a sizable (giant-size) complex which is tyrannizing the personality. The ability to make such a confrontation is evidence of the individual's potential for psychic development ("election"). According to legend[1] Goliath was the son of Orphah, the Moabite sister-in-law of Ruth, who decided not to accompany Ruth and Naomi to Israel. (Ruth 1:14) This would suggest that the complex David had to face concerned his Moabite ancestry which came through his great-grandmother, Ruth. Persons of mixed racial heritage are apt to have a problematic psychology. The opposites are particularly activated, increasing the energy potential of the psyche for good or ill.

David's relationship with Saul begins because he is a musician and can mitigate Saul's dark moods. The symbolism of David here overlaps with that of Orpheus. The Psalms, meant to be accompanied by the psalter, are traditionally attributed to David. The power of the music and poetry of the Psalms to affect the unconscious is beautifully conveyed by legend. Gaer tells us that "the legend of how King David saved the world from

1. Ginzberg, *Legends of the Bible*, p. 536.

another flood appears in many forms and is attributed to various saints, yet all are based on the eloquent psalmic exclamation: the waters saw You. O God, the waters saw You and were afraid (Psalms 77:16)."[2] An example is the following.

> When King David's workmen began to build the House of God, they dug the drain for the altar very deep and inadvertently lifted the shard on the Mouth of the Abyss. Instantly, the Waters of the Deep began to rise to flood the earth. David knew that unless the Mouth of the Abyss were sealed again, the world would be destroyed. He also knew that only a stone with the Ineffable Name upon it could seal the Abyss . . . . David lowered the stone with the Holy name on it sixteen thousand ells, and tightly sealed the Mouth of the Abyss. But it was soon discovered that the earth below had lost its moisture and even the rains were not enough to grow the crops. King David then composed fifteen psalms, and as each psalm was completed, the Waters of the Deep rose one thousand ells. When the waters reached within a thousand ells of the surface of the earth, he offered thanks to God, Who keeps the ground always moist enough for crops, and does not allow the Abyss to sink one iota below, or rise one iota above, one thousand ells.[3]

Another legend says that David's harp had strings made from the gut of the ram sacrificed by Abraham on Mount Moriah and that these strings would vibrate by themselves in the middle of the night and awaken David to study the Torah.[4] The miraculous power of David's music expressed in these legends is due to its connection with the autonomous psyche. The music, although played by the ego (David), comes from the transformed deity itself (the Moriah ram).[5]

Saul's attitude to David soon became one of open hostility. The first-stage ego cannot tolerate the prospect of being supplanted. David must flee to the wilderness where he lives as an outlaw and where "all the oppressed, those in distress, all those in debt, anyone who had a grievance, gathered round him and he became their leader." (I Samuel 22:2) The future ruling principle is a threat to the status quo and, for a time, must exist as an "outsider." However its central integrating power is demonstrated by its bringing together the various rejected aspects of the psyche into a unified whole.

The outlaw period is a time of great danger psychologically. The danger is identification with the shadow and a fall into criminality. This is illustrated in David's encounter with Nabal. (I Samuel 25) Not realizing that he was dealing with naked extortion, Nabal foolishly refused David's demand for "gifts" and would have been murdered by David had not his

2. *The Lore of the Old Testament*, p. 221.
3. Ibid.
4. Ginzberg, *Legends of the Bible*, p. 546.
5. I discuss the Moriah ram as the primitive deity in Edinger, *The Creation of Consciousness*, p. 97.

wife, Abigail, intervened. "Nabal" means fool. "'Brute' is his name and brutish his character." (I Samuel 25:25) David is here encountering his own brutish shadow, and except for the intervention of the anima he would have lapsed into overt criminality and become a psychological fatality.

In flight from Saul, David took refuge among the Philistines and once again barely escaped identification with the shadow. He almost became a traitor to Israel by joining the Philistines in battle against the Israelites, and was saved only by the Philistine leaders who did not trust him to join them in battle. (I Samuel 29:34) On another occasion David was obliged to feign madness. (I Samuel 31:12f) To willingly step over the line between sanity and madness is exceedingly dangerous and suggests how close the outlaw state is to actual psychosis.

David's relation to his first wife, Michal, follows a typical mythological pattern. For his victory over Goliath David wins the hand of the king's daughter. This is the theme of the rescue of the anima from the father, corresponding to the story of Jason and Medea. Michal in turn helps David escape from Saul. (I Samuel 19:11ff) Later, again like Jason and Medea, the relationship sours. Michal ridicules David for dancing before Yahweh as the ark of the covenant arrives. Clearly Michal is envious of the loving attention that David offers Yahweh. As "daughter of the father" she would claim that attention for herself. The helpful anima thus turns into a barren Xantippe ("To the day of her death Michal, the daughter of Saul, had no children"—2 Samuel 6:23). Since she would obstruct the ego's relation to God it turns away from her.

A major episode in the career of David is his encounter with Bathsheba:

> It happened towards evening when David had risen from his couch and was strolling on the palace roof, that he saw from the roof a woman bathing; the woman was very beautiful. David made inquiries about this woman and was told, "Why, that is Bathsheba, Eliam's daughter, the wife of Uriah the Hittite." Then David sent messengers and had her brought. She came to him, and he slept with her . . . . She then went home again. The woman conceived and sent word to David; "I am with child." (2 Samuel 11:2ff)

> David wrote a letter to Joab and sent it by Uriah. In the letter he wrote, "Station Uriah in the thick of the fight and then fall back behind him so that he may be struck down and die." Joab, then besieging the town, posted Uriah in a place where he knew there were fierce fighters. The men of the town sallied out and engaged Joab; the army suffered casualties, including some of David's body guard; and Uriah the Hittite was killed too. (2 Samuel 11:14ff)

> When Uriah's wife heard that her husband Uriah was dead, she mourned for her husband. When the period of mourning was over David sent to have her brought to his house; she became his wife and bore him a son. But what David had done displeased Yahweh. (2 Samuel 11:26f)

This is the story of an anima projection. Bathsheba married to Uriah

corresponds to the theme of the anima married to the shadow.[6] David
would have Bathsheba by killing Uriah, that is, by denial of the shadow.
Such an anima projection is a blissful paradisical illusion that is shattered
by reality. The denied shadow returns as the ego's experience of guilt.
According to a legend,

> One day as David sat in his chamber writing a psalm, Satan came into the
> room disguised as a bird. Its feathers were of pure gold, its beak of dia-
> monds, and its legs of glowing rubies. David dropped his book and tried to
> catch the bird which he thought had come from the Garden of Eden. But
> the bird flew out of the window and settled upon the low branch of a tree
> in a neighboring garden. And under the branch of the tree a young woman
> was washing her hair. She was Bathsheba and David took her by arranging
> the death of her husband Uriah.[7]

This legend, like a dream, underscores the profound evil that David
fell into. It corresponds to the dream of another murderer. In a sensational
crime of the early 1960's an entire Kansas farm family was murdered in
cold blood. The killer reported having the following recurrent dream since
childhood.

> "I'm in Africa, a jungle. I'm moving through the trees toward a tree standing
> all alone. Jesus, it smells bad, that tree; it kind of makes me sick, the way
> it stinks. Only, it's beautiful to look at—it has blue leaves and diamonds
> hanging everywhere. Diamonds like oranges, that's why I'm there—to pick
> a bushel of diamonds. But I know the minute I try to, the minute I reach
> up, a snake is gonna fall on me. A snake that guards the tree . . . . I figure,
> well, I'll take my chances. What it comes down to is I want the diamonds
> more than I'm afraid of the snake. So I go to pick one, I have the diamond
> in my hand, I'm pulling at it, when the snake lands on top of me . . . . He
> is crushing me, you can hear my legs cracking. Now comes the part it makes
> me sweat even to think about. See he starts to swallow me. Feet first. Like
> going down in quicksand . . . . [But a savior arrived in the form of a great
> parrot] taller than Jesus, yellow like a sun flower." . . .
>   Thus, the snake, that custodian of the diamond-bearing tree, never
> finished devouring him but was itself always devoured. And afterward the
> blessed ascent! Ascension to a paradise that in one version was merely "a
> feeling," a sense of power, of unassailable superiority.[8]

This chilling dream has many parallels to the legend: jewels of seduc-
tive beauty, bird, tree and Garden of Eden. Both the legend and the dream

6. Jung says, "Shadow and anima, being unconscious, are then contaminated with each
   other, a state that is represented in dreams by 'marriage' or the like. But if the
   existence of the anima (or the shadow) is accepted and understood, a separation of
   these figures ensues . . . . The shadow is thus recognized as belonging, and the
   anima as not belonging, to the ego." (*Psychology and Alchemy*, CW 12, par. 242,
   note)
7. Gaer, *The Lore of the Old Testament*, p. 225.
8. Truman Capote, *In Cold Blood*, pp. 109f.

describe seduction by Satan, the ultimate evil of possession by the power principle.

The reference to Satan and the Garden of Eden in the legend indicates that David was reliving the original sin. In this case he did not avoid overt criminality and yet was able to escape psychic disaster by profound repentance. According to another legend it was God not David who brought about his crime with Bathsheba in order that God might then say to other sinners, "Go to David and learn how to repent."[9] Whether David's murderous lust be attributed to Satan or to God, in either case the legends indicate that it comes from the non-ego. It is an expression of the primordial psyche—what Jung has called the "not yet transformed God"[10]—and David, as the carrier of kingship, has the task of allowing it to live through him in order that it can be transformed by consciousness.

David's repentance is expressed in Psalm 51, *The Miserere:*

> Have mercy on me, O God, in your goodness,
> in your great tenderness wipe away my faults;
> wash me clean of my guilt,
> purify me from my sin.
> For I am well aware of my faults,
> I have my sin constantly in mind,
> having sinned against none other than you,
> having done what you regard as wrong.
> That you may be found just when you pass judgement on me
>   [alternate reading],
> blameless when you give judgement,
> You know I was born guilty,
> a sinner from the moment of conception. (Psalms 51:1-5)

The phrase "that you may be found just when you pass judgement on me" ("that thou mightest be justified when thou speakest"—AV) was a problem to Augustine[11] and, I suspect, many other commentators. We can now understand that in this passage the astonishing realization is dawning that God is justified by man, that is, that the ego must take responsibility for the evil promptings of the primordial Self in order that it (the Self) may be transformed.

Nathan, the prophet, rebukes David for his sin and announces that, in punishment, Yahweh "will stir up evil for you out of your own House." (2 Samuel 12:11) The evils that came included Ammon's incestuous rape of Tamar, Absalom's murder of Ammon, and finally the rebellion of Absalom. It is as though Absalom were unconsciously assigned the task of avenging Uriah's murder, as happens in Greek tragedy. David's sin has contaminated the psyche of his children.

9.   Ginzberg, *Legends of the Bible,* p. 546.
10.   *C.G. Jung Letters,* vol. 2, p. 314.
11.   "Exposition of the Psalms," *The Nicene and Post-Nicene Fathers,* vol. 8, p. 192.

Uriah appeared in an important dream of Jung's. He dreamt he was in a vast circular building with the great judgment seat of a sultan at the center.

From the centre a steep flight of stairs ascended to a spot high up on the wall . . . . At the top of the stairs was a small door . . . [Then Jung was told] "Now I will lead you into the highest presence." . . . Suddenly I knew . . . that that upper door led to a solitary chamber where lived Uriah, King David's general, whom David had shamefully betrayed for the sake of his wife Bathsheba, by commanding his soldiers to abandon Uriah in the face of the enemy.[12]

Jung says about this dream,

The centre is the seat of Akbar the Great, who rules over a subcontinent, who is a "lord of this world," like David. But even higher than David stands his guiltless victim, his loyal general Uriah, whom he abandoned to the enemy. Uriah is a prefiguration of Christ, the god-man who was abandoned by God. "My God, my God, why has thou forsaken me?" On top of that, David had "taken unto himself" Uriah's wife. Only later did I understand what this allusion to Uriah signified: not only was I forced to speak publicly, and very much to my detriment, about the ambivalence of the God-image in the Old Testament; but also, my wife would be taken from me by death.[13]

The same image of Uriah as higher than David is suggested by a legend.

David went into the desert to repent . . . . God came to him and said: "You shall not be forgiven until Uriah has forgiven you." King David went to Uriah's grave and called: "Uriah, Uriah! Forgive me for my sins against you." . . . "It's not for me to forgive you," answered Uriah, "but for God to judge between us." David left the grave, bowed in deep sorrow. Uriah went up to heaven, and there he saw a palace of great splendor, full of beautiful women, with eyes as black as ravens, preparing for a great feast. "For whom is all this honor intended?" asked Uriah. "For him who forgives his brother even though he has been wronged." "I forgive David his sin against me," said Uriah.[14]

During Absalom's rebellion David is obliged to flee eastward from Jerusalem. During his flight a remarkable incident occurs.

As David was reaching Bahurim, out came a man of the same clan as Saul's family. His name was Shimei son of Gera, and as he came he uttered curse after curse and threw stones at David and at all King David's officers, though the whole army and all the champions flanked the king right and left. The words of his curse were these, "Be off, be off, man of blood, scoundrel! Yahweh has brought on you all the blood of the House of Saul whose sovereignty you have usurped; and Yahweh has transferred that same

12. *Memories, Dreams, Reflections,* p. 219.
13. Ibid., pp. 219ff.
14. Gaer, *The Lore of the Old Testament,* p. 227.

sovereignty to Absalom your son. Now your doom has overtaken you, man of blood that you are." Abishai son of Zeruiah said to the king, "Is this dead dog to curse my lord the king? Let me go over and cut his head off." But the king replied, "What business is it of mine and yours, sons of Zeruiah? Let him curse. If Yahweh said to him, 'curse David,' what right has anyone to say, 'Why have you done this?'" David said to Abishai and all his officers, "Why, my own son, sprung from my body, is now seeking my life; so now how much the more this Benjaminite? Let him curse on if Yahweh has told him to. Perhaps Yahweh will look on my misery and repay me with good for his curse today." (2 Samuel 16:5-12)

David here has the astonishing insight that Yahweh told Shimei to curse him. Psychologically this means that *affect is from the Self* and should not be taken personally. However its highly contagious quality makes objectivity very difficult and David's insight is of the moment only. On his death bed David tells Solomon, "You must not let him [Shimei] go unpunished; you are a wise man and will know how to deal with him to bring his grey head down to Sheol in blood." (1 Kings 2:9)

In the midst of David's reign another example of Yahweh's ambiguity occurs. "The anger of Yahweh once again blazed out against the Israelites and he incited David against them. 'Go,' he said, 'take a census of Israel and Judah.'" (2 Samuel 24:1) In the parallel account of 1 Chronicles 21:1, it is stated that Satan, not Yahweh, instigated the census. The numbering of the people was known to be a crime against Yahweh likely to provoke a pestilence in retaliation. In Exodus 30:11 Yahweh says, "When you take a census and make a register of the sons of Israel, each is to pay Yahweh a ransom for his life, so that no plague comes on them when the census is being made." Soon David regretted the census and said to Yahweh, "I have committed a grave sin." (2 Samuel 24:10) But it was too late and Yahweh sent pestilence on the land.

The primitive taboo against counting is very difficult for the modern mind to understand. However its widespread existence is well established. Frazer discusses the subject and gives the following examples among others.[15] Certain African natives were afraid to count children for fear the evil spirits might hear. They also believed that cattle should not be counted because it would impede the increase of the herd. In Denmark there was the belief that if you counted hatched chickens some would be lost. According to a German belief, if you count your money it will decrease, and in Scotland it was thought that bread cakes baked at home should not be counted because fairies always eat cakes that had been counted. Such superstitions indicate that the unconscious reacts negatively to counting. Yahweh's reaction to the census indicates that it is particularly dangerous when quantitative thinking is applied to man. Quantitative consciousness, the basis of modern science, alienates the ego from the objective psyche

---

15. J.G. Frazer, *Folklore in the Old Testament*, pp. 307ff.

because it promotes statistical thinking which is antithetical to the unique experience of the individual.[16]

The culmination of David's reign is a unique promise from Yahweh.

> Yahweh will make you great; Yahweh will make you a House. And when your days are ended and you are laid to rest with your ancestors, I will preserve the offspring of your body after you and make his sovereignty secure . . . . I will be a father to him and he a son to me; if he does evil, I will punish him with the rod such as men use, with strokes such as mankind gives. Yet I will not withdraw my favor from him, as I withdrew it from your predecessor. Your House and your sovereignty will always stand secure before me and your throne be established for ever. (2 Samuel 7:11-16)

This promise was reaffirmed many times, notably in the Psalms; for instance Psalm 132:11-18:

> Yahweh swore to David
> and will remain true to his word.
> "I promise that your own son
> shall succeed you on the throne.
>
> If your sons observe my covenant,
> the decrees that I have taught them,
> their sons too shall succeed you
> on the throne for evermore."
>
> For Yahweh has chosen Zion,
> desiring this to be his home,
> "Here I will stay for ever,
> this is the home I have chosen.
>
> "I will bless her virtuous with riches,
> provide her poor with food,
> vest her priests in salvation
> and her devout shall shout for joy.
>
> "Here, I will make a horn sprout for David,
> here, I will trim a lamp for my anointed,
> whose enemies I shall clothe in shame,
> while his crown bursts into flower."

Both Christian and Jewish commentators consider these passages to refer to the Messiah, whose synonym is "Son of David." As Isaiah puts it, "A shoot springs from the stock of Jesse,/a scion thrusts from his roots:/on him the spirit of Yahweh rests." (Isaiah 11:1,2) The symbolism of the Messiah will be discussed more fully in the last chapter but here it can be noted that David is his ancestor, that is, the Self (Messiah) is a

---

16. See Jung's discussion of statistical thinking in "The Undiscovered Self," *Civilization in Transition,* CW 10, pars. 488ff.

product or consequence of the second-stage ego. In the paradoxical relationship between ego and Self, the Self is, in part, created by the ego. This necessary willful action of the ego in realizing the Self is suggested by a legend:

> The greatest distinction to be accorded David is reserved for the judgment day, when God will prepare a great banquet in Paradise for all the righteous. At David's petition, God Himself will be present at the banquet, and will sit on His throne, opposite to which David's throne will be placed. At the end of the banquet, God will pass the wine cup over which grace is said, to Abraham, with the words: "Pronounce the blessing over the wine, thou who art the father of the pious of the world." Abraham will reply: "I am not worthy to pronounce the blessing, for I am the father also of the Ishmaelites, who kindle God's wrath" . . . . [God then offers the cup, in turn, to Isaac, Jacob, Moses and Joshua, each of whom deems himself unworthy.] Finally God will turn to David with the words: "Take the cup and say the blessing, thou the sweetest singer in Israel and Israel's king." And David will reply: "Yes, I will pronounce the blessing, for I am worthy of the honor." Then God will take the Torah and read various passages from it, and David will recite a psalm in which both the pious in Paradise and the wicked in hell will join with a loud Amen. Thereupon God will send his angels to lead the wicked from hell to Paradise.[17]

17. Ginzberg, *Legends of the Bible,* p. 551.

10

Solomon

Solomon, the son of David and Bathsheba, succeeded David to the throne as the last king of the united monarchy. He is thus the third and final term in the sequence: Saul, David, Solomon. Symbolically, a temporal sequence of three refers to the opposites and their resolution: thesis, antithesis, synthesis. The forty-year reign of Solomon in all his glory is the fulfillment of the united monarchy. He has become a legendary figure characterized chiefly by his wealth and his wisdom, the temple and palace he built, and by his relations with the Queen of Sheba. He is also traditionally assigned the authorship of Proverbs, Ecclesiastes and The Song of Songs.

Solomon's outstanding quality of wisdom is established at the beginning of the biblical account with a description of his dream:

> At Gibeon Yahweh appeared in a dream to Solomon during the night. God said, "Ask what you would like me to give you." Solomon replied . . . . "Give your servant a heart to understand how to discern between good and evil, for who could govern this people of yours that is so great?" It pleased Yahweh that Solomon should have asked for this. "Since you have asked for this," Yahweh said, "and not asked for long life for yourself or riches or the lives of your enemies, but have asked for a discerning judgement for yourself, here and now I do what you ask. I give you a heart wise and shrewd as none before you has had and none will have after you. What you have not asked I shall give you too: such riches and glory as no other king ever had." (1 Kings 3:5-13)

Solomon is an embodiment of the wisdom archetype and all his major attributes belong to its symbolism. Temple, palace, wealth, glory and the Queen of Sheba are all aspects of this archetype.

> Yahweh gave Solomon immense wisdom and understanding and a heart as vast as the sand on the seashore. . . . He could talk about plants from the cedar in Lebanon to the hyssop growing on the wall; and he could talk of animals and birds and reptiles and fish. (1 Kings 5:9ff)

In legend this passage is interpreted to mean that Solomon could speak *to* plants, animals, birds and reptiles,[1] that is, that like St. Francis he was in communication with the natural levels of the psyche. His connection with

1. Ginzberg, *Legends of the Bible,* p. 558, and Gaer, *The Lore of the Old Testament,* p. 241.

93

natural instinct is illustrated by his well-known response to the two women claiming the same child. (1 Kings 3:16ff) Another example comes from legend:

> One of the puzzles that Solomon was set to solve was how to distinguish between a bunch of natural and a bunch of artificial flowers without leaving his seat to examine them. The king ordered the windows of the room to be opened, and the bees, coming in, alighted on the former and ignored the latter.[2]

Solomon's temple and palace can be considered symbolic synonyms for wisdom. The *Aurora Consurgens* speaks of "the treasure house which wisdom built upon a rock."

> Wisdom hath built herself a house, which if any man enter in he shall be saved and find pastures, as the prophet beareth witness: They shall be inebriated with the plenty of thy house (Psalm 35:9), for better is one day in thy courts above thousands (Psalm 83:11). O how blessed are they that dwell in this house (Psalm 83:5).[3]

> The beauty of this house cannot be told; its walls and streets are of the purest gold, and its gates gleam with pearls and precious stones (Revelation 12:10ff), and its cornerstones are fourteen, containing the principal virtues of the whole foundation.[4]

In alchemy, "the 'treasure-house' of philosophy . . . is a synonym for the *aurum philosophorum,* or lapis. . . . Zosimos . . . describes the lapis as a shining white temple of marble."[5] Solomon's function as builder expresses the *constructive* nature of wisdom, that is, of consciousness based on the Self.[6] The *Aurora* says of wisdom,

> Naught is more precious in nature than she, and God also hath not appointed her to be bought for a price. She it is that Solomon chose to have instead of light, and above all beauty and health . . . . Her fruit is more precious than all the riches of this world, and all the things that are desired are not to be compared with her. . . . She is a tree of life to them that lay hold on her, and an unfailing light. Blessed shall they be who retain her for the science of God shall never perish. He who hath found this science, it shall be his rightful food forever.[7]

According to legend, Solomon's building operations were made possible by a miraculous creature called the *shomeer.*

2. Dummelow, *The One-Volume Bible Commentary,* p. 218.
3. Marie-Louise von Franz, *Aurora Consurgens,* p. 101.
4. Ibid., pp. 105f.
5. Jung, *Mysterium Coniunctionis,* CW 14, par. 2, note 9.
6. "Except the Lord build the house, they labour in vain that build it." (Psalm 127:1, AV)
7. Von Franz, *Aurora Consurgens,* pp. 35f.

According to some sages, the *shomeer* was a worm the size of a grain of wheat, that had the power to hew down trees and split mountains into slabs of stone. These sages said that the *shomeer* was kept in wool, in the Garden of Eden, until Solomon was ready to build the House of God. Then an eagle was sent to carry it to the builders.

Other sages claim that the *shomeer* was a blue stone, the size of a small jewel. And wherever it was placed, and the Ineffable name whispered, the rock beneath would break into the desired shape and size . . . . But the hiding place of the *shomeer* no one knew, excepting Asmodeus, King of Demons, who lived in the Mountains of Darkness.[8]

By trickery, the secret was extracted from Asmodeus and the *shomeer* was obtained to build the temple. On completion, the *shomeer* was given back to the Keeper of the Abyss who "buried it in the Bottomless Sea. And from there no one can obtain it excepting the Creator himself."[9]

The *shomeer's* association to Solomon indicates that it belongs to the symbolism of wisdom. Its ability to split and shape undifferentiated matter gives it a bladelike quality and connects it with the separatio powers of the Logos.[10] As a worm it is the lowest of primordial life. As a blue jewel it is of the highest celestial value. As a stone it is analogous to the Philosophers' Stone and like it is a union of opposites. It initially resided in the Garden of Eden, that is, belonged to the primordial Self; but after being used it was returned to the abyss of the bottomless sea, the depths of the unconscious. The ability to cut and shape undifferentiated matter brings about psychic transformation. Unformed libido bound to inorganic or vegetative matter (stone and wood) is released and made available to the cultural psyche. This theme appears for instance in dreams of felled trees, which often refer to the dissolution of a relationship involving unconscious identification, freeing libido for more differentiated functioning.

The Queen of Sheba

A major symbolic event in the Solomon saga is his meeting with the Queen of Sheba.[11] The canonical account is as follows.

> The fame of Solomon having reached the queen of Sheba . . . she came to test him with difficult questions. She brought immense riches to Jerusalem with her, camels laden with spices, great quantities of gold, and precious stones. On coming to Solomon, she opened her mind freely to him; and

8. Gaer, *The Lore of the Old Testament,* pp. 237f.
9. Ibid., p. 240.
10. See Edinger, *Anatomy of the Psyche,* chapter 7.
11. I am indebted in this section to the excellent essay by Rivkah Schärf Kluger, "The Queen of Sheba in Bible and Legends," *Psyche and Bible,* pp. 85ff.

Solomon had an answer for all her questions, not one of them was too obscure for the king to expound.

When the queen of Sheba saw all the wisdom of Solomon, the palace he had built, the food at his table, the accommodation for his officials, the organisation of his staff and the way they were dressed, his cup-bearers, and the holocausts he offered in the Temple of Yahweh, it left her breathless, and she said to the king, "What I heard in my own country about you and your wisdom was true, then! Until I came and saw it with my own eyes I could not believe what they told me, but clearly they told me less than half: for wisdom and prosperity you surpass the report I heard. How happy your wives are! How happy are these servants of yours who wait on you always and hear your wisdom! Blessed be Yahweh your God who has granted you his favour, setting you on the throne of Israel! Because of Yahweh's ever-lasting love for Israel, he has made you king to deal out law and justice."

And she presented the king with a hundred and twenty talents of gold and great quantities of spices and precious stones: no such wealth of spices ever came again as those given to King Solomon by the queen of Sheba . . . . And King Solomon in his turn, presented the queen of Sheba with all she expressed a wish for, besides those presents he made her out of his royal bounty. Then she went home, she and her servants, to her own country. (1 Kings 10:1-13)

The biblical account has been richly amplified through the centuries by legend. For example Ginzberg gives the following account.

[The hoopoe had informed Solomon that he had found an unknown country] which is not subject to my lord the king . . . . Its trees are from the begin-ning of all time, and they suck up water that flows from the Garden of Eden. The city is crowded with men. On their heads they wear garlands wreathed in Paradise. They know not how to fight, nor how to shoot with bow and arrow. Their ruler is a woman, she is called the Queen of Sheba. [Solomon sends a letter to Sheba by the hoopoe requesting her to visit him and pay him homage and in due time she arrives.]

Benaiah conducted the queen to Solomon, who had gone to sit in a house of glass to receive her. The queen was deceived by an illusion. She thought the king was sitting in water, and as she stepped across to him she raised her garment to keep it dry. On her bared feet the king noticed hair, and he said to her: "Thy beauty is the beauty of a woman, but thy hair is masculine; hair is an ornament to a man, but it disfigures a woman."

Then the queen began and said: "I have heard of thee and thy wisdom; if now I inquire of thee concerning a matter, wilt thou answer me?" He replied: "The Lord giveth wisdom, out of His mouth cometh knowledge and understanding." She then said to him:

1. "Seven there are that issue and nine that enter; two yield the draught and one drinks." Said he to her: "Seven are the days of a woman's defile-ment, and nine the months of pregnancy; two are the breasts that yield the draught, and one the child that drinks it." Whereupon she said to him: "Thou art wise."

2. Then she questioned him further: "A woman said to her son, thy father

is my father, and thy grandfather my husband; thou art my son, and I am thy sister." "Assuredly," said he, "it was the daughter of Lot who spake thus to her son."

3. She placed a number of males and females of the same stature and garb before him and said: "Distinguish between them." Forthwith he made a sign to the eunuchs, who brought him a quantity of nuts and roasted ears of corn. The males, who were not bashful, seized them with bare hands; the females took them, putting forth their gloved hands from beneath their garments. Whereupon he exclaimed: "Those are the males, these the females." [The riddles continued to a total of twenty-two.][12]

We learn from the legend that the Queen of Sheba's realm is a part of original paradise, that is, the anima resides in the original state of unconscious wholeness, the state of nature. Other legends describe the same fact negatively when they say that the Queen of Sheba inhabits a realm of demons. When the ego is identified with spirit, nature becomes demonic— witness the fact that Pan and Dionysus were recast as versions of the devil by Christian mentality. In the biblical account the Queen of Sheba comes to Solomon on her own initiative, indicating that the anima desires a connection with consciousness. Nature wants to be illumined by spirit. In the legend Solomon takes the initiative. He has an intuition (the hoopoe bird) that his dominion is not complete and his power motive is aroused.

The legend's account of the meeting is very interesting psychologically. Solomon received Sheba in a "house of glass." As the queen stepped on the glass floor, thinking it water, she lifted her skirt and revealed a hairy foot. According to some versions it was a goat's foot. Solomon's house of glass is connected symbolically with his traditional wisdom. Glass symbolizes consciousness. Its transparency and its mirror function represent the reflective capacity of self-knowledge as promoted by the transparent vision of the objective, abstract spirit. Sheba, subjected to the scrutiny of the spirit, reveals her unhumanized residue of nature which indicates she is both part animal and part masculine. Nature's original state of the undifferentiated opposites still exists in her.[13] In some versions Sheba's encounter with Solomon transforms and humanizes her foot. Encounter with Solomon as the personification of spirit releases her from her androgynous and demonic residue.

Sheba in turn exerts an effect on Solomon. In the biblical account, "she came to test him with difficult questions." In the legend this becomes a series of twenty-two riddles. The archetypal theme of trial by riddle is widespread. We have already noted this image in the story of Samson. (Judges 14) James A. Kelso mentions other examples:

---

12. Ginzberg, *Legends of the Bible,* pp. 560ff.
13. In the *Zohar,* the Queen of Sheba is identified with Lilith. (Kluger, *Psyche and Bible,* p. 113)

There are modern Greek legends in which the failure to solve a riddle costs a man his life. A monster living in a castle propounds a riddle and gives forty days for its solution. Unfortunate is the person who fails, for the monster devours him. The resemblance to the story of the Sphinx is evident. In the *Mahabharata* the legend takes another form: the hero Yudhishthira frees two brothers from the fetters of a monster by the solution of a riddle. Teutonic legends are of a similar import: in the so-called *Wartburg-Krieg* there is a deadly riddle contest between Odin and the giant Wafthrudhnir, and another instance has been immortalized by Schiller (Turandot).[14]

The outstanding example is the riddle of the Sphinx which Oedipus was required to answer at the risk of his life. Oedipus's victory over Mother Nature was only apparent. She caught him from behind via his unconscious incest tendency. Jung writes,

> Oedipus, thinking he had overcome the Sphinx sent by the mother-goddess merely because he had solved her childishly simple riddle, fell a victim to matriarchal incest . . . . This had all those tragic consequences which could easily have been avoided if only Oedipus had been sufficiently intimidated by the frightening appearance of the "terrible" or "devouring" Mother whom the Sphinx personified.[15]

> It is evident that a factor of such magnitude cannot be disposed of by solving a childish riddle. The riddle was, in fact, the trap which the Sphinx laid for the unwary wanderer. Overestimating his intellect in a typically masculine way, Oedipus walked right into it, and all unknowingly committed the crime of incest. The riddle of the Sphinx was *herself*—the terrible mother-imago, which Oedipus would not take as a warning.[16]

Solomon suffered a fate similar to that of Oedipus, since the Bible tells us, "When Solomon grew old his wives swayed his heart to other gods; and his heart was not wholly with Yahweh his God . . . . Solomon became a follower of Astarte." (1 Kings 11:4,5) In other words Solomon lost his commitment to the masculine spirit principle and regressed to matriarchal "nature" psychology. The Old Testament pictures an early stage of psychological development in which the contrast between the masculine and feminine principles is highly polarized and where an either/ or psychology prevails. However, the underlying symbolism of the Solomon-Sheba story, especially as it is elaborated in legend, points ahead to an ultimate coniunctio of co-equal principles.

The encounter between Solomon and the Queen of Sheba, like the encounter between Oedipus and the Sphinx, represents a meeting of nature and spirit. For Solomon it is an ordeal to test and purify the capacity for

14.   Article on "Riddle," in Hastings, *Encyclopaedia of Religion and Ethics,* vol. 10, p. 769.
15.   *Symbols of Transformation,* CW 5, par. 264.
16.   Ibid., par. 265.

discriminating consciousness. For Sheba it is the opportunity for the humanization and redemption of her bestial and demonic residue. In a woman's psychology this means the humanization of the feminine principle through a conscious relationship to the animus. Rivkah Kluger puts it well:

> If a woman is freed from the animus possession, by uniting as a woman with the animus, instead of *being him,* i.e., *by relating with her feminine feeling to the spirit,* she becomes both more consciously masculine, by accepting and developing her masculinity, and at the same time more feminine, because the accepted animus does not sit anymore on her femininity, twisting or destroying it.[17]

> In our day, because of the obvious shadow side of patriarchal thinking, there is a tendency to depreciate patriarchy and idealize matriarchy. But it should not be forgotten that the shadow side of matriarchal origins is chaos, an undifferentiated swamp which yearns for redemption, an eternal cycle of recurring death and birth, out of which no development would have come without the new principle of Spirit breaking through. The desirable goal, as it appears in myths and legends . . . as well as in dreams, is not a "mother-world" in contrast to the "fatherworld," but the *coniunctio* of feminine and masculine.[18]

In a man's psychology, the transformation of the Queen of Sheba refers to the humanization of his primitive nature-anima. Because of the fluid nature of unconscious imagery, the Queen of Sheba is at one time the content in need of transformation and at another time the agent of transformation. On the one hand she comes to Solomon to be affected by his wisdom, on the other hand she personifies Wisdom herself. She evokes Solomon's wisdom by her riddles and also brings him the wisdom that enables him to answer, for Wisdom is the solver of riddles as Wisdom 8:8 tells us:

> She knows the past, she forcasts the future;
> she knows how to turn maxims and solve riddles;
> she has foreknowledge of signs and wonders,
> of the unfolding of the ages and the times.

Matthew 12:42 links the meeting of Solomon and Sheba with the Last Judgment: "On Judgement day the Queen of the South will rise up with this generation and condemn it, because she came from the ends of the earth to hear the wisdom of Solomon; and there is something greater than Solomon here."

The figure of the Queen of Sheba was used by the Church Fathers. Von Franz writes,

17. *Psyche and Bible,* p. 129.
18. Ibid., p. 130.

In patristic literature the Queen of Sheba was a prefiguration of Mary. On the other hand, in the hermeneutics of the Church Fathers the Queen of the south was also an image for the Church as the "queen" and "concubine" of Christ, who was called the "King of the south." Indeed, this feminine figure was even identified with God himself, who "shall go with the whirlwinds of the south." The south wind is also a symbol of the Holy Spirit, causing the minds of the elect to seethe, "that they may bring about whatsoever good things they desire." The equation of the Holy Spirit with the south wind is presumably due, as Jung points out,[19] to the hot and dry quality of this wind. The Holy Spirit is fiery and causes exaltation. He warms all things with the fire of love. According to Gregory the Great, the "south" signifies "those unfathomed depths of the heavenly country, which are filled with the heat of the Holy Spirit."[20]

The biblical account of the encounter between Solomon and Sheba hints at a coniunctio between nature and spirit but it is not fulfilled. The story ends with Sheba returning to her own country. As Kluger puts it, there "is only *a promise* for the healing of the breach. . . . It was the privilege of a much later time to produce the spiritual blossom of the *coniunctio* between the Queen of Sheba and King Solomon in its deepest form, namely in alchemy."[21] The alchemists used the figures of Solomon and Sheba as personifications of the opposites which are to be united in the alchemical transformation process. For instance, a text says,

> You have the virgin earth, give her a husband who is fitting for her! She is the Queen of Sheba, hence there is need of a king crowned with a diadem— where shall we find him? We see how the heavenly sun gives of his splendour to all other bodies, and the earthly or mineral sun will do likewise, when he is set in his own heaven, which is named the "Queen of Sheba," who came from the ends of the earth to behold the glory of Solomon. So, too, our Mercury has left his own lands and clothed himself with the fairest garment of white, and has given himself to Solomon, and not to any other who is a stranger [*extraneo*] and impure.[22]

This text concerns the coniunctio of Sol and Luna, expressed in this case as a union between the sun (King Solomon) and its containing "mercurial" heaven (Queen of Sheba). Sheba is thus the *medium* within which the sun of King Solomon can shine. "This medium has the nature of Mercurius, that paradoxical being, whose one definable meaning is the unconscious."[23] As Jung tells us, "The union of opposites is a transconscious process and, in principle, not amenable to scientific explanation."[24]

19. *Psychology and Alchemy, CW 12,* par. 473.
20. *Aurora Consurgens,* pp. 158f.
21. Kluger, *Psyche and Bible,* p. 106.
22. Quoted by Jung, *Mysterium Coniunctionis, CW 14,* par. 533.
23. Ibid., par. 534.
24. Ibid., par. 542.

However it can be suggested by a symbolic image such as the meeting of Solomon and Sheba. The *Rosarium* reports King Solomon as saying, "This is my daughter, for whose sake men say that the Queen of the South came out of the east, like the rising dawn, in order to hear, understand, and behold the wisdom of Solomon."[25] Jung remarks,

> The Queen of Sheba, Wisdom, the royal art, and the "daughter of the philosophers" are all so interfused that the underlying psychologem clearly emerges: the art is queen of the alchemist's heart, she is at once his mother, his daughter, and his beloved, and in his art and its allegories the drama of his own soul, his individuation process, is played out.[26]

The coniunctio, which is only hinted at in the story of Solomon and Sheba, receives its full biblical expression later in the Song of Songs.

25. Ibid.
26. Ibid., par. 543.

11

Prophets and Kings

Solomon did not achieve the greater coniunctio indicated by the alchemical symbolism, but rather succumbed to the lesser coniunctio[1] which amounted to a regression. "His wives swayed his heart to other gods" and he "became a follower of Astarte." (1 Kings 11:4,5) In response, upon his death, Yahweh caused his kingdom to be divided into a northern part, Israel, ruled by Jeroboam, and a southern part, Judah, under Solomon's son, Rehoboam.

This event is psychologically significant. On the way to conscious unity, unconscious unity must be split in two, as evidenced by the theme of the hostile brothers. In the process of development the archetypal One is followed by the archetypal Two. Jung writes,

> One is not a number at all; the first number is two. Two is the first number because, with it, separation and multiplication begin, which alone make counting possible. With the appearance of the number two, *another* appears alongside the one . . . . different and distinct . . . . The "One" . . . seeks to hold to its one-and-alone existence, while the "Other" ever strives to be another opposed to the One. . . . Thus there arises a tension of opposites between the One and the Other. But every tension of opposites culminates in a release, out of which comes the "third." In the third the tension is resolved and the lost unity is restored.[2]

The theme of division into two occurs in aborted form in the history of the United States, which has many similarities to the history of Israel. The early settlers thought of America as the new Canaan.[3] Initially there was an exodus from Europe and a dangerous crossing of the sea. During the colonial period the country was a multiplicity of units like the period of the Judges. This was followed by federation and the establishment of a central authority. Secession of the southern states in 1861 threatened division into two which was only avoided by a bloody civil war.

Elijah

We first meet Elijah as he announces to King Ahab a three-and-a-half year drought, the consequences of Yahweh's anger for the introduction of Baal worship. "As Yahweh lives, the God of Israel whom I serve, there shall

---

1. For the distinction between the lesser and the greater coniunctio see Edinger, *Anatomy of the Psyche,* pp. 211ff.
2. "A Psychological Approach to the Dogma of the Trinity," *Psychology and Religion, CW* 11, par. 180.
3. See Sacvan Bercovitch, *The Puritan Origins of the American Self,* passim.

be neither dew nor rain these years except at my order." (1 Kings 17:1) In Leviticus 26:19 Yahweh says, "If you do not listen to me I will break your proud strength, I will give you a sky of iron, an earth of bronze." And in Haggai 1:9,10, "Because while my House lies in ruins you are busy with your own, each one of you. That is why the sky has withheld the rain." In Revelation, a three-and-a-half year drought is part of the Last Judgment. It is proclaimed, "I shall send my two witnesses to prophesy for those 1260 days." (11:3) These witnesses "are able to lock up the sky so that it does not rain as long as they are prophesying." (11:6)[4]

These passages can be understood to refer to the withholding of the "divine water" of the Self from the ego, signifying ego-Self alienation[5] of the country as a whole. For Elijah, whose contact with Yahweh was intact, the time of drought was the occasion for special manifestations of the Self. Like the Israelites in the wilderness (Exodus 16:8,12), Elijah is sent meat in the evenings and bread in the mornings (1 Kings 17:6), and the theme of miraculous provision continues with the widow's jar of meal and jug of oil which replenish themselves with use. These events refer to the psychological fact that the nourishment of the Self only becomes visible at times of emptiness for the ego. It is only then that transpersonal energy-reserves are opened. "Where danger is, grows also the rescuing power."[6]

The widow's reaction to Elijah on the occasion of her son's illness is instructive. "What quarrel have you with me, man of God? Have you come here to bring my sins home to me and to kill my son?" (1 Kings 17:18) As a note tells us, "The woman attributes her misfortune to Elijah's visit: a man of God is like a hostile witness, at his presence secret or unconscious sins are brought to light and draw down retribution."[7] This describes one of the effects of the constellated Self in oneself or another. Since it is a manifestation of wholeness, it challenges all repressed or dissociated complexes. An individual who has a conscious connection to the Self, since there is a reconciliation of opposites within him, is likely to promote harmony in his environment. However, for a person with a highly polarized psyche, unconscious of his own shadow, the presence of a greater consciousness may be very threatening because he now feels accountable for his shadow.

In 1 Kings 18:30-40, a great contest occurs between Elijah and the priests of Baal. Elijah challenges the priests to bring a sacrificial bull to an altar on Mount Carmel; Elijah will do likewise and they will compete to see who can call down fire from heaven to consume his sacrifice. "You must call on the name of your god, and I shall call on the name of mine;

---

4. The "two witnesses" have been associated with Moses and Elijah, the two witnesses of the transfiguration. (*Jerusalem Bible,* p. 435, note 11d)
5. See Edinger, *Ego and Archetype,* pp. 37ff.
6. Hölderlin, "Patmos."
7. *Jerusalem Bible,* p. 445, note 17d.

the god who answers with fire, is God indeed." (18:24) Elijah is the winner. "The fire of Yahweh fell and consumed the holocaust . . . . When all the people saw this they fell on their faces." (18:38,39) At Elijah's command the people then seize the prophets of Baal and help Elijah to slaughter them all.

This astonishing story can be understood psychologically as picturing Elijah's inciting the inflamed mob to lynch the priests of Baal. The ability to call fire from heaven refers to the evocation of transpersonal affect. When this is done in a collective setting it is an act of demagoguery. Playing on the collective (archetypal) passions of a crowd generates the fire of Yahweh and turns the group into a vengeful mob which acts out in an unconscious, collective way the wrath of Yahweh. The slaughtered priests of Baal thus become, in effect, the holocaust to Yahweh.

Quite understandably, Jezebel was upset by the murder of her priests and threatened Elijah with the same fate. Elijah was riding high after the great display of his charisma, so high in fact that "tucking up his cloak he ran in front of Ahab's chariot as far as the outskirts of Jezreel." (1 Kings 18:46) But Jezebel's threat brought him down to earth. He fled for his life and fell into a suicidal depression. Through the guidance of Yahweh he was led through the wilderness—the outer expression of his inner state—until he reached Mount Horeb (Sinai), thus recapitulating the original journey of the Israelites to Sinai. On arrival, he repeats Moses' experience of there meeting Yahweh, who comes to him as the "sound of a gentle breeze" ("still small voice," AV; "low murmuring sound," NEB). The startling assignment Elijah is given is to foment assassination and rebellion. This job was later performed by Elisha (see below).

Elijah's most spectacular performance was his final ascent to heaven. "A chariot of fire appeared and horses of fire . . . and Elijah went up to heaven in the whirlwind." (2 Kings 2:11) This is a sublimatio image, a translation to an upper realm. A concrete, personal (ego) entity is spiritualized, eternalized and transformed into heavenly stuff.[8]

On the basis of his direct ascension to heaven many stories appeared concerning Elijah as an eternal figure who never tasted death. In Malachi Yahweh says,

> I am going to send you Elijah the prophet before my day [the day of Yahweh] comes, that great and terrible day. He shall turn the hearts of fathers towards their children and the hearts of children towards their fathers, lest I come and strike the land with a curse. (3:24)

On the basis of this passage Ecclesiasticus adds, "Blessed is he who shall have seen you before he dies." (48:11, NAB) The New Testament picks up the statement of Malachi and identifies Elijah with John the Baptist, the forerunner of Christ. (Luke 1:17, Matthew 11:14; 17:10-13) Elijah also appears with Christ at the Transfiguration.

8. See Edinger, *Anatomy of the Psyche,* p. 131 and Figs. 5 and 6.

The figure of Elijah takes on great importance in Jewish legend and popular belief. According to Patai,

> Elijah differs from all other Biblical figures in that he alone has remained—in popular belief—a live, charismatic personality who follows with deep paternal concern the fate of Israel in general and of every individual Jew in particular. He is said to have appeared and conversed with many a Talmudic sage, arranged for meetings between them and the Messiah, explained his words to them, and taught them much of the secret lore of the Tora. More important from the point of view of popular psychology is the widely prevalent belief that Elijah is always ready to extend his helping hand to people in distress, has the power to chase away the Angel of Death, and appears to the poor and the troubled in the most unexpected guises—as a beggar, a Persian, an Arab, a horseman, a Roman court official, a harlot, and (in a story by Peretz) a magician. At the Passover Seder meal, he is welcomed in every Jewish home with a large goblet of wine placed in the middle of the festive table especially for him. At circumcision ceremonies the chair on which the *Sandaq* (god-father) holding the child sits is called the Chair of Elijah because the prophet is believed to appear and hold the child.[9]

When misfortune overtakes a good man he says, "If the prophet Elijah were only here he would interpret the meaning of my woes, for he taught us to understand the justice of His ways."[10] The legendary Elijah is a variant of the "Wandering Jew" and sometimes functions as the Moslem El Khidr. Consider for example this parallel to the story of Moses and El Khidr in the 18th sura of the Koran:[11]

> One day a fervent disciple asked Elijah for permission to accompany the prophet on one of his many journeys.
> "You may come with me," said Elijah, "if you promise not to ask any questions about anything I do. For as soon as you ask for an explanation, we must part company."
> The young man promised and they started on their way.
> As night fell they came to the house of a poor man whose only possession was a cow. The man and his wife received Elijah and his young friend gladly, gave them food to eat and a comfortable place in which to sleep.
> Before they left in the morning, Elijah prayed that the poor man's cow should die. The disciple was surprised at the prophet's prayer, but he kept his promise and did not ask any questions.
> The next night they stopped at a mansion. The rich man paid no attention to his guests, offered them nothing to eat or drink, and sent them to sleep in the barn.
> As they were leaving the next morning, Elijah noticed a wall, near the house, that had crumbled away. Elijah prayed that the wall repair itself; and

9. Raphael Patai, *The Messiah Texts*, p. 132.
10. Gaer, *The Lore of the Old Testament*, p. 264.
11. Jung gives an extensive commentary on this story in "Concerning Rebirth," *The Archetypes and the Collective Unconscious*, CW 9i, pars. 240ff.

the wall rose before them complete and whole. Again they went on their way. And again the disciple refrained from asking questions.

The next day they came to a magnificent temple, with pews of gold and pews of silver. But none of the worshipers invited the wayfarers to their home. They went on their way and Elijah prayed that all the worshipers should become leaders. The disciple's bewilderment grew, but again he refrained from asking questions.

At the next town they reached all the people were friendly and welcomed the strangers, offering them food and drink. When they had rested and were ready to leave, Elijah prayed that God should give them one leader.

The disciple could contain himself no longer and asked: "Where is the justice of your prayers, Elijah?"

And Elijah answered: "The poor man's wife was destined to die the day we left them, and I prayed to God to accept the cow as a vicarious sacrifice. Under the crumbling wall of the rich miser was hidden a treasure of gold which he would have discovered had he rebuilt the wall himself. The grudging worshipers in the temple will all become leaders and be ruined by many disputes. But the inhabitants of this good town, united under one wise leader, will always prosper."

"Now," said the disciple humbly, "I see that there is always justice in God's acts, even when the evildoers seem to prosper."

"Yes," said Elijah. "And now, also, since you have asked for an explanation, we must part company."[12]

In this tale Elijah represents the Greater Personality (Self) who operates out of a broader perspective than the ego since it encompasses the opposites. His role as reconciler of the opposites is indicated in this description of his function as forerunner of the Messiah:

> His messianic activity . . . is to be twofold: he is to be the forerunner of the Messiah, yet in part he will himself realize the promised scheme of salvation. His first task will be to induce Israel to repent when the Messiah is about to come, and to establish peace and harmony in the world. Hence he will have to settle all legal difficulties and solve all legal problems, that have accumulated since days immemorial, and decide vexed questions of ritual concerning which authors entertain contradictory views. In short, all differences of opinion must be removed from the path of the Messiah.[13]

The figure of Elijah is still alive in the modern psyche. For instance he appeared to Jung during his confrontation with the unconscious:

> In order to seize hold of the fantasies, I frequently imagined a steep descent. I even made several attempts to get to the very bottom. The first time I reached, as it were, a depth of about a thousand feet; the next time I found myself at the edge of a cosmic abyss. It was like a voyage to the moon, or a descent into empty space. First came the image of a crater, and I had the

---

12.   Gaer, *The Lore of the Old Testament,* pp. 256f.
13.   Ginzberg, *Legends of the Bible,* p. 600.

feeling that I was in the land of the dead. The atmosphere was that of the other world. Near the steep slope of a rock I caught sight of two figures, an old man with a white beard and a beautiful young girl. I summoned up my courage and approached them as though they were real people, and listened attentively to what they told me. The old man explained that he was Elijah, and that gave me a shock. But the girl staggered me even more, for she called herself Salome! She was blind. What a strange couple: Salome and Elijah. But Elijah assured me that he and Salome had belonged together from all eternity, which completely astounded me. . . . They had a black serpent living with them which displayed an unmistakable fondness for me. I stuck close to Elijah because he seemed to be the most reasonable of the three, and to have a clear intelligence. Of Salome I was distinctly suspicious. Elijah and I had a long conversation which, however, I did not understand.[14]

Concerning these figures, Jung writes,

Salome is an anima figure. She is blind because she does not see the meaning of things. Elijah is the figure of the wise old prophet and represents the factor of intelligence and knowledge; Salome, the erotic element. One might say that the two figures are personifications of Logos and Eros. But such a definition would be excessively intellectual. It is more meaningful to let the figures be what they were for me at the time—namely, events and experiences.[15]

Ahab

In an ugly sequence of assassination, butchery and backsliding, 1 Kings: 12-16 describes the succeeding kings who reigned in the divided kingdoms of Israel and Judah. These chronicles of kingship remind us of the tragic and ambiguous burden that is imposed on the human being invested with the mantle of royalty.

In dreams, a king or head of state is a reference to the Self. In history and drama, the king is the ego writ large. He is a limited human being destined to carry a collective, transpersonal meaning. The king is always a more or less tragic figure because he must carry the burden of the opposites: the small and human as contrasted with the large and archetypal. Every king is a failure to some extent, either through passivity—a refusal to take up the kingly burden—or through inflation—arrogance, brutality and hubris. The history of kingship is a picture of ego development. The king was considered quite literally to be God's representative on earth. He is thus an image of the ego's incarnation of the Self, that is, individuation.

Ahab was the seventh king of the northern kingdom of Israel and reigned for twenty-two years. We are told that he

---

14. *Memories, Dreams, Reflections*, p. 181.
15. Ibid., p. 182.

did what was displeasing to Yahweh, and was worse than all his predecessors . . . . He married Jezebel, the daughter of Ethbaal, king of the Sido-
nians and then proceeded to serve Baal and worship him. He erected an
altar to him in the temple of Baal which he built in Samaria. Ahab also put
up a sacred pole and committed other crimes as well, provoking the anger
of Yahweh, the God of Israel, more than all the kings of Israel who were
his predecessors. (1 Kings 16:30-33)

The term Baal (Lord) was the title of the supreme God among the
Canaanites and in the early period was applied also to Yahweh. "After the
time of Ahab, however, the name became associated with the worship and
rites of the Phoenician deity introduced into Samaria by Jezebel, and its
idolatrous associations accordingly caused it to fall into disrepute."[16] Concerning the sacred pole set up by Ahab, Frazer writes,

> We know that at all the old Canaanite sanctuaries, including the sanctuaries
> of Jehovah down to the reformations of Hezekiah and Josiah, the two regular
> objects of worship were a sacred stock and a sacred stone, and that these
> sanctuaries were the seats of profligate rites performed by sacred men
> (*kedeshim*) and sacred women (*kedeshoth*).[17]

Jeremiah speaks of those who say "to a stock, thou art my father; and
to a stone, thou hast brought me forth." (2:27, AV) Frazer considers this
statement to refer to

> the children born of the loose intercourse of the sexes at these places [who]
> were believed to be the offspring or emanations of these uncouth but wor-
> shipped idols . . . . On this view the sacred men and women who actually
> begot or bore the children were deemed the human embodiments of the two
> divinities.[18]

Such practices were variations of the sacred prostitution of the matriarchal
nature religion which Yahweh-worship had supplanted. Ahab was thus
guilty of promoting a religious regression. This was intolerable to Yahweh,
the new spirit principle.

The way Yahweh proceeds to cause Ahab's undoing is chilling to
behold. After listening to a pack of false prophets predict success in his
attack on Ramoth-Gilead, Ahab summons the true prophet, Micaiah, who
makes the following announcement:

> Listen rather to the word of Yahweh. I have seen Yahweh seated on his
> throne; all the array of heaven stood in his presence, on his right and on his
> left. Yahweh said, "Who will trick Ahab into marching to his death at
> Ramoth-gilead?" At which some answered one way, and some another.
> Then the spirit came forward and stood before Yahweh. "I," he said, "I will
> trick him." "How?" Yahweh asked. He replied, "I will go and become a

---

16. *International Standard Bible Encyclopaedia,* vol. 1, p. 346.
17. J.G. Frazer, "Adonis, Attis, Osiris," *The Golden Bough,* part 4, vol. 1, p. 107.
18. Ibid., pp. 107f.

lying spirit in the mouths of all his prophets." "You shall trick him," Yahweh said, "you shall succeed. Go and do it." Now see how Yahweh has put a lying spirit into the mouths of all your prophets here. But Yahweh has pronounced disaster on you. (1 Kings 22:19-23)

This astonishing piece of divine trickery has a parallel in the *Iliad:*

Now the rest of the gods, and men who were lords of chariots,
slept night long, but the ease of sleep came not upon Zeus
who was pondering in his heart how he might bring honour
to Achilleus, and destroy many beside the ships of the Achaians.
Now to his mind this thing appeared to be the best counsel,
to send evil Dream to Atreus' son Agamemnon.
He cried out to the dream and addressed him in winged words:
"Go forth, evil Dream, beside the swift ships of the Achaians.
Make your way to the shelter of Atreus' son Agamemnon;
speak to him in words exactly as I command you.
Bid him arm the flowing-haired Achaians for battle
in all haste; since now he might take the wide-wayed city
of the Trojans. For no longer are the gods who live on Olympos
arguing the matter, since Hera forced them all over
by her supplication, and evils are in store for the Trojans."
    So he spoke, and Dream listened to his word and descended.
Lightly he came down beside the swift ships of the Achaians
and came to Agamemnon the son of Atreus. He found him
sleeping within his shelter in a cloud of immortal slumber.
Dream stood then beside his head in the likeness of Nestor,
Neleus' son, whom Agamemnon honoured beyond all
elders beside. In Nestor's likeness the divine Dream spoke to him:
"Son of wise Atreus breaker of horses, are you sleeping?
He should not sleep night long who is a man burdened with counsels
and responsibility for a people and cares so numerous.
Listen quickly to what I say, since I am a messenger
of Zeus, who far away cares much for you and is pitiful.
Zeus bids you arm the flowing-haired Achaians for battle
in all haste; since now you might take the wide-wayed city
of the Trojans. For no longer are the gods who live on Olympos
arguing the matter, since Hera forced them all over
by her supplication, and evils are in store for the Trojans
from Zeus. Keep this thought in your heart then, let not forgetfulness
take you, after you are released from the kindly sweet slumber."
    So he spoke and went away, and left Agamemnon
there, believing things in his heart that were not to be accomplished.
For he thought that on that very day he would take Priam's city;
fool, who knew nothing of all the things Zeus planned to accomplish,
Zeus, who yet was minded to visit tears and sufferings
on Trojans and Danaans alike in the strong encounters.[19]

---

19. Homer, *Iliad,* trans. Richard Lattimore, book 2, lines 1-40.

These examples demonstrate in a shocking way the ambiguous trickster nature of the unconscious. The God that requires man not to bear false witness (Exodus 20:16) has no qualms on that score about himself. Micaiah's vision of military defeat—"I have seen all Israel scattered on the mountains like sheep without a shepherd" (1 Kings 22:17)—can also be applied to those who have an innocent, "good shepherd" attitude toward Yahweh. He is a union of opposites, evil as well as good. *"God can be loved but must be feared."*[20]

For those who would claim that such ambiguities apply only to the Old Testament God and not to the God of Love of the New Testament, I would remind them of the Lord's Prayer where we find these words: "Lead us not into temptation but deliver us from evil." (Matthew 6:13, AV) About this request Jung observes,

> God is asked not to entice us outright into doing evil, but rather to deliver us from it. The possibility that Yahweh . . . might yet revert to his former ways is not so remote that one need not keep one eye open for it. At any rate, Christ considers it appropriate to remind his father of his destructive inclinations towards mankind and to beg him to desist from them.[21]

Concerning the relation between the Old Testament and New Testament God, I was once brought an interesting dream:

> I am listening to a lecture concerning God's relation to man. The speaker drew a chart on the blackboard, a sort of graph that signified the dealings of God with men. The graph was described as showing the dynamics of God's love and His punishment, the dramatic shifts from pole to pole of His activity. It was pointed out that the activity was less dramatic at the time of Jesus and the New Testament than it was "later" in the Old Testament. I suddenly saw that there was psychological wisdom in what was being presented.

The dreamer drew the following "graph" in explanation.

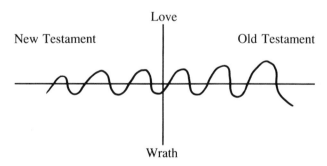

Love

New Testament   Old Testament

Wrath

20. Jung, "Answer to Job," *Psychology and Religion,* CW 11, par. 732.
21. Ibid., par. 651.

Jung tells us that, to understand it psychologically, the Tibetan Book of the Dead should be read backwards.[22] The same remark applies also to the Bible. The Bible pictures the totality of the psyche—the latest is the closest to consciousness, the earliest is the most remote. What the Bible presents as a sequence in time represents successive strata of deposits in the objective psyche. The empirical exploration of the psyche is very similar to an archeological dig. The upper layers are the most recent in time and the lower layers more remote. In the process of excavation the upper layers appear first and the deeper layers appear "later." Thus it is that the psychological realization of the Old Testament Yahweh comes "later."

Although Ahab was doomed to an ignominious end because of his idolatry, the immediate cause of his downfall was, surprisingly, an act of mercy. After defeating Ben-hadad the king of Aram in battle, Ahab accepted his pleas for mercy and made a treaty with him. Yahweh then announced to Ahab, "Since you have let the man escape who was under my ban, your life will pay for his, your people for his people." (1 Kings 20:42) And Ahab fell in battle against Ben-hadad who had not honored the treaty.

Ahab has reappeared to the modern mind through the imagination of Herman Melville in his novel *Moby-Dick*. Captain Ahab is a central figure and Elijah puts in a marginal appearance as a crazed seer.[23]

Elisha

The mantle of Elijah is passed on to Elisha who performs many miracles. A particularly instructive one is the healing of Naaman.

> Naaman, army commander to the king of Aram, was a man who enjoyed his master's respect and favour, since through him Yahweh had granted victory to the Aramaeans. But the man was a leper. Now on one of their raids, the Aramaeans had carried off from the land of Israel a little girl who had become a servant of Naaman's wife. She said to her mistress, "If only my master would approach the prophet of Samaria. He would cure him of his leprosy." Naaman went and told his master. "This and this," he reported, "is what the girl from the land of Israel said." "Go by all means," said the king of Aram. "I will send a letter to the king of Israel."
>
> So Naaman left, taking with him ten talents of silver, six thousand shekels of gold and ten festal robes. He presented the letter to the king of Israel. It read: "With this letter, I am sending my servant Naaman to you for you to cure him of his leprosy." When the king of Israel read the letter, he tore his garments. "Am I a god to give death and life," he said, "that he sends

22. "Psychological Commentary on 'The Tibetan Book of the Dead,'" *Psychology and Religion,* CW 11, par. 844.
23. See Edinger, *Melville's Moby-Dick,* pp. 49ff.

a man to me and asks me to cure him of his leprosy? Listen to this, and take note of it and see how he intends to pick a quarrel with me."

When Elisha heard that the king of Israel had torn his garments, he sent word to the king, "Why did you tear your garments? Let him come to me, and he will find there is a prophet in Israel." So Naaman came with his team and chariot and drew up at the door of Elisha's house. And Elisha sent him a messenger to say, "Go and bathe seven times in the Jordan, and your flesh will become clean once more." But Naaman was indignant and went off, saying, "Here was I thinking he would be sure to come out to me, and stand there, and call on the name of Yahweh his God, and wave his hand over the spot and cure the leprous part. Surely Abana and Pharpar, the rivers of Damascus, are better than any water in Israel? Could I not bathe in them and become clean?" And he turned round and went off in a rage.

But his servants approached him and said, "My father, if the prophet had asked you to do something difficult, would you not have done it? All the more reason, then when he says to you, 'Bathe, and you will become clean.'" So he went down and immersed himself seven times in the Jordan, as Elisha had told him to do. And his flesh became clean once more like the flesh of a little child.

Returning to Elisha with his whole escort, he went in and stood before him. "Now I know," he said, "that there is no God in all the earth except in Israel. Now, please, accept a present from your servant." But Elisha replied, "As Yahweh lives, whom I serve, I will accept nothing." Naaman pressed him to accept, but he refused. Then Naaman said, "Since your answer is 'No,' allow your servant to be given as much earth as two mules may carry, because your servant will no longer offer holocaust or sacrifice to any god except Yahweh. Only—and may Yahweh forgive your servant—when my master goes to the temple of Rimmon to worship there, he leans on my arm, and I bow down in the temple of Rimmon when he does, may Yahweh forgive your servant this act!" "Go in peace," Elisha answered.

Naaman had gone a small distance, when Gehazi, the servant of Elisha, said to himself, "My master has let this Aramaean Naaman off lightly, by not accepting what he offered. As Yahweh lives, I will run after him and get something out of him." So Gehazi set off in pursuit of Naaman. When Naaman saw him running after him, he jumped down from his chariot to meet him. "Is all well?" he asked. "All is well," he said. "My master has sent me to say, 'This very moment two young men of the prophetic brotherhood have arrived from the highlands of Ephraim. Be kind enough to give them a talent of silver.'" "Please accept two talents," Naaman replied, and pressed him, tying up the two talents of silver in two bags and consigning them to two of his servants who carried them in front of Gehazi. When he reached Ophel, he took them from their hands and put them away in the house. He then dismissed the men, who went away.

He, for his part, went and presented himself to his master. Elisha said, "Gehazi, where have you been?" "Your servant has not been anywhere," he replied. But Elisha said to him, "Was not my heart present there when someone left his chariot to meet you? Now you have taken the money, you can buy gardens with it, and olive groves, sheep and oxen, male and female slaves. But Naaman's leprosy will cling to you and to your descendants for ever." And Gehazi left his presence a leper, white as snow. (2 Kings 5:1-27)

This story can serve as a paradigm for the process of depth psychotherapy. Naaman, the ego, is ill. He learns of the possibility of healing from the foreign anima who comes from Yahweh's holy land (the unconscious). He decides to seek out the healer-prophet of Israel, that is, he decides to visit an analyst. Naaman presents his letter to the king of Israel, but the king is alarmed by his extravagant expectation. "Am I a god to give death and life?" Thus will the analyst's ego react to the patient's assumption that the analyst has the power to heal him. Jung often told his patients that he didn't know how to help them but there is a two-million-year-old man within them; *he* will know what to do.[24] This old wise man is a personification of the instinctual wisdom of the unconscious and corresponds to the figure of Elisha. Elisha's invitation for Naaman to visit him indicates that inner archetypal wisdom has been constellated and help from the unconscious is forthcoming.

The prescription is to bathe seven times in the Jordan river. This is a recipe for solutio.[25] He is to immerse himself in the waters of the unconscious and experience the death and rebirth that is implied by that image. In other words he must open himself to the effects of his dreams and fantasies and allow their wisdom to "dissolve" his problem. Seven is the number of initiation, transformation and creative action completed. Seven rungs of the planetary ladder stand between earth and heaven and creation took seven days. Naaman reacts to this prescription with rage. He had expected a "treatment" from Elisha who should "wave his hand over the spot and cure the leprous part." The idea that one should consult the unconscious is an offense to the rational ego. However, his servants counseled a wiser course. They represent the lowly, modest aspects of the personality in better touch with psychic reality.

Naaman does immerse himself in the Jordan seven times and is healed. This image condenses a process that, in practical psychotherapy, may take years. The experience of the unconscious often does lead to a transformation. Jung says,

> Analysis should release an experience that grips us or falls upon us as from above, an experience that has substance and body such as those things which occurred to the ancients. If I were going to symbolize it I would choose the annunciation.[26]

Naaman's baptism in the Jordan, like Christ's, brought about such an experience. This is followed naturally by the appearance of a religious attitude ("Now I know . . . that there is no God in all the earth except in Israel") and by an outpouring of gratitude to the man who made the experience possible. The latter is indicated by Naaman's offer to give Elisha a gift. This signifies a transference projection whereby the patient, Naaman,

24. *C.G. Jung Speaking*, p. 89.
25. See Edinger, *Anatomy of the Psyche*, chapter 3.
26. *Seminar 1925*, p. 111.

would attribute a psychic value to the analyst Elisha that does not properly belong to him. Elisha wisely declines the gift. To accept it would mean identification with the transference projection. Elisha would then take personal credit for Naaman's healing. That act of hubris would have disastrous consequences, for it would make him responsible for Naaman's destiny as a whole. This latter consequence is represented by Gehazi who accepted Naaman's gift and received with it his leprosy as well.

The load of earth transported from Israel to Naaman's homeland becomes the ground on which an altar to Yahweh is built. Earth is a coagulatio image[27] and in this context refers to a *realization* of the transpersonal psyche which becomes the ground on which a living religious attitude is constructed. This attitude is the factor that heals.

Hazael and Jehu

In 1 Kings Yahweh tells Elijah on Mount Horeb,

> You are to go and annoint Hazael as king of Aram. You are to annoint Jehu son of Nimshi as king of Israel . . . . Anyone who escapes the sword of Hazael will be put to death by Jehu; and anyone who escapes the sword of Jehu will be put to death by Elisha. (19:15-17)

These assignments were carried out by Elisha. He visited Hazael, a subordinate of King Ben-hadad, and cunningly incited him to assassination. Like the witches in *Macbeth* he told the ambitious Hazael, "In a vision from Yahweh . . . I have seen you king of Aram." (2 Kings 8:13) Thus Elisha fulfilled Yahweh's assignment to "annoint" Hazael. In this account, inciting his ambition to seize the throne is symbolically equivalent to annointing him king.

A similar annointing was done to Jehu. Elisha dispatched a young prophet who

> poured the oil on his head, saying, "Yahweh the God of Israel says this, 'I have annointed you king over the people of Yahweh, king of Israel. You are to strike down the family of Ahab your master, and I will avenge the blood of my servants the prophets and of all the servants of Yahweh on Jezebel and the whole family of Ahab.'" (2 Kings 9:6-8)

In other words, Yahweh puts out a murder contract against King Jehoram, Jezebel and the entire royal family, which bloody deed was duly carried out.

The "annointings" of Hazael and Jehu signify psychologically an influx from the unconscious which tells the ego to kill the current king or ruling principle and seize power. This message is presented as "God's will."

---

27. See Edinger, *Anatomy of the Psyche,* chapter 4.

Such an occasion is a moment of terrible ambiguity. The assignment is an individuation imperative and to ignore it can be fatal. But to take concretely and literally a *symbolic* message can be equally fatal. Orestes in Aeschylus's drama was in such a position and barely escaped with his sanity. Vengeance belongs to God (Psalm 94:1), that is, revenge is from the Self. But the Self needs the ego to realize it and if that "realization" amounts to a literal crime the ego is left holding the bag.

A modern pathological version of the annointing of Jehu was reported some years ago in the newspaper. An adolescent boy was told by God in a hallucinatory vision to kill his family. He laid in wait for them in the bushes and shot them all with a rifle. Jung is reported to have said that if God told him to murder someone he wouldn't do it, but instead would interpose himself against God and die if necessary. As Jung says, "God *is* a most shocking problem."[28]

12

Exile and Return

The Chosen People

"You are a people consecrated to Yahweh your God, and Yahweh has chosen you to be his very own people out of all the peoples on the earth." (Deuteronomy 14:2) Here and in many other places throughout the Old Testament Yahweh announces the special, elect status of the Jews. This is a central theme of individuation. Its application to Israel marks the nation as a collective carrier of individuation symbolism and helps to explain the awesome history of this peculiar people.[1]

To feel oneself chosen is one of the features of the ego's encounter with the Self. There are several aspects of this experience.

1. *One is given a task, an assignment, a transpersonal purpose.* This process operates more or less unconsciously in normal living whenever one follows a desire, a talent or an attachment into some life consequence such as a work, a vocation, a cause or a relationship. In the second half of life, as individuation becomes conscious, these libido manifestations take on a different quality. They become imperatives of the Self which one is enjoined to honor in the conscious pursuit of wholeness.

2. *One is singled out as separate, special, different.* In other words one is made into an *individual,* brought out from the state of collective *participation mystique.* As Rivkah Kluger demonstrates, Yahweh separates out one special people to be his in order to bring about his own separation from the many gods of polytheism:

> The Godhead Yahweh, who has, so to speak, grown together from many polytheistic god-figures into a God-personality, has become thereby a *distinct* God, who stands out from all the other gods. This distinct God now chooses for himself an equally distinct people as his vis-à-vis. Here we see, projected onto a people, the birth of the idea of the *individual* who is removed from the anonymous existence in the cycle of nature and placed into a personal, unique fate.[2]

As a separate, distinct people crystallizes out among the nations, simultaneously Yahweh is differentiated from the multiplicity of gods. This refers to the parallel aspect of the ego-Self relationship. The Self, seeking its own discrimination, offers the ego a special, chosen status. By accepting that offer and living it out, the ego helps to create the actualized Self.

---

1. See Rivkah Kluger's excellent essay, "The Idea of the Chosen People," *Psyche and Bible.*
2. Ibid., p. 19.

The chosen people are "the elect," which term has an ambiguous double meaning. The elect ones have been elected for a special status and also they have elected to assume that special role.

To be set apart as a special one has both positive and negative aspects.[3] To be specially favored is flattering and inflating, analogous to the spoiled child who expects everything to be according to his wishes. Such Israelites say, "No misfortune will ever touch us, nor even come anywhere near us." (Amos 9:10) "Is not Yahweh in our midst? No evil is going to overtake us." (Micah 3:11) These remarks indicate unconscious assumptions of the infantile psyche. When these assumptions are contradicted by reality they generate bitter resentment such as the complaints of the Israelites to Moses. "Why did we not die at Yahweh's hand in the land of Egypt, when we were able to sit down to pans of meat and could eat bread to our hearts content! As it is, you have brought us to this wilderness to starve this whole company to death." (Exodus 16:3) However, if the status of special one is accepted consciously and maturely it is expressed in the attitude of Samuel: "Speak, Yahweh, your servant is listening." (1 Samuel 3:10)

3. *One is marked out as consecrated, a possession of God.* "You are a people consecrated to Yahweh your God; it is you that Yahweh our God has chosen to be his very own people out of all the peoples on the earth." (Deuteronomy 7:6) Psychologically this means that one is required to pay constant attention to the inner authority, the Self. One has become its possession so to speak. This state of affairs exposes one to the twin experiences symbolized by "God's love" and "God's punishment." "If Yahweh set his heart on you and chose you, it was not because you outnumbered other peoples; you were the least of peoples. It was for love of you." (Deuteronomy 7:7) On the other hand, Yahweh announces, "You only have I known of all the families of the earth; therefore I will punish you for all your iniquities." (Amos 3:2) When the Self has been activated, one must diligently consider its requirements. Its approval and disapproval manifest clearly and the ego becomes painfully aware that it is not master in its own house.

4. *One is chosen to be known by God and to know him.* "I knew you in the wilderness." (Hosea 15:3, alternate reading) "You only have I known of all the families of the earth." (Amos 3:2) Other passages allude to Yahweh's need to be known, for instance, "I will adopt you as my own people, and I will be your God. Then you shall *know* that it is I Yahweh your God who has freed you from the Egyptians' burdens." (Exodus 6:6, italics added) This is a very important issue psychologically. Rivkah Kluger notes that the Hebrew word *yāda* (to know, to become conscious of), also is used for sexual intercourse, which indicates the connection of meaning between love and knowledge. She then makes this important observation.

3. See Edinger, *Ego and Archetype*, pp. 170ff.

Yahweh *knows* (chooses) the people *so that it may know him.* Suggested here is the idea . . . that God needs his vis-à-vis in order to become conscious of himself. This could not be stated more clearly than in Isaiah 48:9-11: "For the sake of my name I deferred my anger . . . . And now I have put you in the fire like silver, I have tested you in the furnace of distress. *For my sake and my sake only have I acted.*"[4]

We are now in a position to understand such passages. The Self desperately needs the ego to know it.[5]

5. *One is chosen to be redeemed by God and to redeem him.* Knowing and being known belongs to the phenomenon of *consciousness, and* this is redeeming. When Yahweh speaks of choosing Israel he usually mentions at the same time redeeming them from slavery. "It was for love of you and to keep the oath he swore to your fathers that Yahweh brought you out with his mighty hand and redeemed you from the house of slavery." (Deuteronomy 7:8) Encounter with the Self has a redeeming or rescuing effect on the ego because it releases one from an unconscious state and reveals meaning. The reciprocal process, in which the Self is redeemed by the ego, is also hinted in the Old Testament. Kluger has ferreted out the major passage. "For my sake and my sake only have I acted," says Yahweh in explaining why he afflicted the Israelites. This states explicitly that Yahweh *needs* Israel's awareness of Him. A Midrash to Psalm 91:16[6] says, "This is one of the difficult verses, which identify God's salvation with the salvation of Israel."[7] Thus, Israel's fate is Yahweh's fate. This idea parallels the alchemical opus which was an effort to redeem the divine substance hidden in the darkness of the prima materia.[8]

The Babylonian Captivity

The Bible and history make clear that to be chosen by Yahweh is a very dubious distinction. Rivkah Kluger addresses the question: Why did Yahweh choose Israel?

> It was a poor peasant people, eternally oppressed by the surrounding great kingdoms, Egypt and Babylon: It could make room for itself only inwardly, and was thereby peculiarly suited to take upon itself the misery and dignity, the curse and blessing, of God's election. It was, so to speak, *God's easiest prey.*[9]

The grave ambiguity of being God's elect is demonstrated in the down-

---

4. Kluger, *Psyche and Bible,* p. 23, italics mine. I have changed the Isaiah passage to the version in the *Jerusalem Bible.*
5. See Edinger, *The Creation of Consciousness,* pp. 52ff.
6. "With long life will I satisfy him, and show him my salvation." (AV)
7. Cited by Kluger, *Psyche and Bible,* p. 24.
8. See Edinger, *Anatomy of the Psyche,* chapter 1.
9. Kluger, *Psyche and Bible,* p. 41.

fall of Israel and Judah and the Babylonian exile. In response to their infidelities, Yahweh reacts to the chosen people with the rage of a jealous husband. The northern kingdom of Israel fell to the invading Assyrians in 721 BC and its population was deported. In 598 and 587 Jerusalem fell to Babylon, followed by deportations to Babylon. These disasters were specifically attributed to Yahweh's wrath at the worship of Baal and Astarte.

> Since Manasseh king of Judah has done these shameful deeds, acting more wickedly than all the Amorites did before him, and has led Judah itself into sin with his idols, Yahweh, the god of Israel, says this, "Look, I will bring such disaster as to make the ears of all who hear of it tingle. I will stretch over Jerusalem the same measuring line as over Samaria, the same plumb-rule as for the house of Ahab; I will scour Jerusalem as a man scours a dish and having scoured it, turns it upside down. I will cast away the remnant of my inheritance, delivering them into the power of their enemies, and making them serve as prey and booty to all their enemies, because they have done what is displeasing to me and have provoked my anger from the day their ancestors came out of Egypt until now." (2 Kings 21:11-15)

This terrible passage describes the ghastly consequences of being God's chosen one, his vessel or dish. It represents the stark and brutal reality of one aspect of individuation. Once a conscious connection with the Self has been made (the covenant or choosing) one has very little margin for error. The ego is now committed to being a vessel to contain transpersonal meaning. If it shirks its task it will be scoured.

The disaster struck; Jerusalem fell to the attacking Babylonians; King Zedekiah was captured, and we are confronted with the aweful image of utter defeat. The king of Babylon passed sentence on Zedekiah at Riblah. "He had the sons of Zedekiah slaughtered before his eyes, then put out Zedekiah's eyes and, loading him with chains, carried him off to Babylon." (2 Kings 24:7) As it happened to her king, so it happened to all of Judah and she was carried off to seventy years of Babylonian captivity.

Babylonian captivity represents the mortificatio phase of Israel's sacred history.[10] Like the prima materia of the alchemists, the Israelites are subjected to torturous operations to bring about their transformation. Elsewhere Yahweh says, "I have put you in the fire like silver, I have tested you in the furnace of distress." (Isaiah 46:10) The symbolism of the Babylonian captivity refers not only to mortificatio but also to coagulatio.[11] Von Franz tells us,

> The captivity is an important concept in the *Turba* and there it symbolizes the intentional "fixing" (solidifying) of a volatile spirit or soul for the purpose of transformation. "The soul is held fast like a slave, so that she cannot flee, and she falleth into sickness and rust and perisheth. But because she

10. See Edinger, *Anatomy of the Psyche,* chapter 6.
11. Ibid., chapter 4.

fleeth not, she is made free and gaineth her spouse." The fixing is called *katochē* (imprisonment) in Greek alchemy.[12]

Chapter eight of the alchemical treatise *Aurora Consurgens* is entitled, "Of the Gate of Brass and Bar of Iron of the Babylonish Captivity."[13] This text, with elaborate biblical amplifications, equates the Israelites' rescue from the Babylonian captivity with the alchemical solutio:

> God hath anointed me with the oil of gladness that there may dwell in me *the virtue of penetration and of liquifaction* in the day of my resurrection, when I shall be glorified (by) God. For this generation cometh and passeth away, until he come that is to be sent, who also taketh away the yoke of our captivity, wherein we sate seventy years by the rivers of Babylon.[14]

The image of Babylon appears in Revelation 17:3-6:

> I saw a woman riding a scarlet beast which had seven heads and ten horns and had blasphemous titles written all over it. The woman was dressed in purple and scarlet, and glittered with gold and jewels and pearls, and she was holding a gold wine cup filled with the disgusting filth of her fornication; on her forehead was written a name, a cryptic name: "Babylon the Great, the mother of all the prostitutes and all the filthy practices on the earth." I saw that she was drunk, drunk with the blood of the saints, and the blood of the martyrs of Jesus.

The immediate reference is to Rome but she is presented as a manifestation of the archetype, Babylon. The symbolism of Babylon is very similar to that of Egypt, signifying secular, fleshly existence oblivious to God. Psychologically it represents secular egohood living unconsciously at the expense of transpersonal energies ("drunk with the blood of the saints"). Although, at one phase of development, the "captivity" of Egypt or Babylon is a necessary coagulatio, at a later phase it becomes bestial and blasphemous. The gold cup, in its contents, is a negative version of the Holy Grail, but its presence, together with the gold, jewels and pearls, indicates that the supreme value of the psyche is being manifest.

The archetypal image of Babylon appears historically in the description of the period from 1309-1377 when the papacy was moved from Rome to Avignon, France. This period was called the Babylonian captivity of the papacy. Petrarch describes the Avignon of the popes as,

> The impious Babylon, the hell on earth, the soul of vice, the sewer of the world. There is in it neither faith nor charity or religion nor the fear of God . . . . All the filth and wickedness of the world have run together here . . . . Old men plunge hot and headlong into the arms of Venus; forgetting their age, dignity, and powers, they rush into every shame, as if all

12. *Aurora Consurgens*, p. 269.
13. Ibid., p. 73.
14. Ibid., p. 75, italics mine.

their glory consisted not in the cross of Christ but in feasting, drunkenness, and unchastity . . . . Fornication, incest, rape, adultery are the lascivious delights of the pontifical games.[15]

What Petrarch describes so negatively, psychologically considered, is a necessary step in the development of the collective Western psyche. It is a "return of the repressed" for the purpose of assimilation.

The Return

As predicted by Jeremiah, Judah and Jerusalem were turned into a "formless waste" (*tohu wa bohu*). (Jeremiah 4:23)

> Yes, thus speaks Yahweh,
> "The whole land shall be laid waste,
> I will make an end of it once for all;
> at which the earth will go into mourning,
> and the heavens above grow dark.
> For I have spoken and will not change my mind,
> I have decided and will not go back on it." (Jeremiah 4:27,28)

The nation was plunged into the mortificatio of exile expressed so poignantly in Lamentations. Zion has been widowed; the princess is now a vassal.

> She passes her nights weeping;
>   the tears run down her cheeks.
> Not one of all her lovers
>   remains to comfort her.
> Her friends have all betrayed her
>   and become her enemies. (Lamentations 1:2)

But the same prophet who announced the destruction of Israel also prophesied its restoration. "But look, I will hasten their recovery and their cure; I will cure them and let them know peace and security in full measure. I will restore the fortunes of Judah and Jerusalem and build them again as they were before." (Jeremiah 33:6,7) The great thirty-first chapter of Jeremiah announces the reconciliation which is to come between Israel and Yahweh:

> Yahweh says this:
> They have found pardon in the wilderness,
> those who have survived the sword.
> Yahweh has appeared to him from afar:
> I have loved you with an everlasting love,
> so I am constant in my affection for you.
> I build you once more; you shall be rebuilt,

15. *Cambridge Medieval History,* vol. 7, p. 288.

virgin of Israel.
Adorned once more, and with your tambourines,
you will go out dancing gaily.
You will plant vineyards once more
on the mountains of Samaria
(the planters have done their planting: they will
gather their fruit).
Yes, a day will come when the watchmen shout
on the mountains of Ephraim,
"Up! Let us go up to Zion,
to Yahweh our God!"
For Yahweh says this:
Shout with joy for Jacob!
Hail the chief of nations!
Proclaim! Praise! Shout:
"Yahweh has saved his people,
the remnant of Israel!"
See, I will bring them back
from the land of the North
and gather them from the far ends of earth;
all of them: the blind and the lame,
women with child, women in labour:
a great company returning here.
They had left in tears,
I will comfort them as I lead them back;
I will guide them to streams of water,
by a smooth path where they will not stumble.
For I am a father to Israel,
and Ephraim is my first-born son. (Jeremiah 31:2-9)

Ephraim replies in 31:18:

You have disciplined me, I accepted the discipline
like a young bull untamed.
Bring me back, let me come back,
for you are Yahweh my God!
Yes, I turned away, but have since repented.

The reference to the disciplining of a young bull reminds us of the yoke symbolism used in Chapter 27. Jeremiah is there told to "make yourself ropes and a yoke and put them on your neck." (verse 2) The message in this symbolic action is that all must bow their necks to the yoke of Nebuchadnezzer, whom Yahweh speaks of as "my servant." (27:7) Otherwise they will be banished from the soil. Because Israel would not submit to a willing yoke she was subjected to the harsher yoke of exile.

The theme of taming the young bull occurs in the *I Ching,* Hexagram 26, "The Taming Power of the Great." The commentary speaks of gelding a boar or fastening a headboard to the horns of a young bull. These images are applied to the strengthening of character:

The superior man acquaints himself with many sayings of antiquity and many deeds of the past, in order to strengthen his character thereby.

. . . In the words and deeds of the past there lies hidden a treasure that men may use to strengthen and elevate their own characters. The way to study the past is not to confine oneself to mere knowledge of history but, through application of this knowledge, to give actuality to the past.[16]

The Babylonian captivity can be seen as a taming or cultivating process whereby primitive psychic energies are domesticated. The willful arrogance of the young ego (bull) is yoked to the service of a transpersonal purpose. Once Israel had accepted the exile as the yoke of Yahweh, she "found pardon in the wilderness." As Yahweh says, "On that day . . . I will break the yoke on their necks and snap their chains. They will be no longer the servants of aliens, but will serve Yahweh their God." (Jeremiah 30:8,9) In other words, servitude to man is replaced by servitude to God. Psychologically this means that the ego accepts its limitations as coming from the Self. This generates a religious attitude which no longer kicks against the goad. In the words of Emerson,

We should not postpone and refer and wish, but do broad justice where we are, by whomsoever we deal with, accepting our actual companions and circumstances, however humble or odious, as the mystic officials to whom the universe has delegated its whole pleasure for us.[17]

Just as bondage in Egypt and the wandering in the wilderness was followed by Yahweh's covenant with Israel at Mount Sinai, so the bondage and exile in Babylon is followed by a new covenant announced by Jeremiah:

See, the days are coming—it is Yahweh who speaks—when I will make a new covenant with the House of Israel (and the House of Judah), but not a covenant like the one I made with their ancestors on the day I took them by the hand to bring them out of the land of Egypt. They broke that covenant of mine, so I had to show them who was master. It is Yahweh who speaks. No, this is the covenant I will make with the House of Israel when those days arrive—it is Yahweh who speaks. Deep within them I will plant my Law, writing it on their hearts. Then I will be their God and they shall be my people. There will be no further need for neighbor to try to teach neighbor, or brother to say to brother, "Learn to know Yahweh!" No, they will all know me, the least no less than the greatest—it is Yahweh who speaks—since I will forgive their iniquity and never call their sin to mind. (Jeremiah 31:31-34)

An important feature of the new covenant is that Yahweh's relation to man will be *individualized*. "In those days people will no longer say: 'The

---

16. *The I Ching or Book of Changes*, p. 105.
17. "Experience," *The Selected Writings of Ralph Waldo Emerson*, pp. 350f.

fathers have eaten unripe grapes;/the children's teeth are set on edge.' But each is to die for his own sin. Every man who eats unripe grapes is to have his own teeth set on edge." (Jeremiah 31:29,30) The announcement that Yahweh's Law will be written "on their hearts" means nothing less than the recognition of the *psychic reality* of religious and metaphysical images.

Ezekiel's Vision

It was during the Babylonian captivity, the nadir of Israel's existence according to the Old Testament records, that Ezekiel's magnificent vision occurred.

> I looked; a stormy wind blew from the north, a great cloud with light around it, a fire from which flashes of lightning darted, and in the centre a sheen like bronze at the heart of the fire. In the centre I saw what seemed four animals. They looked like this. They were of human form. Each had four faces, each had four wings. Their legs were straight; they had hooves like oxen, glittering like polished brass. Human hands showed under their wings; the faces of all four were turned to the four quarters. Their wings were spread upwards; each had two wings that touched, and two wings that covered his body; and they all went straight forward; they went where the spirit urged them; they did not turn as they moved.
>
> Between these animals something could be seen like flaming brands or torches, darting between the animals; the fire flashed light, and lightning streaked from the fire. And the creatures ran to and fro like thunderbolts.
>
> I looked at the animals; there was a wheel on the ground by each of them, one beside each of the four. The wheels glittered as if made of chrysolite. All four looked alike and seemed to be made one inside the other. They went forward four ways and kept their course unswervingly. Their rims seemed enormous when I looked at them and all four rims had eyes all the way round. When the animals went forward, the wheels went forward beside them; and when the animals left the ground, the wheels too left the ground. Where the spirit urged them, there the wheels went, since the spirit of the animal was in the wheels. Over the heads of the animals a sort of vault, gleaming like crystal, arched above their heads; under this vault their wings stretched out to one another, and each had two covering his body. I heard the noise of their wings as they moved; it sounded like rushing water, like the voice of Shaddai, a noise like a storm, like the noise of a camp; when they halted, they folded their wings, and there was a noise.
>
> Above the vault over their heads was something that looked like a sapphire; it was shaped like a throne and high up on this throne was a being that looked like a man. I saw him shine like bronze, and close to and all around him from what seemed his loins upwards was what looked like fire; and from what seemed his loins downwards I saw what looked like fire, and a light all round like a bow in the clouds on rainy days; that is how the surrounding light appeared. It was something that looked like the glory of

Yahweh. I looked, and prostrated myself, and I heard a voice speaking.
(Ezekiel 1:4-28)

This great vision, writes Jung, "is made up of two well-ordered compound quaternities, that is, conceptions of totality, such as we frequently observe today as spontaneous phenomena."[18] It is the culmination of the Old Testament considered as a psychological document. Just as a numinous mandala-image of the Self often expresses the consummation of an individual analysis, so this vision of Ezekiel completes the collective process of individuation of which the Old Testament is a record.

This vision has played a central role in the psychological development of the Western psyche. The four "animals" of the vision were taken over by Christian iconography to represent the four evangelists, who appear in Christian mandalas as the four pillars of the throne of Christ. It was the central image in early Jewish mysticism, so-called *Merkabah* or throne-mysticism. Scholem writes,

> The earliest Jewish mysticism is throne-mysticism. Its essence is not absorbed contemplation of God's true nature, but perception of His appearance on the throne, as described by Ezekiel, and cognition of the mysteries of the celestial throne-world . . . . God's pre-existing throne, which embodies and exemplifies all forms of creation, is at once the goal and the theme of his mystical vision.[19]

Ezekiel's vision was also important in the speculations of the Kabbalists and finally was brought into connection with the modern mind when Jung used it as a model for his most differentiated formula of the Self.[20]

Jung emphasizes the fact that the figure on the throne is "a being that looked like a man." "Here Ezekiel has seen the essential content of the unconscious, namely *the idea of the higher man* by whom Yahweh was morally defeated [in his encounter with Job] and who he was later to become."[21] And Jung continues,

> Ezekiel grasped, in a symbol, the fact that Yahweh was drawing closer to men. This is something which came to Job as an experience but probably did not reach his consciousness. That is to say, he did not realize that his consciousness was higher than Yahweh's, and that consequently God wants to become man. What is more, in Ezekiel we meet for the first time the title "Son of Man," which Yahweh significantly uses in addressing the prophet, presumably to indicate that he is a son of the "Man" on the throne, and hence a prefiguration of the much later revelation in Christ.[22]

18. "Answer to Job," *Psychology and Religion*, CW 11, par. 665.
19. Scholem, *Major Trends in Jewish Mysticism*, p. 44.
20. See *Aion*, CW 9ii, pars. 259ff, and *C.G. Jung Letters*, vol. 2, p. 118.
21. "Answer to Job," *Psychology and Religion*, CW 11, par. 665.
22. Ibid., par. 667.

In a letter Jung elaborates further the development of the "Son of Man" image. He writes,

> The immediate source and origin of the myth projected upon the teacher Jesus is to be found in the then popular Book of Enoch and its central figure of the "Son of Man" and his messianic mission. From the Gospel texts it is even manifest that Jesus identified himself with this "Son of Man." Thus it is the spirit of his time, the collective hope and expectation, which caused this astounding transformation and not at all the more or less insignificant story of the man Jesus. The true *agens* is the archetypal image of the God-man, appearing in Ezekiel's vision (Ezekiel 1:26) for the first time in Jewish history, but in itself a considerably older figure in Egyptian theology, viz., Osiris and Horus.[23]

And finally he summarizes the essence of Ezekiel's vision in these words:

> The encounter with the creature changes the creator. . . . The two main climaxes are formed firstly by the Job tragedy, and secondly by Ezekiel's revelation. Job is the innocent sufferer, but Ezekiel witnesses the humanization and differentiation of Yahweh. By being addressed as "Son of Man," it is intimated to him that Yahweh's incarnation and quaternity are, so to speak, the pleromatic model for what is going to happen, through the transformation and humanization of God, not only to God's son as foreseen from all eternity, but to man as such.[24]

Jung's linking of Job's experience with Ezekiel's vision draws our attention to the parallel between Job's ordeal and Israel's collective ordeal in the Babylonian exile. By enduring the wrath of Yahweh during the catastrophic events of defeat and captivity, and by diligently seeking the meaning of these events through the vision of her prophets, Israel is granted a supreme revelation of the ground plan of the psyche through Ezekiel's vision and thereby contributes to the humanization and transformation of God.

*

The redemption of the nation which is presaged by Jeremiah and Ezekiel is realized by Cyrus whom Yahweh calls "my shepherd" (Isaiah 44:28) and my "annointed" (Isaiah 45:1). The captives are freed and instructed to "go up to Jerusalem in Judah to build the Temple of Yahweh." (Ezra 1:3) In due time the temple was rebuilt and this was followed by the restitution of the community and the rebuilding of the walls in Jerusalem through the efforts of Ezra and Nehemiah.

The reborn community and restored temple can be seen as symbolic

---

23. *C.G. Jung Letters,* vol. 2, pp. 205f.
24. "Answer to Job," *Psychology and Religion,* CW 11, par. 686.

expressions of Jeremiah's "new covenant" and Ezekiel's revelation of the new humanized Yahweh, which culminate in the Old Testament. Thus the Hebrew scriptures according to the Jewish arrangement end with the Book of Chronicles whose final verse reads,

> Thus speaks Cyrus king of Persia, "Yahweh, the God of heaven, has given me all the kingdoms of the earth; he has ordered me to build him a Temple in Jerusalem, in Judah. Whoever there is among you of all his people, may his God be with him! Let him go up." (2 Chronicles 36:23)

13

Emergence of the Feminine

Immediately following the biblical account of the restoration of Israel from Babylonian captivity comes Esther, Job and the Wisdom literature. As previously suggested, the Book of Job is the central point of the Old Testament.[1] On either side of Job stand the two great female figures of the Old Testament, Esther and Divine Wisdom as she appears in Psalms, Proverbs and personified as the Shulamite in the Song of Songs. Job's great transformative encounter with Yahweh has its prelude in Esther's encounter with King Ahasuerus.

Esther

Throughout their three-thousand-year history the Jews have been a visible symbol of the fate of the Godly soul required to live in a pagan world. The essence of this historical symbolism is caught in the remarkable Book of Esther.

The story takes place at the court of Ahasuerus (Xerxes, reigned 485-465 B.C.) in Susa, where Jews of the Diaspora were also living. The drama begins when the drunken king while banqueting orders Queen Vashti to appear in order that he may show off her beauty. The queen refuses and in his wrath Ahasuerus banishes her. Psychologically, this pictures the unconscious condition of the ruling psychic dominant (king) whose arrogant assumptions are challenged by refusal to obey them. The power principle, the essential feature of paganism, is frustrated by the feminine eros principle which requires equal consideration. This conflict between the opposites (power and love) opens up a space for a new element to enter the picture. The king must choose a new queen and his choice falls on Esther.

As a Jewess, Esther represents the godly or transpersonal factor. This means that the issue of individuation has made its appearance. The relation between the opposites and between man and woman can no longer be governed by power but must now be determined by the requirement of wholeness. However this transformation is not achieved without the overcoming of great resistance.

Soon after Esther became queen a plot by eunuchs to assassinate the king was discovered by Mordecai, Esther's uncle, and reported to the king by Esther. (Esther 2:21-23) Remembering that *post hoc ergo propter hoc*

---

1. For commentary on the psychological significance of Job see Edinger, *Creation of Consciousness*, chapter 3, and *Encounter with the Self*.

128

is proper to the interpretation of dreams and myths, we can understand the conspiracy of the eunuchs to symbolize the dangerous state of the realm which is rescued from disaster by Esther's coming to the throne. The eunuchs, incapable of relating to women, represent the king's tyrannical attitude which allows no autonomy for the feminine principle and no room for the interplay of the opposites. This attitude threatened to destroy the king, who was saved only by Mordecai and Esther who brought transpersonal consciousness.

Characteristically, this increase of consciousness is followed by a counterthrust from the unconscious. Haman now becomes the image of the willful power motive and, in revenge for Mordecai's refusal to bow to him, plots the annihilation of the Jews. To avoid this catastrophe Esther is required to carry out her heroic act of confrontation.

In his plot to massacre the Jews, Haman deceives the king and gets his permission to issue orders for the slaughter of a "certain unassimilated nation scattered among the other nations throughout the provinces of your realm." (Esther 3:8) The letter drafted by Haman, in the name of the king, reads in part as follows:

> Mixed in with all the races throughout the world, there is one people of bad will, which by its laws is opposed to every other people and continually disregards the decrees of kings, so that the unity of empire blamelessly designed by us cannot be established. Having noted therefore, that this most singular people is continually at variance with all men, lives by divergent and alien laws, is inimical to our interests and commits the worst crimes, so that stability of government cannot be obtained, we hereby decree that all those who are indicated to you in the letters of Haman, who is in charge of the administration and is a second father to us, shall, together with their wives and children, be utterly destroyed by the fourteenth day of the twelfth month, Adar, of the current year. (Esther 3:B:1-6, NAB)[2]

This letter clearly establishes the Jews as symbolizing individuation. As carriers of God-consciousness they are intolerable obstacles to all tyranny. Subordination to the Self is detestable to the power-driven ego, and it resorts to violence in a desperate effort to retain its position. The king himself was not aware of who it was he was allowing Haman to exterminate. It is as though Haman, the king's power-shadow, had pulled the wool over his eyes and was functioning outside of the royal consciousness. In this situation it was necessary that the facts be brought to the attention of the king. Mordecai thus urged Esther "to go to the king and implore his favour and plead with him for her people." (Esther 4:8)

Esther is placed in a desperate quandry. She is asked to approach the king in spite of the fact that "for a man or woman who approaches the

---

2. This passage derives from the Septuagint and is not part of the Hebrew and Protestant canon.

king in the inner court without being summoned there is one penalty: death, unless, by pointing his golden sceptre towards him, the king grants him his life." (Esther 4:11) Esther courageously decides to take the risk. She will begin with a fast, "after which I shall go to the king in spite of the law; and if I perish, I perish." (Esther 4:16)

> Having passed through door after door, she found herself in the presence of the king. He was seated on the royal throne, dressed in all his robes of state, glittering with gold and precious stones—a formidable sight. Raising his face, afire with majesty, he looked on her, blazing with anger. The queen sank down. She grew faint and the colour drained from her face, and she leaned her head against the maid who accompanied her.
>
> But God changed the king's heart, inducing a milder spirit. He sprang from his throne in alarm and took her in his arms until she recovered, comforting her with soothing words. "What is the matter, Esther?" he said. "I am your brother. Take heart; you will not die; our order only applies to ordinary people. Come to me." And raising his golden sceptre he laid it on her neck, embraced her and said, "Speak to me."
>
> "My lord," she said, "you looked to me like an angel of God, and my heart was moved with fear of your majesty. For you are a figure of wonder, my lord, and your face is full of graciousness." But as she spoke she fell down in a faint. The king was distressed, and all his attendants tried their best to revive her. "What is the matter, Queen Esther?" the king said. "Tell me what you desire; even if it is half my kingdom, I grant it you." "Would the king be pleased," Esther replied, "to come with Haman today to the banquet I have prepared for him?" (Esther 5)[3]

With fear and trembling the feminine soul confronts the masculine *numinosum* which appears "like an angel of God" to her. Like Psyche gazing upon Eros, Esther disobeys the law and approaches the forbidden. However Esther's action is on a much more conscious level than Psyche's, and for that reason does not have the negative consequences that Psyche's action had. Instead, Esther's act has the immediate effect of increasing the king's consciousness. While reading the book of royal chronicles he is reminded of Mordecai's loyalty and the fact that he had not been rewarded for discovering the plot against the king.

The consequence of this increase in consciousness is that Haman and Mordecai reverse positions. Mordecai becomes prime minister and Haman is hanged on the gallows meant for Mordecai. The tyrannical shadow is unmasked and the Jews, the representatives of individuation, are saved.

Divine Wisdom

In "Answer to Job" Jung demonstrates that Yahweh's encounter with Job had an effect on Yahweh.

---

3.   This passage includes the apocryphal additions from the Septuagint.

At about the same time, or a little later, it is rumoured what has happened: he has remembered a feminine being who is no less agreeable to him than to man, a friend and playmate from the beginning of the world, the first-born of all God's creatures, a stainless reflection of his glory and a master workman, nearer and dearer to his heart than the late descendants of the protoplast, the original man, who was but a secondary product stamped in his image. There must be some dire necessity responsible for this anamnesis of Sophia: things simply could not go on as before, the "just" God could not go on committing injustices, and the "Omniscient" could not behave any longer like a clueless and thoughtless human being. Self-reflection becomes an imperative necessity, and for this Wisdom is needed. Yahweh has to remember his absolute knowledge; for, if Job gains knowledge of God, then God must also learn to know himself. It just could not be that Yahweh's dual nature should become public property and remain hidden from himself alone. Whoever knows God has an effect on him.[4]

In the canonical literature Wisdom is described chiefly in Proverbs. There she describes herself as equivalent to the preexistent Logos, the playmate of God the creator:

Yahweh created me when his purpose first unfolded,
    before the oldest of his works.
From everlasting I am firmly set,
    from the beginning, before earth came into being.
The deep was not, when I was born,
    there were no springs to gush with water.
Before the moutains were settled,
    before the hills, I came to birth;
    . . . .
    When he laid down the foundations of the earth,
I was by his side, a master craftsman,
    delighting him day after day,
    ever at play in his presence,
at play everywhere in his world,
    delighting to be with the sons of men. (Proverbs 8:22-31)

Another source for the biography of Wisdom is Ecclesiasticus, where she equates herself with the Divine Presence of Yahweh. "I came forth from the mouth of the most High, / and I covered the earth like a mist. / I had my tent in the heights, / and my throne in a pillar of cloud." (24:3f) This passage equates Wisdom with the Shekinah, the glory of Yahweh, who is described in Psalms 19:1-4:

The heavens declare the glory of God,
the vault of heaven proclaims his handiwork;
day discourses it to day,
night to night hands on the knowledge.

---

4. *Psychology and Religion,* CW 11, par. 617.

No utterance at all, no speech,
no sound that anyone can hear;
Yet their voice goes out through all the earth,
and their message to the ends of the world.

In other words, Wisdom is the *anima mundi,* a matrix or invisible network that maintains interconnections among all things. Her role as world creator is based on the idea that she contains the original patterns or models of all things. According to von Franz,

In patristic literature she was mostly interpreted as Christ, the preexistent Logos, or as the sum of the *rationes aeternae* (eternal forms), of the "self-knowing primordial causes," exemplars, ideas, and prototypes in the mind of God. She was also considered the *archetypus mundus,* "that archetypal world after whose likeness this sensible world was made," and through which God becomes conscious of himself. *Sapientia Dei* is thus the sum of archetypal images in the mind of God.[5]

Thomas Aquinas expresses the same idea:

Divine wisdom devised the order of the universe residing in the distinction of things, and therefore we must say that in the divine wisdom are the models of all things, which we have called *ideas*—i.e., exemplary forms existing in the divine mind.[6]

It is exceedingly significant psychologically that Divine Wisdom makes her appearance only after Job's encounter with Yahweh. This means that the ego's conscious realization of the nature of the primordial psyche—the virgin state, untouched by conscious reflection—causes a transformation within the unconscious itself. Divine Wisdom is the creator and preexistent source of the manifest world (ego) but it happens unconsciously. She does not know it and does not come into visible existence until the ego has discovered the unconscious, distinguished itself from it and perceived its objective nature. Thus Job is obliged to remind Yahweh that He created him.

You, who inquire into my faults
    and investigate my sins,
you know very well that I am innocent,
    and that no one can rescue me from your hand.
Your own hands shaped me, modelled me;
    and would you now have second thoughts and destroy me?
You modelled me, remember, as clay is modelled,
    and would you reduce me now to dust?
Did you not pour me out like milk,

---

5. *Aurora Consurgens,* pp. 155f.
6. *Summa Theologica* I, q. 44, art. 4.

and curdle me then like cheese;
Clothe me with skin and flesh,
    and weave me of bone and sinew?
And then you endowed me with life,
    watched each breath of mine with tender care. (Job 10:6-12)

Job's "righteousness" or "integrity" consists in the fact that he never forgets that *the ego does not create itself*. The unconscious creates the ego but forgets it, or rather never knew it. This knowledge comes only when the ego reaches sufficient development that it can refuse to take responsibility for everything in the psyche. At that point the ego is no longer identical with the psyche, the psyche becomes an objective reality and Divine Wisdom can awaken to awareness of her existence. The ego has become a reflecting mirror for the emerging consciousness of the Self.

The rescue of Wisdom from her dark embrace with matter is a prominent Gnostic myth. Jung writes,

In Simon Magus it is Helen, the *mētēr* and *ennoia* who "descended to the lower regions . . . and generated the inferior powers, angels, and firmaments." She was forcibly held captive by the lower powers (Irenaeus I, 27, 1-4). She corresponds to the much later alchemical idea of the "soul in fetters" . . . . "The soul once turned towards matter, fell in love with it, and burning with desire to experience bodily pleasures, was no longer willing to tear herself away from it. So was the world born." . . . [In the *Pistis Sophia*, Sophia] deluded by the false light of the demon Authades . . . falls into imprisonment in chaos.[7]

Dreams may picture the encounter with Divine Wisdom (the *anima mundi*) as light shining out of the darkness; for example, this dream by a middle-aged man:

There is a darkness, but with a luminosity in it, not describable. A darkness somehow glowing. Standing in it is a beautiful golden woman, with an almost Mona Lisa face. Now I realize that the glow is emanating from a necklace she is wearing. It is of great delicacy: small cabochons of turquoise, each circled in reddish gold. It has great meaning for me, as if there were a message in the complete image if only I could break through its elusiveness.[8]

Wisdom shares with Aphrodite and the Holy Ghost the symbolism of the dove. The Gnostics say, according to Irenaeus, "In the form of a dove, she [Sophia] descended into the water and begot Saturn, who is identical with Yahweh."[9] A personal dream of Jung makes use of this image. Around Christmas of 1912 he dreamed,

---

7. *Aion*, CW 9ii, par. 307, note 33.
8. For a fuller discussion of this dream see Edinger, *Ego and Archetype*, pp. 217f.
9. Quoted by Jung, *Aion*, CW 9ii, par. 307.

I found myself in a magnificent Italian loggia with pillars, a marble floor, and a marble balustrade. I was sitting on a gold Renaissance chair; in front of me was a table of rare beauty. It was made of green stone, like emerald. There I sat, looking out into the distance, for the loggia was set high up on the tower of a castle. My children were sitting at the table too.

Suddenly a white bird descended, a small sea-gull or a dove. Gracefully, it came to rest on the table, and I signed to the children to be still so that they would not frighten away the pretty white bird. Immediately, the dove was transformed into a little girl, about eight years of age, with golden blond hair. She ran off with the children and played with them among the colonnades of the castle.

I remained lost in thought, musing about what I had just experienced. The little girl returned and tenderly placed her arms around my neck. Then she suddenly vanished; the dove was back and spoke slowly in a human voice. "Only in the first hours of the night can I transform myself into a human being, while the male dove is busy with the twelve dead." Then she flew off into the blue air and I awoke.[10]

This dream presaged Jung's encounter with the collective unconscious. I consider the dove-girl to be a manifestation of Divine Wisdom incarnating in Jung. The fact that she ran off to play with the children is probably a reference to Jung's initial connection with the unconscious by playing childhood games.[11]

The goal of the alchemical opus was called the Philosophers' Stone, that is, the stone created by the lovers of Wisdom. It is in fact Wisdom incarnate. An alchemist exclaims,

From the beginning of my birth have I sought her out and knew not that she was the mother of all sciences that went before me. And she bestowed on me innumerable riches, which I have learned without guile and will communicate without envy, and without hiding her worth. For she is an infinite treasure to all men . . . . Senior likewise saith: For there is a stone, which he that knoweth layeth it upon his eyes, but he that doth not, casteth it upon the dung hill, and it is a medicine which putteth poverty to flight, and after God hath man no better thing.[12]

Divine Wisdom is the feminine personification of the unconscious who yearns to be known by her son or daughter, the ego, and thus achieve realization.

Wisdom brings up her own sons,
  and cares for those who seek her.
Whoever loves her loves life,
  those who wait on her early will be filled with happiness.
Whoever holds her close will inherit honor,

10. *Memories, Dreams, Reflections*, pp. 171f.
11. Ibid., pp. 173f.
12. Quoted by von Franz, *Aurora Consurgens*, pp. 43f.

and wherever he walks the Lord will bless him.
Those who serve her minister to the Holy One,
   and the Lord loves those who love her.
Whoever obeys her judges aright,
   and whoever pays attention to her dwells secure.
If he trusts himself to her he will inherit her,
   and his descendants will remain in possession of her;
for though she takes him at first through winding ways,
   bringing fear and faintness on him,
plaguing him with her discipline until she can trust him,
   and testing him with her ordeals,
in the end she will lead him back to the straight road,
   and reveal her secrets to him. (Ecclesiasticus 4:11-20)

14

Coniunctio: The Song of Songs

The Song of Songs is a coniunctio poem, a love drama expressing the union of opposites.[1] The lovers have been given various identifications during centuries of commentary,[2] all of which can be subsumed under the image of the coniunctio as the reconciliation of opposites in the process of individuation. The Jewish sage Saadia stated that "the Song of Songs resembles locks to which the keys have been lost."[3] The lost key has now been found by depth psychology.

The poem describes the vicissitudes of two lovers, the Bridegroom and his Beloved, the Shulamite. For the purpose of exposition I shall divide the story into a sequence of ten pictures.

1. *The Shulamite, burned black by the sun, labors in her brothers' vineyards and yearns for the Bridegroom.* (1:1-2:7) The story begins in a state of servitude.

> I am black but lovely, daughters of Jerusalem,
> like the tents of Kedar,
> like the pavilions of Salmah.
> Take no notice of my swarthiness,
> it is the sun that has burnt me.
> My mother's sons turned their anger on me,
> they made me look after the vineyards.
> Had I only looked after my own! (1:5,6)

The Bride and Bridegroom, strictly speaking, represent the opposites that constitute the Self and are, or should be, quite separate from the ego. In practice, however, the ego is more or less identified with one or both, as the archetypal drama unfolds in the individual soul.

The initial condition is one of blackness and captivity corresponding to the alchemical *nigredo*. Jewish commentators associated the blackness of the Shulamite to the sins of Israel. According to a Targum, "When the House of Israel made the calf, their faces grew dark like the Ethiopians who dwell in the tents of Qedar. And when they turned in penitence, and their guilt was pardoned them, the precious radiance of their faces increased like the angels."[4] R. Levi ben Haytha interpreted the blackness

---

1. Jung says, "The factors which come together in the coniunctio are conceived as opposites, either confronting one another in enmity or attracting one another in love." (*Mysterium Coniunctionis,* CW 14, par. 1)
2. See Marvin H. Pope, ed., "Song of Songs," *Anchor Bible,* Introduction. I am indebted to Pope for his comprehensive gathering of relevant material.
3. Ibid., p. 84.
4. Ibid., p. 320.

to mean, "I am black on the days of the week and comely on the Sabbath; black all the days of the year and comely on the Day of Atonement; black in this world and comely in the world to come."[5] According to Pope,

> The Greek Fathers, applying this verse to the whole Church, related the blackness to the Gentile element and the comeliness to the Hebrew. The black and the beautiful was also applied to the mixture of saints and sinners which comprise the Church. The Virgin Mary also had her dark days and her beautiful moments, as when her reputation was blackened by slander because of her premarital pregnancy, though she was full of grace; and black too, as Mother of Sorrows, when she stood by the cross and was despised with her Son, but beautiful in the joy of His Resurrection.[6]

The alchemists used the image of the black Shulamite as "the feminine personification of the prima materia in the *nigredo* state."[7] One text quotes her as attributing her blackness to the original sin of Eve: "O that the serpent roused up Eve! To which I must testify with my black colour that clings to me."[8] Jung says, "Psychologically this dark figure is the unconscious anima."[9] She represents the *anima mundi* or Gnostic Sophia caught in the dark embrace of *physis*.

The Shulamite tells us she is a captive of her brothers, forced to work in their vineyards. Her "brothers" have been understood as "the Chaldeans of Nebuchadnezzer who destroyed Jerusalem and took Judah captive."[10] Psychologically, forced labor in the brothers' vineyards symbolizes subordination of the feminine principle to the masculine, or the subordination of the living psyche to abstract rationality. This initial condition calls out for rescue or redemption.

2. *The Bridegroom comes to the Shulamite like the coming of spring.* (2:8-17)

> I hear my Beloved.
> See how he comes
> leaping on the mountains,
> bounding over the hills.
> My Beloved is like a gazelle,
> like a young stag.
>
> See where he stands
> behind our wall.
> He looks in at the window,
> he peers through the lattice.
>
> My Beloved lifts up his voice,

5. Ibid., p. 321.
6. Ibid.
7. Jung, *Mysterium Coniunctionis*, CW 14, par. 592.
8. Ibid., par. 591.
9. Ibid., par. 592.
10. Pope, "Song of Songs," p. 323.

he says to me,
"Come then, my love,
my lovely one, come.
For see, winter is past,
the rains are over and gone.
The flowers appear on the earth.
The season of glad songs has come,
the cooing of the turtledove is heard
in our land." (2:8-12)

With the coming of the Bridegroom, the Shulamite gets the first glimpse of her redemption. A Targum applied the "leaping" and "bounding" to the Jews' release from bondage in Egypt. "They leaped over the terminal date by virtue of the merit of their fathers (mountains) and skipped over the time of servitude a hundred and ninety years for the righteousness of their mothers, who are likened to the hills."[11] Christian commentators considered the voice of the Beloved to be that of Christ just before His Advent, or the voice was the "call to resurrection before the second coming."[12] Again, "Christ comes leaping to us as we study Holy Scripture, in passage after passage on the hills of the Old Testament, and on the higher and more conspicuous mountains of the New Testament."[13]

The Bridegroom is identified with spring, bringing flowers and "blessed greenness" ("all green is our bed"—1:16). The miraculous growth of flowers and greenery are a feature of the coniunctio. It occurs for instance with the union of Zeus and Hera in Book XIV of the *Iliad:*

His eager arms around the Goddess threw.
Glad Earth perceives, and from her bosom pours
Unbidden herbs, and voluntary flowers;
Thick new-born violets a soft carpet spread,
And clust'ring lotus swell'd the rising bed,
And sudden hyacinths the Turf bestrow.
And flamy crocus made the mountain glow.[14]

The Philosophers' Stone is credited with the power of the vegetation principle to promote trees, plants, flowers and "how to produce and make them grow, flourish and bear fruit; how to increase them in colour and smell, and when and where we please."[15] An alchemical text quotes the black Shulamite (prima materia) as saying, "I am alone among the hidden; nevertheless I rejoice in my heart, because I can live privily, and refresh myself in myself. But under my blackness I have hidden the fairest green."[16] Jung comments on this passage as follows:

11. Ibid., p. 390.
12. Ibid.
13. Ibid.
14. Lines 394-400, Alexander Pope transl.
15. *Theatrum Chemicum Britannicum*, in Edinger, *Ego and Archetype*, p. 272.
16. See Jung, *Mysterium Coniunctionis*, par. 622.

The state of imperfect transformation, merely hoped for and waited for, does not seem to be one of torment only, but of positive, if hidden, happiness. It is the state of someone who, in his wanderings among the mazes of his psychic transformation, comes upon a secret happiness which reconciles him to his apparent loneliness. In communing with himself he finds not deadly boredom and melancholy but an inner partner; more than that, a relationship that seems like the happiness of a secret love, or like a hidden springtime, when the green seed sprouts from the barren earth, holding out the promise of future harvests. It is the alchemical *benedicta veriditas,* the blessed greenness, signifying on the one hand the "leprosy of the metals" (verdigris), but on the other the secret immanence of the divine spirit of life in all things.[17]

3. *The lonely Shulamite rises from her bed and searches the streets for her Beloved.* (3:1-3)

On my bed, at night, I sought him
whom my heart loves.
I sought but did not find him.
So I will rise and go through the city;
in the streets and the squares
I will seek him whom my heart loves.
. . . I sought but did not find him. (3:1-3)

The encounter in chapter two was only fleeting and now again the Shulamite is searching for the Bridegroom. Some have suggested that seeking him in "bed at night" refers to a dream.[18] A Targum identified the missing Beloved as the Holy Presence which had forsaken Israel:

Said the Israelites one to the other: "Let us rise and go and surround the appointment-tent which Moses spread outside the camp, and let us request instruction from YHWH and the Holy Presence which has been removed from us." Then they went around in the towns, in the streets and squares, but could not find (the Holy Presence).[19]

Christian commentators have usually understood the object of the quest to be Christ, especially the search for the dead Christ in John 20:11-18. A remarkable alchemical text applies the plight of the Shulamite to the alchemical opus.

Be turned to me with all your heart and do not cast me aside because I am black and swarthy, because the sun hath changed my colour and the waters covered my face and the earth hath been polluted and defiled in my works; for there was darkness over it, because I stick fast in the mire of the deep and my substance is not disclosed. Wherefore out of the depths have I cried, and from the abyss of the earth with my voice to all you that pass by the way. Attend and see me, if any shall find one like unto me, I will give into

17. Ibid., par. 623.
18. Pope, "Song of Songs," p. 415.
19. Ibid., p. 419.

his hand the morning star. For behold in my bed by night I sought one to comfort me and I found none, I called and there was none to answer me.— Therefore will I arise and go into the city, seeking in the streets and broad ways a chaste virgin to espouse, comely in face, more comely in body, most comely in her garments, that she may roll back the stone from the door of my sepulchre and give me wings like a dove, and I will fly with her into heaven and then say: I live forever.[20]

In this passage, the Philosophers' Stone identified with the Shulamite, buried in the prima materia, calls for redemption by its conscious realization in the coniunctio.

4. *The Shulamite finds the Bridegroom. He comes like a royal procession of King Solomon.* (3:4-11)

> What is this coming up from the desert
> like a column of smoke,
> breathing of myrrh and frankincense
> and every perfume the merchant knows?
>
> See, it is the litter of Solomon.
> Around it are sixty champions,
> the flower of the warriors of Israel;
> all of them skilled swordsmen,
> veterans of battle.
> Each man has his sword at his side,
> against alarms by night.
>
> King Solomon
> has made himself a throne
> of wood from Lebanon.
> The posts he has made of silver,
> the canopy of gold,
> the seat of purple;
> the back is inlaid with ebony. (3:6-10)

This passage presents the second encounter with the Self. This time he is not wild and leaping, but solemn and regal. Commentators equate the "column of smoke" with the column of cloud by day and fire by night which indicated the divine presence during the Israelites' wandering in the wilderness.[21] "Solomon" is considered to symbolize either Yahweh or the Messiah.[22] The "throne" of Solomon (*appiryon*, chariot, AV) is a *hapax legomenon*[23] and seems to designate some sort of litter or portable throne.[24] Jewish interpreters related the term to the Tabernacle or the

20. Quoted by von Franz, *Aurora Consurgens*, pp. 133f.
21. Pope, "Song of Songs," p. 426.
22. Ibid., p. 432.
23. This means "a word that occurs only once."
24. Pope, "Song of Songs," p. 442.

Temple and Christian commentators applied it to the Church. According to Philo of Carpasia, "As Christ made His own human body first to be the litter in which the Godhead is borne, so He made the Church the vehicle in which He, the man-God, would be carried in procession among the people to whom He comes as King and Conqueror."[25]

5. *The Bride and Bridegroom meet in the garden. The Bridegroom praises the Bride but is wounded by her.* (4:1-5:1)

How beautiful you are, my love,
how beautiful you are!
Your eyes, behind your veil,
are doves;
Your hair is like a flock of goats
frisking down the slopes of Gilead.
Your teeth are like a flock of shorn ewes
as they come up from the washing,
Each one has its twin,
not one unpaired with another.
Your lips are a scarlet thread
and your words enchanting.
Your cheeks, behind your veil,
are halves of pomegranate.
Your neck is the tower of David
built as a fortress,
hung round with a thousand bucklers,
And each the shield of a hero.
Your two breasts are two fawns,
twins of a gazelle,
that feed among the lilies. (4:1-5)

For Jewish interpreters, the beauty of the Bride refers to Israel's devotion to the law. For Christians the reference is either to the Church or to the contemplative soul kindled with longing for God.[26] For Jews, her two breasts looking to the past are Moses and Aaron; looking to the future, they are the two messiahs. For Christians they are the two Testaments, the twin precepts, love of God and love of neighbor, the blood and water which flowed from the side of the crucified Christ, etc.[27]

The encounter in the garden includes pain as well as pleasure. The Bridegroom is wounded:

You ravish my heart,
My sister, my promised bride,
You ravish my heart
with a single one of your glances. (4:9)

25. Ibid., p. 443.
26. Ibid., p. 461.
27. Ibid., p. 471.

The Douay Version says, "Thou hast wounded my heart with one of thy eyes." This image refers to the wounding effect of *being seen by the "other."* One aspect of the coniunctio is that the opposites are seen by each other—the ego is seen by the Self and the Self is seen by the ego. Each becomes an object of knowledge and perception by the other, which has a wounding or violating effect.[28] As Jung tells us, "the integration of contents that were always unconscious and projected involves a serious lesion of the ego."[29] Likewise, the Self in its original unconscious state is wounded in the process of conscious realization. Just as the ego is "emptied" by encounter with the "other," so also is the Self. This theme is expressed in the doctrine of *kenosis,* based on Philippians 2:6,7 which describes the incarnation of Christ as a process of emptying. "His state was divine,/yet he did not cling/to his equality with God/but emptied himself/to assume the condition of a slave,/and became as men are." The theme of "emptying" also appears in the concept of *Tsimtsum* as developed in the Kabbala of Isaac Luria. Scholem describes *Tsimtsum* as follows:

> It means briefly that the existence of the universe is made possible by a process of shrinkage in God . . . . If God is "all in all," how can there be things which are not God. . . . [Thus] God was compelled to make room for the world by, as it were, abandoning a region within Himself, a kind of mystical primordial space from which He withdrew in order to return to it in the act of creation and revelation.[30]

Thus the encounter between God and world (Self and ego) involves a wounding or diminishment of God. Honorius applies this image to Christ and the Church.

> So was Christ upon the cross wounded for love by his Church: "Thou didst first wound my heart when I was scourged for thy love, that I might make thee my sister . . . . Again thou didst wound my heart with one of thine eyes when, hanging upon the cross, I was wounded for love of thee that I might make thee my bride to share my glory."[31]

6. *The Bridegroom knocks at the Shulamite's door but she is slow in answering and he is gone.* (5:2-5:6)

> I sleep, but my heart is awake,
> I hear my Beloved knocking.
> "Open to me, my sister, my love,
> my dove, my perfect one,
> for my head is covered with dew,
> my locks with the drops of night."

28. See Edinger, *The Creation of Consciousness,* pp. 41ff.
29. "The Psychology of the Transference," *The Practice of Psychotherapy,* CW 16, par. 472.
30. Scholem, *Major Trends in Jewish Mysticism,* pp. 260f.
31. Quoted by Jung, *Mysterium Coniunctionis,* CW 14, par. 25.

—"I have taken off my tunic,
am I to put it on again?
I have washed my feet,
am I to dirty them again?"
My Beloved thrust his hand
through the hole in the door;
I trembled to the core of my being,
Then I rose
to open to my Beloved,
myrrh ran off my hands,
pure myrrh off my fingers,
on to the handle of the bolt.

I opened to my Beloved,
but he had turned his back and gone!
My soul failed at his flight. (5:2-5:6)

The reference to sleeping suggests that this passage may refer to a dream.[32] Certainly a knock on the door which one is reluctant to answer is a common dream theme, representing an unconscious content trying to gain admission to consciousness. The coniunctio is both desired and dreaded. From a distance it is the source of all yearning,[33] but knocking at our door it is an object of terror. Once seen and then lost it is occasion for despair.

7. *The Shulamite again goes in search of the lost Bridegroom.* (5:6)

I sought him but I did not find him,
I called to him but he did not answer. (5:6)

The Divine Presence has removed itself from Israel[34] or Wisdom neglected has departed.

Then they shall call to me, but I will not answer,
    they shall seek me eagerly and shall not find me. (Proverbs 1:28)

8. *The watchmen beat the Shulamite and steal her cloak.* (5:7)

The watchmen came upon me
as they made their rounds in the City,
They beat me, they wounded me,
they took away my cloak,
they who guard the ramparts. (5:7)

For Jews the "watchmen" were the Chaldeans who besieged Jerusalem. For Christians they were "the pagan Roman rulers who persecuted the

---

32. Pope, "Song of Songs," p. 510.
33. Jung writes, "What is behind all this desirousness? A thirsting for the eternal." (*Mysterium Coniunctionis*, CW 14, par. 192)
34. Pope, "Song of Songs," p. 526.

Church and stripped the martyrs of that outer vest of flesh which covered their souls."[35] Psychologically they are the guardians of the ramparts of the status quo which is always an enemy of individuation. In 4:9 the Bridegroom was wounded, now it is the Bride's turn. The opposites cannot meet without wounding each other.

9. *Bride and Bridegroom find each other and unite in the garden of pomegranates. (6:1-8:3)*

> Come, my Beloved,
> let us go to the fields.
> We will spend the night in the villages,
> And in the morning we will go to the vineyards.
> We will see if the vines are budding,
> if their blossoms are opening,
> if the pomegranate trees are in flower.
> Then I shall give you
> the gift of my love. (7:11-13)

The coniunctio is consummated with the union of Bride and Bridegroom symbolizing all the pairs of opposites. Now is established the eternal alliance between Yahweh and Israel, the millenial marriage between Christ and his Church, or, according to the Kabbala, the sacred union between "the Holy one, blessed be He and His Shekinah."[36] Rabbi Simon ben Jochai, the presumed author of the *Zohar*, described the sacred coniunctio on his death-bed in these words:

> When . . . the mother is separated and conjoined with the King face to face in the excellence of the Sabbath, all things become one body. And then the Holy one—blessed be he!—sitteth on His throne and all things are called the Complete Name, the Holy Name. Blessed be His Name for ever and unto the ages of the ages . . . . When this Mother is conjoined with the King, all the worlds receive blessing, and the universe is found to be in joy.[37]

Jung had a similar coniunctio vision while convalescing from a near-fatal illness. He describes it as follows:

> Everything around me seemed enchanted. At this hour of the night the nurse brought me some food she had warmed—for only then was I able to take any, and I ate with appetite. For a time it seemed to me that she was an old Jewish woman, much older than she actually was, and that she was preparing ritual kosher dishes for me. When I looked at her, she seemed to have a blue halo around her head. I myself was, so it seemed, in the Pardes Rimmonim, the garden of pomegranates, and the wedding of Tifereth with Malchuth was taking place. Or else I was Rabbi Simon ben Jochaï, whose

35. Ibid., p. 528.
36. Scholem, *Major Trends in Jewish Mysticism*, p. 227.
37. Mathers, *The Kabbalah Unveiled*, p. 337.

wedding in the afterlife was being celebrated. It was the mystic marriage as it appears in the Cabbalistic tradition. I cannot tell you how wonderful it was. I could only think continually, "Now this is the garden of pomegranates! Now this is the marriage of Malchuth with Tifereth!" I do not know exactly what part I played in it. At bottom it was myself; I was the marriage. And my beatitude was that of a blissful wedding.

Gradually the garden of pomegranates faded away and changed. There followed the Marriage of the Lamb, in a Jerusalem festively bedecked. I cannot describe what it was like in detail. These were ineffable states of joy. Angels were present, and light. I myself was the "Marriage of the Lamb."

That, too, vanished, and there came a new image, the last vision. I walked up a wide valley to the end, where a gentle chain of hills began. The valley ended in a classical amphitheatre. It was magnificently situated in the green landscape. And there, in this theatre, the *hierosgamos* was being celebrated. Men and women dancers came on stage, and upon a flower-decked couch All-father Zeus and Hera consummated the mystic marriage, as it is described in the *Iliad*.

All these experiences were glorious. Night after night I floated in a state of purest bliss, "thronged round with images of all creation."[38]

10. *The united lovers are sealed to each other in eternal love.* (8:5-7)

Set me like a seal on your heart,
like a seal on your arm.
For love is strong as Death,
jealousy[39] relentless as Sheol. (8:6)

This final image corresponds to the creation of the Philosophers' Stone, the immortal body "strong as death." It symbolizes the eternal, atemporal fruits of individuation.[40] The opposites that were torn apart at the birth of consciousness in the Garden of Eden are reunited and "sealed" as belonging to each other. This new condition is symbolically equivalent to the Messianic age. Thus the verse,

I should lead you, I should take you
into my mother's house, and you would teach me!
I should give you special wine to drink,
juice of my pomegranates (8:2)

was applied to the Messianic Banquet.

I will lead you, O King Messiah, and bring you up to my Temple; and you will teach me to fear before YHWH and to walk in His ways. And there we shall partake of the feast of Leviathan and will drink old wine preserved

---

38. *Memories, Dreams, Reflections*, p. 294. The final phrase is from Goethe's *Faust*, part 2.
39. *Qinah*, also passion, zeal.
40. See Edinger, *The Creation of Consciousness*, pp. 23ff.

in the grape since the day the world was created and from the pomegranates and fruits prepared for the righteous in the Garden of Eden.[41]

The united opposites generate "love" and "jealousy" (*ahabah* and *qinah*, rendered in the Septuagint as *agapē* and *zēlos*). These terms correspond to the two poles of cosmogonic libido. To unite them in consciousness corresponds to Jung's description of "the moral task of alchemy" which is "to bring the feminine, maternal background of the masculine psyche, seething with passions, into harmony with the principle of the spirit—truly a labour of Hercules!"[42]

---

41.   From a Targum quoted by Pope, "Song of Songs," p. 660.
42.   *Mysterium Coniunctionis,* CW 14, par. 35.

15

Messiah: The Self Realized

The Coming King

Throughout the Old Testament are many references to a coming king or annointed one who will deliver Israel from her enemies and establish a perpetual kingdom. The first clear reference to this figure is found in Genesis 49:10-12:

> The sceptre shall not pass from Judah,
> nor the mace from between his feet,
> until he come to whom it belongs,
> to whom the peoples shall render obedience.
> He ties up his young ass to a vine,
> to its stock the foal of his she-ass.
> He washes his coat in wine,
> his cloak in the blood of the grape;
> his eyes are cloudy [AV, red] with wine
> his teeth are white with milk.

This passage has been understood concretely as a prophecy of a Judaic king who is to rule over the nations. More generally it is considered to refer to the Messiah by both Jewish and Christian commentators. The theme of wine and milk finds a parallel in Joel 3:18 (4:18, JB).

> When that day comes,
> the mountains will run with new wine
> and the hills flow with milk,
> and all the river beds of Judah
> will run with water.
> A fountain will spring from the house of Yahweh
> to water the wadi of Acacias.

Washing garments in blood appears in Revelation 7:14. "These are the people who have been through the great persecution, and because they have washed their robes white again in the blood of the Lamb, they now stand in front of God's throne and serve him day and night in his sanctuary." The theme of red and white is reminiscent of the alchemical coniunctio between the red man and white woman (Sol and Luna).

The next passage considered to refer to the Messiah appears in Numbers 24:17ff, in Balaam's prophecy.

> I see him—but not in the present,
> I behold him—but not close at hand;

a star from Jacob takes the leadership,
a sceptre arises from Israel.
It crushes the brows of Moab
the skulls of all the sons of Sheth.

The Qumran community applied this text to "the Interpreter of the Law,"[1] and it was the source of the name of the last chief of the Zealot movement, Bar Kokhba, son of the Star.[2] The patristic writers made much of this passage, applying it to Christ's nativity star.[3]

In Deuteronomy 18:15 Moses announces Yahweh's promise to "raise up for you a prophet like myself, from among yourselves, from your own brothers; to him you must listen." This was understood to be a prophecy of the Messiah as a second Moses. The promise was repeated to David.

Yahweh will make you great; Yahweh will make you a House. And when your days are ended and you are laid to rest with your ancestors, I will preserve the offspring of your body after you and make his sovereignty secure . . . . I will be a father to him and he a son to me . . . . Your House and your sovereignty will always stand secure before me and your throne be established for ever. (2 Samuel 7:11-16)

This promise is repeated in the Psalms, for instance Psalm 132.

Yahweh swore to David
And will remain true to his word,
"I promise that your own son
shall succeed you on the throne." (v. 11)

For Yahweh has chosen Zion,
desiring this to be his home,
"Here I will stay for ever,
this is the home I have chosen." (v. 13)

"Here, I will make a horn sprout for David,
here, I will trim a lamp for my annointed,
whose enemies I shall clothe in shame,
while his crown bursts with flower." (v. 17,18)

These promises are the source of the term "Son of David" applied to the Messiah. The history of Israel soon made it clear that they could not be taken literally. Psalm 89 bemoans Yahweh's broken promise as taken concretely. Jeremiah postpones the promise to the future:

See, the days are coming—it is Yahweh who speaks—
when I will raise a virtuous Branch for David,
who will reign as true king and be wise,
practising honesty and integrity in the land.

1. *Damascus Document* VIII, 19. See G. Vermes, *The Dead Sea Scrolls in English,* p. 104.
2. Jean Daniélou, *The Theology of Jewish Christianity,* p. 219.
3. Ibid.

In his days Judah will be saved
and Israel dwell in confidence.
And this is the name he will be called:
Yahweh-our-integrity. (Jeremiah 23:5,6)

Similarly, Ezekiel prophesies against the ill-fated Zedekiah:

And thou, profane wicked prince of Israel, whose day is come, when
iniquity shall have an end, thus saith the Lord God; Remove the diadem,
and take off the crown: this shall not be the same: exalt him that is low,
and abase him that is high. I will overturn, overturn, overturn, it: and it
shall be no more, until he come whose right it is; and I will give it him.
(Ezekiel 21:25-27, AV)

He "whose right it is" echoes the words of Genesis 49:10, and like the
latter has been understood as a messianic prophecy. As F.F. Bruce puts it,

It might have been thought at one time that the establishment of the Davidic
monarchy exhausted the terms of the promise in Judah's blessing; again,
with the fall of that monarchy it might have been thought that the promise
had been annulled. But Ezekiel declares that the prophecy neither found its
ultimate fulfillment in the rise of David's house nor met its final frustration
in the ruin of that house. Another David, a true shepherd to Israel, is yet
to come, the one to whom the sovereignty belongs by right, and in him all
the promises made to Judah's tribe and David's house will be perfectly
satisfied.[4]

Several Psalms speak explicitly of a future ideal king, an annointed
one, who will rule forever.

Like sun and moon he will endure,
   age after age,
welcome as rain that falls on the pasture,
   and showers to thirsty soil.
In his days virtue will flourish,
   a universal peace till the moon is no more;
his empire shall stretch from sea to sea,
   from the river to the ends of the earth. (Psalm 72:5-8)

He will carry supreme authority. Yahweh tells him, "Sit at my right
hand and I will make your enemies a footstool for you." (Psalm 110:1)
His absolute sovereignty is described most fully in Psalm 2:

Why this uproar among the nations?
Why this impotent muttering of pagans—
kings on earth rising in revolt,
princes plotting against Yahweh and his annointed,
"Now let us break their fetters!
Now let us throw off their yoke!"

---

4. F.F. Bruce, *New Testament Development of Old Testament Themes*, p. 74. I am
indebted to this book for the ordering of some of the material in this chapter.

The One whose throne is in heaven sits laughing,
Yahweh derides them.
Then angrily he addresses them,
in a rage he strikes them with panic,
"This is my king, installed by me
on Zion, my holy mountain."

Let me proclaim Yahweh's decree:
he has told me, "You are my son,
today I have become your father.
Ask and I will give you the nations for your heritage,
the ends of the earth for your domain.
With iron sceptre you will break them,
shatter them like potter's ware."

So now, you kings, learn wisdom,
earthly rulers, be warned:
serve Yahweh, fear him,
tremble and kiss his feet,
or he will be angry and you will perish,
for his anger is very quick to blaze.

Happy all who take shelter in him.

The phrase "Thou art my Son; this day have I begotten thee" (verse 7, AV) establishes the Messiah as "Son of Yahweh." Other passages call him "Son of David" and later, "Son of Man." This double parentage suggests that the Self consciously realized (Messiah) is begotten by *both* the original Self *and* the ego. The same twofold symbolism occurs in alchemy where the Philosophers' Stone is described both as the gift of God and also as the "Son of the Philosophers," that is, the product of the efforts of the alchemists.

The Day of Yahweh

In the writings of the prophets the imagery of a coming Messiah is overlapped with the idea of a "Last Day," "the Day of the Lord," in which Divine Judgment will be meted out to the sinful world. Many of these prophetic passages refer primarily to the coming invasions of Israel and Judah by Assyria and Babylon. However they have taken on or had projected into them a secondary eschatological meaning. Isaiah exclaims,

Howl! For the day of Yahweh is near,
bringing devastation from Shaddai.
At this, every arm falls limp . . .
The heart of each man fails him,
they are terrified,
pangs and pains seize them,
they writhe like a woman in labour.
They look at one another

with feverish faces.
The day of Yahweh is coming, merciless,
with wrath and fierce anger,
to reduce the earth to desert
and root out the sinners from it.
For the stars of the sky and Orion
shall not let their light shine;
the sun shall be dark when it rises,
and the moon not shed her light.
I will punish the world for its evil-doing,
and the wicked for their crime,
to put an end to the pride of arrogant men
and humble the pride of the despots. (Isaiah 13:6-11)

Zephaniah sounds the same theme:

The great day of Yahweh is near,
near, and coming with all speed.
How bitter the sound of the day of Yahweh,
the day when the warrior shouts his cry of war.
A day of wrath, that day,
a day of distress and agony,
a day of ruin and of devastation,
a day of darkness and gloom,
a day of cloud and blackness,
a day of trumpet blast and battle cry
against fortified town
and high corner-tower.
I am going to bring such distress on men
that they will grope like the blind
(because they have sinned against Yahweh);
their blood will be scattered like dust,
their corpses like dung.
Neither their silver nor their gold
will have any power to save them.
On the day of the anger of Yahweh,
in the fire of his jealousy,
all the earth will be consumed.
For he means to destroy, yes, to make an end
of all the inhabitants of the earth. (Zephaniah 1:14-18)[5]

The terrible image of unmitigated destruction is finally softened in
Zechariah with a glimpse of the messianic age which will follow the day
of Yahweh's wrath.

When that day comes, there will be no more cold, no more frost. It will be
a day of wonder—Yahweh knows it—with no alternation of day and night;
in the evening it will be light. When that day comes, running waters will

5. Other passages on the "Day of Yahweh" include Isaiah 2:12, 34:8; Ezekiel 13:5,
30:3; Joel 1:15, 2:1; Amos 5:18.

issue from Jerusalem, half of them to the eastern sea, half of them to the western sea; they will flow summer and winter. And Yahweh will be king of the whole world. (Zechariah 14:6-9)

Psychologically, the "Day of Yahweh" is a particular example of the more general archetypal image of the "Last Judgment" which is found in many religions, usually projected into the afterlife or into an eschatological future.[6] This image refers to a major encounter between the ego and the Self in which the former experiences a devastating insight into its defects and unacknowledged reality. It is the experience of "being seen" by an Other, often symbolized by the eye of God.[7] The image of widespread destruction refers to those aspects of the personality which are not grounded in psychic reality and therefore cannot survive transpersonal scrutiny. If, in this encounter, the ego holds, it is followed by an enlargement of personality. Jung describes the experience in these words:

> When a summit of life is reached, when the bud unfolds and from the lesser the greater emerges, then, as Nietzsche says, "One becomes Two," and the greater figure, which one always was but which remained invisible, appears to the lesser personality with the force of a revelation. He who is truly and hopelessly little will always drag the revelation of the greater down to the level of his littleness, and will never understand that the day of judgment for his littleness has dawned. But the man who is inwardly great will know that the long expected friend of his soul, the immortal one, has now really come, "to lead captivity captive" [Ephesians 4:8]; that is, to seize hold of him by whom this immortal had always been confined and held prisoner, and to make his life flow into that greater life—a moment of deadliest peril![8]

The Suffering Servant of Yahweh

While some Messiah texts picture the Messiah as an invincible king, others represent him as a humble suffering servant—for instance Psalm 22:

> My God, my God, why have you deserted me?
> How far from saving me, the words I groan!
> I call all day, my God, but you never answer,
> all night long I call and cannot rest.
> . . . .
> Yet here am I, now more worm than man,
> scorn of mankind, jest of the people,
> all who see me jeer at me,
> they toss their heads and sneer,
> "He relied on Yahweh, let Yahweh save him!

6. Relevant material has been gathered by S.G.F. Brandon, *The Judgment of the Dead.*
7. For more on this subject see Edinger, *The Creation of Consciousness,* pp. 41ff.
8. "Concerning Rebirth," *The Archetypes of the Collective Unconscious,* CW 9i, par. 217.

If Yahweh is his friend, let Him rescue him!"
. . . .
I am like water draining away,
my bones are all disjointed,
my heart is like wax,
melting inside me;
my palate is drier than a potsherd
and my tongue is stuck to my jaw.
A pack of dogs surrounds me,
a gang of villains closes me in;
they tie me hand and foot
and leave me lying in the dust of death.
I can count every one of my bones,
and there they glare at me, gloating;
they divide my garments among them
and cast lots for my clothes. (Psalms 22:1-18)

These words are considered to be spoken by the Messiah. The first line
was uttered by Christ on the cross and some think he recited the entire
Psalm on that occasion.

The other major text is the so-called "Fourth song of the servant of
Yahweh," found in Isaiah:

See, my servant will prosper,
he shall be lifted up, exalted, rise to great heights.
. . . .
"Who could believe what we have heard,
and to whom has the power of Yahweh been revealed?"
Like a sapling he grew up in front of us,
like a root in arid ground.
Without beauty, without majesty (we saw him),
no looks to attract our eyes;
a thing despised and rejected by man,
a man of sorrows and familiar with suffering,
a man to make people screen their faces;
he was despised and we took no account of him.

And yet ours were the sufferings he bore,
ours the sorrows he carried.
But we, we thought of him as someone punished,
struck by God, and brought low.
Yet he was pierced through our faults,
crushed for our sins.
On him lies a punishment that brings us peace,
and through his wounds we are healed.
. . . .
Yahweh has been pleased to crush him with suffering.
If he offers his life in atonement,
he shall see his heirs, he shall have a long life
and through him what Yahweh wishes will be done.

His soul's anguish over
he shall see the light and be content.
By his sufferings shall my servant justify many,
taking their faults on himself.

Hence I will grant whole hordes for his tribute,
he shall divide the spoil with the mighty,
for surrendering himself to death
and letting himself be taken for a sinner,
while he was bearing the faults of many
and praying all the time for sinners. (Isaiah 52:13-53:12)

The "Servant of Yahweh" here described was first introduced in Isaiah 42:1-4.

Here is my servant whom I uphold,
my chosen one in whom my soul delights.
I have endowed him with my spirit
that he may bring true justice to the nations.

He does not cry out or shout aloud,
or make his voice heard in the streets.
He does not break the crushed reed,
nor quench the wavering flame.[9]

Faithfully he brings true justice;
he will neither waver, nor be crushed
until true justice is established on earth,
for the islands are awaiting his law.

The phrase "I have endowed him with my spirit" indicates the servant is an "annointed one,"[10] thus in some sense a Messiah. In the New Testament this passage was applied to Christ who was annointed by the Holy Spirit at his baptism. F. F. Bruce has pointed out that members of the Qumran Community "were conscious of a vocation to fulfill the commission of the Servant of Yahweh."[11] He cites a passage in the tractate Sanhedrin of the Babylonian Talmud:

The Messiah . . . what is his name? . . . Our rabbis say "the Leper of the house of Rabbi (house of learning) is his name," as it is said: "Surely he has borne our sicknesses and carried our pains, yet we esteemed him a leper (Heb. *nāgūa,* "stricken"), smitten by God, and afflicted." (TB Sanhedrin 98)[12]

He also quotes "a hymn by the poet Eleazar ben Qalir (variously dated

---

9. Jung used this verse as a motto for *Psychology and Alchemy,* CW 12.
10. "The spirit of the Lord Yahweh has been given to me, for Yahweh has annointed me." (Isaiah 61:1) Christ applied this text to himself in Luke 4:16ff. "Messiah" means "annointed one."
11. Bruce, *New Testament Development of Old Testament Themes,* p. 93.
12. Ibid., p. 94.

from the late seventh to the tenth century A.D.) which is included in the additional prayers for the Day of Atonement":

> Our righteous Messiah had departed from us;
> we are horror-stricken, and there is none to justify us.
> Our iniquities and the yoke of our transgressions
> he carries, and is wounded for our transgressions.
> He bears on his shoulder our sins
> to find pardon for our iniquities
> may we be healed by his stripes.[13]

The "Suffering Servant" is a personification of redeeming consciousness. He takes on himself the voluntary role of the scapegoat. As part of the great annual ritual of atonement, a scapegoat was loaded with the sins of the community and sent into the wilderness. (Leviticus 16:20-22) The Suffering Servant of Yahweh performs a similar function since he was "crushed for our sins" and "through his wounds we are healed." This figure emerges in the process of individuation as an image of "consciousness of wholeness." Although experienced by the ego, the ego must not identify with it. It is rather a manifestation of the Self consciously realized which brings with it a reconciliation of opposites (redemption). A dream of a young man illustrates this figure.

> I dreamed I saw a modern Christ figure. He was traveling in a bus with a group of his disciples. Then I sensed there was danger. He was going to be betrayed. It happened and the bus rocked with violence. He was set upon and subdued. I looked in and saw that they had apparently tied ropes to each of his hands and feet and had pulled him tight, spread-eagled in four directions. I knew they would kill him that way. Then it appeared when I looked at him more closely that he was not tied by the hands but was grasping with each hand a wooden bar attached to the rope. He was cooperating in his own death! At the end of the dream came an image of a magnetic field of force which looked like this drawing:[14]

This dream marked a life transition and change in vocation. It represents a new energy configuration forming at the center of the psyche, brought about by a willing sacrifice of the Self.

The theme of voluntary suffering appears in a remarkable passage of a

13. Ibid.
14. See also Edinger, *Ego and Archetype,* pp. 138f.

letter by Jung. He writes to an unknown recipient, "I consciously and intentionally made my life miserable, because I wanted God to be alive and free from the suffering man has put on him by loving his own reason more than God's secret intentions."[15] Jung is here speaking out of the Suffering Servant archetype. A willing acceptance of suffering is an aspect of consciousness of wholeness since it includes a painful awareness of the opposites. Jung puts it starkly:

> Without the experience of the opposites there is no experience of wholeness and hence no inner approach to the sacred figures. . . . Although insight into the problem of opposites is absolutely imperative, there are very few people who can stand it in practice . . . . The reality of evil and its incompatibility with good cleave the opposites asunder and lead inexorably to the crucifixion and suspension of everything that lives. Since "the soul is by nature Christian" this result is bound to come as infallibly as it did in the life of Jesus: we all have to be "crucified with Christ," i.e., suspended in a moral suffering equivalent to veritable crucifixion.[16]

The Son of Man

We encounter the term "Son of Man" for the first time in the Old Testament in Ezekiel. At the time of his great mandala vision Ezekiel is addressed by Yahweh as "Son of Man" (Ezekiel 2:1), "presumably to indicate that he is a son of the 'Man' on the throne [in the vision]."[17] It shows up again in a vision of Daniel, this time clearly identified as the Messiah.

> I gazed into the visions of the night.
> And I saw, coming in the clouds of heaven,
> one like a son of man.
> He came to the one of great age
> and was led into his presence.
> On him was conferred sovereignty,
> glory and kingship.
> And men of all peoples, nations and languages became his servants.
> His sovereignty is an eternal sovereignty
> which shall never pass away,
> nor will his empire ever be destroyed. (Daniel 7:13,14)

The same term is used in the Book of Enoch which gives an extensive description of the messianic "Son of Man."

> And in that place I saw the fountain of righteousness
> Which was inexhaustible:
> And around it were many fountains of wisdom:

---

15. Quoted by Gerhard Adler, "Aspects of Jung's Personality and Work," p. 12.
16. *Psychology and Alchemy*, CW 12, par. 24.
17. Jung, "Answer to Job," *Psychology and Religion*, CW 11, par. 667.

And all the thirsty drank of them,
And were filled with wisdom,
And their dwellings were with the righteous and holy and elect.
And at that hour that Son of Man was named
In the presence of the Lord of Spirits,
And his name before the Head of Days.
Yea, before the sun and the signs were created,
Before the stars of the heaven were made,
His name was named before the Lord of Spirits.
He shall be a staff to the righteous whereon to stay themselves and not fall,
And he shall be the light of the Gentiles
And the hope of those who are troubled in heart.
All who dwell on earth shall fall down and worship before him,
And will praise and bless and celebrate with Song the Lord of Spirits.
And for this reason hath he been chosen and hidden before Him,
Before the creation of the world and for evermore. (Enoch 48:1-6)[18]

Jung comments on Enoch's vision,[19] noting that,

> When Yahweh addressed Ezekiel as "Son of Man," this was no more at first than a dark and enigmatic hint. But now it becomes clear: the man Enoch is not only the recipient of divine revelation but is at the same time a participant in the divine drama, as though he were at least one of the sons of God himself. This can only be taken as meaning that in the same measure as God sets out to become man, man is immersed in the pleromatic process. He becomes, as it were, baptized in it and is made to participate in the divine quaternity (i.e., is crucified with Christ).[20]

Man's being "made to participate in the divine quaternity" refers to Ezekiel's fourfold vision of the divine chariot (Ezekiel 1:4ff) and to Enoch's vision of the "four presences" or "angels" who "stood before the Lord of Spirits." (Enoch 40:1ff)[21]

Thus, to the extent that one participates in the divine quaternity—which is the essence of individuation—one is incarnating the archetype of the Son of Man. Christ repeatedly identified himself with the "Son of Man,"[22] and on that evidence alone becomes a symbol of the Self. The term "Son of Man" is symbolically analogous to the alchemical term *Filius Philosophorum*, Son of the Philosophers, which is a synonym for the Philosophers' Stone. The phrase "Son of the Philosophers" indicates that the Philosophers' Stone is a product of the efforts of the alchemists. Likewise, "Son of Man" implies that the Messiah (Self) is, in part, created by the ego.

18. R.H. Charles, *The Apocrypha and Pseudepigrapha of the Old Testament in English,* vol. 2, p. 216.
19. "Answer to Job," *Psychology and Religion,* pars. 669ff.
20. Ibid., par. 677.
21. Charles, *The Apocrypha,* p. 211.
22. See Matthew 8:20, 9:6, 10:23, 11:19, 12:8, 16:27f, 19:28, 24:30, 25:31, 26:64, etc.

The Messianic Age

The coming of the Messiah will inaugurate an ideal age of peace and piety. It is alluded to in the Old Testament and developed more fully in the legends. In that day,

> The wolf lives with the lamb,
> the panther lies down with the kid,
> calf and lion cub feed together
> with a little boy to lead them.
> The cow and the bear make friends,
> their young lie down together.
> The lion eats straw like the ox.
> The infant plays over the cobra's hole;
> into the viper's lair
> the young child puts his hand.
> They do no hurt, no harm,
> on all my holy mountain,
> for the country is filled with the knowledge of Yahweh
> as the waters swell the sea. (Isaiah 11:6-9)[23]

According to Hosea,

> When that day comes I will make a treaty on her behalf with the wild animals,
> with the birds of heaven and the creeping things of the earth;
> I will break bow, sword and battle in the country,
> and make her peace secure.
> I will betroth you to myself for ever,
> betroth you with integrity and justice,
> with tenderness and love;
> I will betroth you to myself with faithfulness,
> and you will come to know Yahweh. (Hosea 2:18-20)

And Micah,

> They will hammer their swords into ploughshares,
> their spears into sickles.
> Nation will not lift sword against nation,
> there will be no more training for war.
> Each man will sit under his vine and his fig tree,
> with no one to trouble him. (Micah 4:3,4)

In the Messianic Age the opposites will be reconciled. The conflicts between animals, between man and animals, between man and man and between man and God will be resolved. This describes a state of totality in which the divisions of the psyche have been harmonized by conscious-

23.   See also Isaiah 35.

ness of the whole. According to legend there will be a great Messianic Banquet at which the flesh of Behemoth and Leviathan will be eaten and the Garden of Eden state will be restored:

> In that hour the Holy One, blessed be He, will set table and slaughter Behemoth and Leviathan . . . and prepare a great banquet for the pious. And He will seat each one of them according to his honor . . . . And the Holy One, blessed be He, will bring them wine that was preserved in its grapes since the six days of creation . . . . And He fulfills the wishes of the pious, rises from the Throne of Glory, and sits with them . . . . And He brings all the fine things of the Garden of Eden.[24]

The primordial deity (Behemoth and Leviathan) will be humanized and transformed as it is assimilated by consciousness. This restores the original state of wholeness (Garden of Eden) on a new conscious level. Then a new Torah will be taught and the dissociation between heaven and hell will be healed.

> And the Holy One, blessed be He, will expound to them the meanings of a new Torah which He will give them through the Messiah . . . . In that hour the Holy One, blessed be He, takes the keys of Gehenna and, in front of all the pious, gives them to Michael and Gabriel, and says to them: "Go and open the gates of Gehenna, and bring them up from Gehenna" . . . . And Gabriel and Michael stand over them [the wicked] in that hour, and wash them, and annoint them with oil, and heal them of the wounds of gehenna, and clothe them in beautiful and good garments, and take them by their hand, and bring them before the Holy One, blessed be He.[25]

The final state of wholeness is expressed in the image of a new Jerusalem. Patai writes,

> In the Talmud and Midrash, the heavenly Jerusalem is a standard Aggadic notion, presented in great detail and in many variants. In them, the undying love of the Jewish people for Jerusalem, the Holy City, the city of the temple and the royal seat of David, finds eloquent expression in limitless flights of fantasy describing the glories of the future Jerusalem in the days of the Messiah. This Messianic Jerusalem, which will descend in its entirety from heaven, will comprise a thousand towers, fortresses, street corners, pools, and cisterns, it will extend as far as Damascus, its height will increase by miles, its gates will be huge precious stones, jewels and pearls will be scattered all over its streets and environs like pebbles, and its radiance will light up the whole world and will rise up to God's Throne of Glory.[26]

In the spirit of this collective Jewish fantasy is the great mandala vision of the New Jerusalem recorded in Revelation:

24. Patai, *The Messiah Texts*, pp. 238f.
25. Ibid., pp. 252f.
26. Ibid., pp. 221f.

Then I saw a new heaven and a new earth; the first heaven and the first earth had disappeared now, and there was no longer any sea. I saw the holy city, and the new Jerusalem, coming down from God out of heaven, as beautiful as a bride all dressed for her husband. Then I heard a loud voice call from the throne, "You see this city? Here God lives among men. He will make his home among them; they shall be his people, and he will be their God."

. . . .

In the spirit, he took me to the top of an enormous high mountain, and showed me Jerusalem, the holy city, coming down from God and out of heaven. It had all the radiant glory of God and glittered like some precious jewel of crystal-clear diamond. The walls of it were of a great height, and had twelve gates; at each of the twelve gates there was an angel, and over the gates were written the names of the twelve tribes of Israel; on the east there were three gates, on the north three gates, on the south three gates, and on the west three gates. The city walls stood on twelve foundation stones, each one of which bore the name of one of the twelve apostles of the Lamb.

The angel that was speaking to me was carrying a gold measuring rod to measure the city and its gates and wall. The plan of the city is perfectly square, its length the same as its breadth. He measured the city with his rod and it was twelve thousand furlongs in length and in breadth, and equal in height. He measured its wall, and this was a hundred and forty-four cubits high—the angel was using the ordinary cubit. The wall was built of diamond, and the city of pure gold, like polished glass. The foundations of the city wall were faced with all kinds of precious stone: the first with diamond, the second lapis lazuli, the third turquoise, the fourth crystal, the fifth agate, the sixth ruby, the seventh gold quartz, the eighth malachite, the ninth topaz, the tenth emerald, the eleventh sapphire and the twelfth amethyst.

The twelve gates were twelve pearls, each gate being made of a single pearl, and the main street of the city was pure gold, transparent as glass. I saw that there was no temple in the city since the Lord God Almighty and the Lamb were themselves the temple, and the city did not need the sun or the moon for light, since it was lit by the radiant glory of God. (Revelation 21:1-23)

This grand image of totality is a fitting conclusion to our survey of individuation symbolism in the Old Testament. Jung interprets it as follows:

The city is Sophia, who was with God before time began, and at the end of time will be reunited with God through the sacred marriage. As a feminine being she coincides with the earth, from which, so a Church Father tells us, Christ was born, and hence with the quaternity of the four living creatures in whom God manifests himself in Ezekiel. In the same way that Sophia signifies God's self-reflection, the four seraphim represent God's consciousness with its four functional aspects. The many perceiving eyes [Ezekiel 1:18] which are concentrated in the four wheels point in the same direction. They represent a fourfold synthesis of unconscious luminosities, corresponding to the tetrameria of the *lapis philosophorum,* of which the description of the heavenly city reminds us: everything sparkles with precious gems, crystal, and glass, in complete accordance with Ezekiel's vision of God. And just as the *hieros gamos* unites Yahweh with Sophia (Shekinah in the Cabala), thus restoring the original pleromatic state, so the parallel description of God and city points to their common nature: they are originally one, a single hermaphroditic being, an archetype of the greatest universality.[27]

27. "Answer to Job," *Psychology and Religion,* CW 11, par. 727.

Bibliography

Adler, Gerhard. "Aspects of Jung's Personality and Work." *Psychological Perspectives,* vol. 6, no. 1 (Spring 1975).

Aid to Bible Understanding. Brooklyn: Watchtower Bible and Tract Society, 1971.

The Ante-Nicene Fathers. 10 vols. Ed. Alexander Roberts and James Donaldson. Grand Rapids, Mich.: Eerdmans, 1977.

Aquinas, Thomas. *Basic Writings of St. Thomas Aquinas.* 2 vols. Ed. Anton C. Pegis. New York: Random House, 1945.

Aristotle. *The Basic Works of Aristotle.* Ed. Richard McKeon. New York: Random House, 1941.

Augustine. *The City of God.* Trans. Marcus Dods. New York: Modern Library, Random House, 1950.

————. "Exposition on the Book of Psalms," *The Nicene and Post-Nicene Fathers,* vol. 8. Ed. Philip Schaff and A. Cleveland Coxe. Grand Rapids, Mich.: Eerdmans, 1979.

Bercovitch, Sacvan. *The Puritan Origins of the American Self.* New Haven, Conn.: Yale University Press, 1975.

Blake, William. "The Marriage of Heaven and Hell," *The Poetry and Prose of William Blake.* Ed. David Erdman. Garden City, N.Y.: Doubleday Anchor, 1970.

Brandon, S.G.F. *The Judgment of the Dead.* New York: Scribner's, 1967.

Briggs, W.A. and W.R. Bénet, eds. *Great Poems of the English Language.* New York: Tudor, 1944.

Bruce, F.F. *New Testament Development of Old Testament Themes.* Grand Rapids, Mich.: Eerdmans, 1982.

Cambridge Medieval History. 8 vols. New York: Macmillan, 1924f.

Capote, Truman. *In Cold Blood.* New York: Signet, New American Library, 1965.

Charles, R.H., ed. *The Apocrypha and Pseudepigrapha of the Old Testament in English.* 2 vols. London: Oxford University Press, 1968.

Cornford, F.M. *From Religion to Philosophy.* New York: Harper Torchbooks, 1957.

Daniélou, Jean. *The Theology of Jewish Christianity.* Trans. John A. Baker. Philadelphia: The Westminster Press, 1978.

Dante. *The Divine Comedy.* Trans. Laurence Grant White. New York: Pantheon Books, 1948.

Davidson, Gustav. *A Dictionary of Angels.* New York: Free Press, 1971.

Dummelow, J.R., ed. *The One-Volume Bible Commentary.* New York: Macmillan, 1975.

Edinger, Edward F. *Anatomy of the Psyche.* La Salle, Ill.: Open Court, 1985.

————. *The Creation of Consciousness: Jung's Myth for Modern Man.* Toronto: Inner City Books, 1984.

————. *Ego and Archetype: Individuation and the Religious Function of the Psyche.* New York: Putnam's, 1972.

————. *Encounter with the Self: A Jungian Commentary on William Blake's Illustrations of the Book of Job.* Toronto: Inner City Books, 1986.

————. *The Living Psyche.* In preparation.

————. *Melville's Moby-Dick: A Jungian Commentary.* New York: New Directions, 1978.

Emerson, Ralph Waldo. *The Selected Writings of Ralph Waldo Emerson.* New York: Modern Library, Random House, 1950.

Frazer, J.G. *Folklore in the Old Testament.* New York: Macmillan, 1923.

————. *The Golden Bough.* 3rd ed. 13 vols. London: Macmillan, 1919.

Gaer, Joseph. *The Lore of the Old Testament.* New York: Grosset and Dunlap, 1966.

Ginzberg, Louis. *Legends of the Bible.* New York: Simon and Schuster, 1956.

Graves, Robert. *The Greek Myths.* 2 vols. New York: George Braziller, 1955.

Gubitz, Myron B. "Amalek: The Eternal Adversary." *Psychological Perspectives,* vol. 8, no. 1 (Spring 1977).

Hastings, James, ed. *Encyclopaedia of Religion and Ethics.* 13 vols. New York: Scribners, 1922.

Heidel, Alexander. *The Babylonian Genesis.* Chicago: Phoenix Books, University of Chicago Press, 1951.

Homer. *Iliad.* Trans. Alexander Pope. *The Complete Poetical Works of Pope.* Cambridge, Mass.: Houghton Mifflin, 1931.

————. *Iliad.* Trans. Richard Lattimore. Chicago: University of Chicago Press, 1961.

The I Ching or Book of Changes. Trans. Richard Wilhelm. Princeton: Princeton University Press, 1967.

International Standard Bible Encyclopaedia. 4 vols. Ed. James Orr. Grand Rapids, Mich.: Eerdmans, 1980.

James, M.R. *The Apocryphal New Testament.* London: Oxford University Press, 1960.

Jerusalem Bible. Garden City, N.Y.: Doubleday and Co., 1966.

Jonas, Hans. *The Gnostic Religion.* Boston: Beacon Press, 1958.

Jung, C.G. *The Collected Works* (Bollingen Series XX). 20 vols. Trans. R.F.C. Hull. Ed. H. Read, M. Fordham, G. Adler, Wm. McGuire. Princeton: Princeton University Press, 1953-1979.

————. *C.G. Jung Letters* (Bollingen Series XCV). 2 vols. Ed. Gerhard Adler and Aniela Jaffé. Trans. R.F.C. Hull. Princeton: Princeton University Press, 1973-1975.

————. *C.G. Jung Speaking* (Bollingen Series XCVII). Ed. Wm. McGuire and R.F.C. Hull. Princeton: Princeton University Press, 1977.

————. *Interpretation of Visions.* 12 vols. Mimeographed Notes of Seminar, Zurich, 1930-1934.

————. *Memories, Dreams, Reflections.* Ed. Aniela Jaffé. Trans. Richard and Clara Winston. New York: Pantheon Books, 1963.

————. *Seminar 1925.* Mimeographed Notes of Seminar, March 23-July 6, 1925, Zurich.

————. *The Visions Seminars.* 2 vols. (Abridged Version of *Interpretation of Visions,* above). Zurich: Spring Publications, 1976.

Kluger, H. Yechezkel. "Ruth: A Contribution to the Study of the Feminine Principle in the Old Testament." *Spring 1957.*

Kluger, Rivkah Schärf. "The Image of the Marriage between God and Israel." *Spring 1950.*

————. *Psyche and Bible.* Zurich: Spring Publications, 1974.

————. *Satan in the Old Testament.* Evanston, Ill.: Northwestern University Press, 1967.

Mathers, S.L. MacGregor, trans. *The Kabbalah Unveiled.* London: Routledge and Kegan Paul, 1962.

Meister Eckhart. Ed. Franz Pfeiffer. Trans. C. de B. Evans. London: John M. Watkins, 1956.

Milton, John. "Samson Agonistes," *Milton: Complete Poetry and Selected Prose.* Ed. E.H. Visiak. Glasgow: The Nonesuch Library, 1969.

The Nag Hammadi Library. Ed. James M. Robinson. San Francisco: Harper and Row, 1977.

Neumann, Erich. *The Origins and History of Consciousness* (Bollingen Series XLII). Trans. R.F.C. Hull. New York: Pantheon Books, 1954.

New American Bible. New York: P.J. Kenedy and Sons, 1970.

Nietzsche, Friedrich. *My Sister and I.* Trans. Oscar Levy. New York: Bridgehead Books, Boar's Head Books, 1965.

Otto, Rudolf. *The Idea of the Holy.* Trans. John W. Harvey. London: Oxford University Press, 1950.

Patai, Raphael. *The Messiah Texts.* New York: Avon Books, 1979.

Philo. *The Essential Philo.* Ed. Nahum N. Glatzer. New York: Schocken Books, 1971.

Pistis Sophia. Trans. G.R.S. Meade. London: John M. Watkins, 1947.

Plato. *The Collected Dialogues.* Ed. Edith Hamilton and Huntington Cairns. New York: Pantheon Books, 1961.

————. *Plato I.* Trans. Harold North Fowler. Cambridge, Mass.: Loeb Classical Library, Harvard University Press, 1960.

Pope, Marvin H., trans. and ed. "Song of Songs," *Anchor Bible.* Garden City, N.Y.: Doubleday and Co., 1977.

Pritchard, James E., ed. *The Ancient Near East.* Princeton: Princeton University Press, 1958.

Rahner, Hugo. *Greek Myths and Christian Mystery.* New York: Harper and Row, 1963.

Rank, Otto. *The Myth of the Birth of the Hero.* New York: Vintage Books, 1959.

Scholem, Gershom G. *Major Trends in Jewish Mysticism.* New York: Schocken Books, 1954.

Smith, W. Robertson. *The Religion of the Semites.* New York: Meridian Books, 1956.

Vermes, G. *The Dead Sea Scrolls in English.* New York: Penguin Books, 1975.

Von Franz, Marie-Louise. *Aurora Consurgens.* Trans. R.F.C. Hull and A.S.B. Glover. New York: Pantheon Books, 1966.

Waite, A.E. *The Hermetic and Alchemical Writings of Paracelsus.* 2 vols. New Hyde Park, N.Y.: University Books, 1967.

———. *The Holy Kabbalah.* New Hyde Park, N.Y.: University Books, n.d.

Wellisch, Erich. *Isaac and Oedipus.* London: Routledge and Kegan Paul, 1954.

Index

Studies in Jungian Psychology by Jungian Analysts

LIMITED EDITION PAPERBACKS

Prices quoted are in U.S. dollars (except for Canadian orders)

1. **The Secret Raven: Conflict and Transformation.**
   Daryl Sharp (Toronto). ISBN 0-919123-00-7. 128 pages. $10

A concise introduction to the application of Jungian psychology. Focuses on the creative personality—and the life and dreams of the writer Franz Kafka —but the psychology is relevant to anyone who has experienced a conflict between the spiritual life and sex, or between inner and outer reality. (Knowledge of Kafka is not necessary.) Illustrated. Bibliography.

2. **The Psychological Meaning of Redemption Motifs in Fairytales.**
   Marie-Louise von Franz (Zurich). ISBN 0-919123-01-5. 128 pages. $10

A unique account of the significance of fairytales for an understanding of the process of individuation, especially in terms of integrating animal nature and human nature. Particularly helpful for its symbolic, nonlinear approach to the meaning of typical dream motifs (bathing, beating, clothes, animals, etc.), and its clear description of complexes and projection.

3. **On Divination and Synchronicity: Psychology of Meaningful Chance.**
   Marie-Louise von Franz (Zurich). ISBN 0-919123-02-3. 128 pages. $10

A penetrating study of the meaning of the irrational. Examines time, number, and methods of divining fate such as the I Ching, astrology, Tarot, palmistry, random patterns, etc. Explains Jung's ideas on archetypes, projection, psychic energy and synchronicity, contrasting Western scientific attitudes with those of the Chinese and so-called primitives. Illustrated.

4. **The Owl Was a Baker's Daughter: Obesity, Anorexia Nervosa, and the Repressed Feminine.**
   Marion Woodman (Toronto). ISBN 0-919123-03-1. 144 pages. $10

A pioneer work in feminine psychology, with particular attention to the body as mirror of the psyche in eating disorders and weight disturbances. Explores the personal and cultural loss—and potential rediscovery—of the feminine principle, through Jung's Association Experiment, case studies, dreams, Christianity and mythology. Illustrated. Glossary. Bibliography.

5. **Alchemy: An Introduction to the Symbolism and the Psychology.**
   Marie-Louise von Franz (Zurich). ISBN 0-919123-04-X. 288 pages. $16

A lucid and practical guide to what the alchemists were really looking for— emotional balance and wholeness. Completely demystifies the subject. An important work, invaluable for an understanding of images and motifs in modern dreams and drawings, and indispensable for anyone interested in relationships and communication between the sexes. 84 Illustrations.

6. **Descent to the Goddess: A Way of Initiation for Women.**
   Sylvia Brinton Perera (New York). ISBN 0-919123-05-8. 112 pages. $10

A timely and provocative study of women's freedom and the need for an inner, female authority in a masculine-oriented society. Based on the Sumerian goddess Inanna-Ishtar's journey to the underworld, her transformation through contact with her dark "sister" Ereshkigal, and her return. Rich in insights from dreams, mythology and analysis. Glossary. Bibliography.

7. **The Psyche as Sacrament: C.G. Jung and Paul Tillich.**
   John P. Dourley (Ottawa). ISBN 0-919123-06-6. 128 pages. $10

An illuminating, comparative study showing with great clarity that in the depths of the soul the psychological task and the religious task are one. With a dual perspective, the author—Jungian analyst and Catholic priest—examines the deeper meaning, for Christian and non-Christian alike, of God, Christ, the Spirit, the Trinity, morality and the religious life. Glossary.

8. **Border Crossings: Carlos Castaneda's Path of Knowledge.**
   Donald Lee Williams (Boulder). ISBN 0-919123-07-4. 160 pages. $12

The first thorough psychological examination of the popular don Juan novels. Using dreams, fairytales, and mythic and cultural parallels, the author brings Castaneda's spiritual journey down to earth, in terms of everyone's search for self-realization. Special attention to the psychology of women. (Familiarity with the novels is not necessary.) Glossary.

9. **Narcissism and Character Transformation: The Psychology of Narcissistic Character Disorders.**
   Nathan Schwartz-Salant (New York). ISBN 0-919123-08-2. 192 pp. $13

An incisive and comprehensive analysis of narcissism: what it looks like, what it means and how to deal with it. Shows how an understanding of the archetypal patterns that underlie the individual, clinical symptoms of narcissism can point the way to a healthy restructuring of the personality. Draws upon a variety of psychoanalytic points of view (Jungian, Freudian, Kohutian, Kleinian, etc.). Illustrated. Glossary. Bibliography.

10. **Rape and Ritual: A Psychological Study.**
    Bradley A. Te Paske (Minneapolis). ISBN 0-919123-09-0. 160 pp. $12

An absorbing combination of theory, clinical material, dreams and mythology, penetrating far beyond the actual deed to the impersonal, archetypal background of sexual assault. Special attention to male ambivalence toward women and the psychological significance of rape dreams and fantasies. Illustrated. Glossary. Bibliography.

11. **Alcoholism and Women: The Background and the Psychology.**
    Jan Bauer (Zurich). ISBN 0-919123-10-4. 144 pages. $12

A major contribution to an understanding of alcoholism, particularly in women. Compares and contrasts medical and psychological models, illustrates the relative merits of Alcoholics Anonymous and individual therapy, and presents new ways of looking at the problem based on case material, dreams and archetypal patterns. Glossary. Bibliography.

12. **Addiction to Perfection: The Still Unravished Bride.**
    Marion Woodman (Toronto). ISBN 0-919123-11-2. 208 pages. $12

A powerful and authoritative look at the psychology and attitudes of modern woman, expanding on the themes introduced in *The Owl Was a Baker's Daughter*. Explores the nature of the feminine through case material, dreams and mythology, in food rituals, rape symbolism, perfectionism, imagery in the body, sexuality and creativity. Illustrated.

13. **Jungian Dream Interpretation: A Handbook of Theory and Practice.**
    James A. Hall, M.D. (Dallas). ISBN 0-919123-12-0. 128 pages. $12

A comprehensive and practical guide to an understanding of dreams in light of the basic concepts of Jungian psychology. Jung's model of the psyche is described and discussed, with many clinical examples. Particular attention to common dream motifs, and how dreams are related to the stage of life and individuation process of the dreamer. Glossary.

14. The Creation of Consciousness: Jung's Myth for Modern Man.
Edward F. Edinger, M.D. (Los Angeles). ISBN 0-919123-13-9. 128 pp. $12
An important new book by the author of *Ego and Archetype.* Explores the
significance of Jung's work, the meaning of human life and the pressing need
for humanity to become conscious of its dark, destructive side. Illustrated.

15. The Analytic Encounter: Transference and Human Relationship.
Mario Jacoby (Zurich). ISBN 0-919123-14-7. 128 pp. $12
A sensitive study illustrating the difference between relationships based on
projection and those characterized by psychological objectivity and mutual
respect. Shows how complexes manifest in dreams and emotional reactions.

16. Change of Life: Dreams and the Menopause.
Ann Mankowitz (Santa Fe). ISBN 0-919123-15-5. 128 pp. $12
A moving account of a menopausal woman's Jungian analysis, revealing this
crucial period as a time of rebirth – a rare opportunity for psychological
integration, increased strength and specifically feminine wisdom.

17. The Illness That We Are: A Jungian Critique of Christianity.
John P. Dourley (Ottawa). ISBN 0-919123-16-3. 128 pp. $12
A radical study by Catholic priest and analyst, exploring Jung's views that
the Gnostic, mystical and alchemical traditions contain the necessary
compensation for the essentially masculine ideals of Christianity.

**18. Hags and Heroes: A Feminist Approach to Jungian
Psychotherapy with Couples.** ISBN 0-919123-17-1. 192 pp. $14
Polly Young-Eisendrath (Philadelphia)
A highly original integration of feminist views with the concepts of Jung
and Harry Stack Sullivan. Detailed strategies and techniques; emphasis on
revaluing the feminine and re-assessing the nature of female authority.

19. Cultural Attitudes in Psychological Perspective. 128 pp. $12
Joseph L. Henderson, M.D. (San Francisco). ISBN 0-919123-18-X.
A thoughtful new work by the co-author of *Man and His Symbols.* Examines
the nature and value of social, religious, aesthetic and philosophic attitudes, showing how the concepts of analytical psychology can give depth and
substance to an individual *Weltanschauung.* Illustrated.

20. The Vertical Labyrinth: Individuation in Jungian Psychology.
Aldo Carotenuto (Rome). ISBN 0-919123-19-8. 144 pp. $12
A guided journey through the analytic process, following the dreams of one
man who over a lengthy period of analysis finds new life and inner purpose;
an individual journey that yet echoes the universal themes of humanity.

**21. The Pregnant Virgin: A Process of Psychological Transforma-
tion.** Marion Woodman (Toronto). ISBN 0-919123-20-1. 208 pp. $15
A major new work about the struggle to become conscious of our own unique
truth and inner potential. Explores the wisdom of the body, relationships,
dreams, initiation rituals, addictions (food, drugs, work, etc.). Illustrated.

Add $1 per book (bookpost) or $3 per book (airmail)

INNER CITY BOOKS
Box 1271, Station Q, Toronto, Canada M4T 2P4   (416) 927-0355